Essays on freedom of action

Edited by

Ted Honderich

D1308156

Routledge & Kegan Paul

London and Boston

First published 1973
by Routledge & Kegan Paul Ltd
Broadway House, 68–74 Carter Lane
London EC4V 5EL and
9 Park Street,
Boston, Mass. 02108, U.S.A.
Printed in Great Britain by
The Camelot Press Ltd, London and Southampton
© Routledge & Kegan Paul Ltd 1973
No part of this book may be reproduced in
any form without permission from the
publisher, except for the quotation of brief
passages in criticism
ISBN 0 7100 7392 5
Library of Congress Catalogue Card No. 72–93516

Essays on freedom of action

Contents

Introduction

The essays in this book, all of them new, have to do with the freedom that is thought to be bound up with moral responsibility. This freedom is also integral to other things, including our view of ourselves as persons, and, perhaps, it is of more immediate significance for this reason. It is what traditionally has been called the Freedom of the Will. The Will, conceived as one among several faculties, is no longer much with us. As a consequence, the term 'freedom of action' has come to have a place in philosophical usage and is most appropriate as a description of the subject-matter of the essays.

They are of individual natures and give evidence of different intellectual commitments. Each of them, I think, can be said to take up some new ground. Despite this, and for good reason, they have relations with what has gone before, and I have paid attention to traditional categories in putting them into an order.

The first three essays are concerned with rather affirmative conceptions. Mary Warnock writes of Sartre's assertion of our freedom and responsibility, the role of the imagination in it, and the seemingly conflicting proposition that we are destined to pursue a certain end. John Watling examines closely and critically Stuart Hampshire's argument against determinism, which rests on a view of the explanation of our beliefs. David Wiggins, in the hope at least of salvaging its insights, advances a characterisation of libertarianism. He considers its logic and its ramifications.

The fourth, fifth, sixth and seventh essays, in different ways, bear on the tradition of thought which asserts the compatibility of causation and freedom. Harry Frankfurt examines coercion, whose absence has been thought, in that tradition, to be sufficient for freedom. His essay, since absence of coercion is taken by others to be a necessary condition of responsibility, also has a wider relevance. Anthony Kenny argues that it is unproven that causation and freedom are incompatible, despite the fact that certain attempts to establish compatibility are wanting. David Pears suggests that explanation of actions in terms of an agent's reasons moves towards an ideal of deterministic explanation.

His essay thus gives support to a premiss, if not necessarily the conclusion, of the tradition in question. Donald Davidson, finally, offers a resolution of a dilemma which arises when it is claimed that freedom to act is a causal power of agents which comes into play when certain conditions are fulfilled. He considers among others, the arguments of J. L. Austin in 'Ifs and Cans'.

Daniel Dennett's essay and my own, the seventh and eighth, have in common the view that reflections on freedom of action must at least be limited by an awareness of the physical nature of a person. Professor Dennett resists the supposition that mechanism drives out purpose and intentionality. My own essay is an attempt to sketch the premisses, principally based on neurophysiology, and also the conclusions, of one determinism.

T. H.

Freedom in the early philosophy of J.-P. Sartre

Mary Warnock

Freedom in the early philosophy of J.-P. Sartre

It is well known that at one time Sartre was a true and full-blooded Existentialist; it is also perhaps the best-known fact about Existentialism that it is concerned with human freedom, and that according to its central doctrine, man has no essence which could determine what he shall do. He is free to choose to *become* anything, since it is only what he freely chooses to *do* which determines what he is. But Sartre, notoriously, also wrote, in *Being and Nothingness*, that man was a useless passion; and this meant that he necessarily aimed for something which was contradictory, and could therefore never be attained. He necessarily hated and feared the hollowness within himself, which was the consequence of his having no essence; he felt anguish at the freedom with which he was burdened, and he longed to evade it, and to become a thing, subject to none but causal laws, and determined by its essence. He longed in fact to be a thing, but a human thing, and this was impossible.

But if it was supposed by Sartre that people had necessarily to adopt this particular attitude to themselves and their life, how was it possible for him to accept, at the same time, the Existentialist doctrine of total freedom? Not only does he say that freedom is a case of all or nothing; one must be totally free or not free at all; but he also seems to claim that it is intuitively obvious that man is free; indeed that the concept of human action entails the concept of freedom. And yet he regards men as bound, by an apparently ineluctable necessity, to aim at certain (gloomily impossible) ends. The question at issue, then, is simply this: was Sartre or was he not a defender of the existence of free will? Did he or did he not, in his Existentialist phase, think of free choice as an illusion?

To this simple question I shall argue that there is a relatively simple answer, namely that Sartre was confused, and sometimes believed himself to have solved the problem of freedom, but at other times did not. Particularly I shall argue that he was over-impressed by one phenomenon, which he took to be a fact, namely, that the human imagination at least is free.

We must examine in turn the two conflicting views with which we started, first, that all choice is free, and second, that people are bound to choose in a certain way, because of what they, all of them, necessarily aim at. Both items of this pair of statements can be derived from the Existentialist theory of the nature of consciousness. There is, according to this theory, an absolute distinction between conscious and unconscious things. Unconscious beings are essentially whatever they are; they can, in principle, be totally explained, and their behaviour totally predicted by reference to their nature and function. Given sufficient knowledge and ingenuity, one could predict everything that could possibly happen to such a being, in accordance with causal laws. Conscious beings, on the other hand, are characterised by not only being aware of other objects in the world, but by being at the same time always aware of themselves. They are Beings-For-Themselves. Consciousness is, by definition, directed onto an object: but its most important feature is that it is directed at one and the same time upon *two* objects, itself and something else. There is at the least a minimal self-consciousness which accompanies all other awareness whatever. The perceiving man does not think of himself as an object of his own attention (or does not necessarily do so). But he is aware of himself, none the less, as that self who is perceiving. This feature of consciousness carries with it the consequence that at any moment of perception in the world, the perceiving subject is aware that he is different from what he is perceiving. The distinction between subject and object is made immediately. He therefore knows that apart from exceptional cases of introspection, he is not what he perceives. The suggestion then is that a negative judgment enters into perception immediately and necessarily, and there could be no perception without it, or rather no consciousness without it. But the negative judgment does not consist only in the subject's saying 'I am not the object I perceive'. It goes further. The fact that the perceiving conscious subject is in this way set at a distance from the object of his perception means that he is in a position to raise questions about it.

It seems fairly plain that in Sartre's view consciousness is coextensive with the use of language. A language-user not only names the object before him, but describes it, and can raise a question as to whether his description is right or wrong. If he says of an object that it is sweet, he is therefore capable of entertaining certain reflections, 'Is it *really* sweet?' 'How else should I describe it?' 'At least I can say that it is not sour.' Sartre quotes from Spinoza in support of the view that every specification of an object entails negation. If we are prepared to identify being conscious with being able to use some language, then there is great plausibility in the theory that consciousness entails the power to form negative judgments.

But it is this combination of self-awareness with negative judgment that determines what it is that conscious beings must necessarily aim for. To be conscious is to be aware that whatever one may say of oneself is not completely true. One is conscious that, though other people may describe one, from the outside, as of a particular kind, this is not a *proper* or *complete* description, simply because one has possibilities . . . other things may become true of one at any time.

It is difficult to separate empirical from metaphysical statement at this point, as so often in Sartre. On the one hand, he seems to be calling attention to the psychological fact that we never feel that anyone's version, or even our own version, of our character is complete. We can happily say of someone else, 'he is jealous' or 'he was too tired to go on', but it never seems that we ourselves are properly or completely described by such statements. Sartre is particularly concerned with the difference, at an empirical level, between the things we say of other people, or they say of us, and our own version of ourselves. But on the other hand he is also saying that it is of the nature of self-conscious Beings-For-Themselves to be aware of their own possibilities and to be aware that whatever they are, they are not that thing completely. The only way to specify a conscious being is by his acts. But one does not act unless one has a project, unless, that is, one can see that something is *not yet true* which might be true, or that some state of affairs is *not* as it conceivably *could be*. Into the notion of the project itself, therefore, the negative judgment enters as an essential element.

In order to act, therefore, a conscious being must see that he is not yet anything, and he must attempt to become something determinate, a tidy describable object, through his actions. This, then, is the complex source of the 'useless passion'. It is a project to *be* something or other completely, so that one could be properly and fully described as something or other. Going with this fundamental project, there is also a sense of fear, that if one did become thing-like one would lose one's whole identity, that one would, in short, lose one's consciousness. The only way to be completely thing-like is to be a corpse. So one is necessarily liable to be overcome by loathing for the mode of being of things, their actual glutinous, uncontrollable, unmanageable existence. This attitude, along with the fundamental project, is, according to

Sartre, written into the nature of consciousness. There is no freedom from such aims nor from such attitudes.

But the concept of free choice is also built into the idea of consciousness in just this very aspect, that consciousness can frame negative judgments. A man is a physical object, as well as a consciousness, and this means that he exists in space and time. His existence consists in actions which take place in time, and, being also conscious, he is aware of a future for himself in every act which he performs. Now thinking of the future is itself thinking of a state of affairs which is *not yet actual*. Therefore any intentional act is motivated by the negative judgment that something or other is not yet true, and could be made true. Sartre appears to think that this possibility of envisaging a future is identical with, or is an important part of, the imagination. And he also holds that a man is entirely free to envisage anything in any way that he wishes, simply because this envisaging is negative. It consists in forming an image, or of otherwise thinking, of what *is not*, and this is unlimited. Thus, in the view of Sartre, a man must be capable of intentional action if he is conscious at all; and being capable of intentional action means being capable of freely forming a project, of envisaging any future whatever, as long as it is different from the present.

In examining this part of the theory, two questions arise. First, has Sartre shown that the imagination, working as it does through the concept of non-existence, is completely free? and second, if he had shown that, would that have had the consequence he thought it had for human *action*? To put the question another way: would the fact, if it were one, that the imagination is free, entail that action is so? Could one not be bound by necessity in such a way that one *could* not put one's imagined projects into practice?

The difficulty in answering the first question is that, in *The Psychology of the Imagination*, in which Sartre discusses the imagination in the greatest detail, it is genuinely unclear exactly what he thinks the function of the imagination is, and why he thinks it must be free. I may, he says, either conceive of a fictitious object, a golden mountain, for example, or envisage it. If I conceive of it I merely conjoin in my thoughts the property of being mountainous with that of being golden. But if I actually imagine or envisage the golden mountain, then I must first *decide* that this is what I will do, and then begin to think of the golden mountain in a new way. I have no physical representation of the mountain, no photograph or picture, nor do I necessarily have a perception of a real mountain which I try to think of as golden when it is not. So how do I think of it? Sartre seems to say that, though there can exist no such thing as a mental image in the mind, yet I do form a kind of picture, which is an *analogical representation* of the golden mountain. There is some content of the mind, at the moment of imagining, which I take to be significant of, or to stand for, the golden mountain. He says, 'We can conclude that the act of imagining envisages an absent or non-existent object in its corporality through a physical or psychical content, which is given, not for its own sake, but only as an analogical representation of the object envisaged.' It does not matter whether we think of absent or past or future objects by means of actual pictures or by means of images. Whatever we use has no importance of its own, and images literally have no independent existence of their own, apart from their *function* of representation or analogy. So, in being imaginatively aware of a future condition which does not yet exist but which, let us say, I should like to bring into being, I know that what I am aware of is *nothing*. Imagination just is the grasping and positing of what is not. The image carries its non-existence with it, as its essence. Moreover, we know an image for what it is, because, Sartre says, there is nothing in the image except what we put into it ourselves. We cannot be taken by surprise by an image, we cannot learn anything new from it; it is simply what we have made it to be, and it has the meaning, no more and no less, that we have endowed it with.

There is a different, and perhaps more interesting, kind of imagining, in which we can see an existent object in the world, and imagine it to be other than it is. Here, as in the first case, we deliberately decide to interpret the existent object in a certain way, to give it particular significance. Sartre has an elaborate example in *The Psychology of the Imagination* of this kind of imagining. He discusses our understanding of impersonation. He sets the scene in a theatre, where there is an act consisting of Franconay impersonating Maurice Chevalier. The representation, in such a case, is bound to be very approximate: Franconay is not trying to make us think that she *is* Maurice Chevalier, in any literal sense. Rather, she is trying to make us see Maurice Chevalier, through the medium of herself; to see her as Maurice Chevalier. The task of consciousness is to answer the question of whom she is impersonating, and 'to realise the object of the impersonation as an image, through the person imitating'. When the first question is answered, and we realise, perhaps from the hat or the stick, that

Maurice Chevalier is intended, then we deliberately change our mode of awareness of Franconay herself. We begin to see her vaguely, as a kind of opaque background for what we mean to see, but know is not there, namely for Maurice Chevalier. In the end, we begin to experience emotions connected, not with Franconay, but with the object of the impersonation, and then the trick is complete; we are fully imagining her as she intends that we should. Going with this condition of imagination, there is, Sartre says, a sense of spontaneity or freedom, because we realise that it is open to us to see the person on the stage in either of two ways, or in both ways at once. We can see her as we choose. Sartre himself likens the imaginative seeing of one thing as significant of another, to the seeing of trick pictures, like Wittgenstein's Duck-Rabbit. Once you know that it is a trick picture, then by a deliberate choice, you can see either as a duck or as a rabbit. In seeing things in the world, or in our mind's eye, as significant, we exercise the same kind of choice. They may signify for us one thing or another. We are free to decide upon the significance.

Now the bearing of this imaginative envisaging upon our actions is clear. If we see our future as conspicuously lacking something, then this lack becomes a motive to us for action. But we may always decide how to see the future, whether as lacking one thing or another. It is here that our freedom, according to Sartre, is absolute. In *Being and Nothingness* he argues that the freedom of the imagination consists in the fact that it freely withdraws itself from the real, and chooses to envisage the possible or the ideal. An ideal state is always proposed as a negation of an existent state, and the act of disengaging oneself from one's present moment in time to envisage a future in one of an infinite number of possible ways is a free act. However, he merely *states* that this act is free.

In the end, the argument that the imagination is free seems to turn on the subjective sense that it is so. There seems to be no serious reason, and certainly none is offered by Sartre, against saying that we are conditioned or determined to envisage the future as we do by our situation, or our past experience or the way we have been brought up.

Sartre appears to be beguiled by the fact that if I consciously think, for example, that the walls of my room might one day be painted green, I am also capable of realising that they might be painted red instead. The fact that I may envisage either green or red, and that *I* know that I may, is the root of the idea that the imagination is free. To go back, he believes that if I say to myself 'My walls need not always be the colour they are now' this is the first, and negative, step in the deliberate detachment of myself from the bare contemplation of things as they are. This is the basic freedom of imagination. Consciousness of the present, in his sense of the word (with self-consciousness as part of it), and imagination of the future are both incomplete notions without the notion of freedom as part of them. The trouble with this part of the argument is that Sartre presents a plausible picture of consciousness, and offers an analysis of it as containing freedom. But such plausibility does not really attain the status of a proof.

Turning now to the second question proposed above, what are we to say is the connexion between the alleged freedom of the imagination and man's freedom in general? As we have seen, Sartre regards freedom, plausibly enough, as a matter of all or nothing. So, in a sense, to show that one area of human activity or thought is free should be enough to prove that the whole is so. But Sartre also wishes to assert a positive connexion between imagination and action, through the concept of motive. We are never motivated to act, he says, by the mere facts of a case, but only by the facts as seen and interpreted by ourselves. We are able to interpret facts just because we are able imaginatively to envisage a future in which these facts do not obtain. It is this imagination of an ideal future which changes our present state into a 'situation', in which we can form a project of action. Thus, if I am too cold, and cannot envisage the possibility of getting warm, I do nothing. But the moment that I envisage a future in which I am warm, I experience my present cold as an unbearable *situation*, and form a definite project of action. I interpret the present as unbearable just because I can grasp imaginatively the possibility of getting another blanket for my bed. Sartre says, in *Being and Nothingness*, 'It is by fleeing a situation towards our possibility of changing it that we organise this situation into complexes of causes and motives.' It is impossible to separate the motive from the action: the envisaging the future, the interpreting the present as deficient and unbearable, the organisation of the situation in the light of my imagined ideal, all these aspects must be taken together as the complete act. And if the part which the imagination plays in framing the whole project is shown to be free, it follows that the act as a whole is free. This is the argument.

It cannot be too strongly emphasised that what Sartre is saying we are free to do, is to interpret our position in the world and in time in a particular light (just as we are free to interpret the trick picture as either a duck or a rabbit). We need not go in for conscious deliberation in order to be taken to be acting freely. Indeed, often our acts or semi-acts appear un-thought-out and spontaneous, but are nevertheless free in this particular sense. For, according to Sartre, even what we *feel* in a particular situation is determined by the meaning we attach to that situation, and therefore ultimately to our detachment from it and description of it. Emotion, he thought, though it may certainly be said to overwhelm us, is nevertheless our *chosen way of behaving* in a situation, envisaged by us in a certain light. If I suffer acute panic fear in some situation, so that I become incapable of coherent thought or action, nevertheless there is a sense in which I freely adopted this attitude and decided that rational solutions were impossible for me, so that I must have recourse to magic, to the pretence that by blotting out the horrors before me by paralysing myself, I should somehow magic them out of existence. I could have interpreted the possibilities otherwise, and not experienced the panic.

Sartre is not saying that we can always bring about that which we envisage, nor that we are not often frustrated in our actions by circumstances which we did not choose and cannot change. He is saying two things: one is that wherever we do act, we act freely according to a chosen way of interpreting our situation and future; the second is that our freedom does in fact extend over a great deal more of our life than we are sometimes prepared to accept. (We may find freedom terrifying or burdensome, and by numerous devices of bad faith pretend to be bound when we are not.) Whether he is thinking of fully-fledged acts, interventions in the ordinary world of things to change the way they are, or whether he is thinking of the vestigial acts which constitute emotions, the dependence on the imagination is the same. The imagination is needed to set the agent apart from the facts, to turn his position into a *situation* and to enable him to envisage a project in the face of it. Therefore the degree to which Sartre has succeeded in showing that we are free depends on the degree to which he can be thought to have *proved* that the imagination is free. And this, in my opinion, he has failed to do.

However that may be, he himself certainly held that the imagination was free and that therefore human action was so. And if he thought this, then we are still left with the contradiction with which we started. How can he assert both that individual human projects are totally free, and also that the overriding human project – 'the original project' – is necessarily identical for all of us, and is something from which we cannot escape? The fundamental human project is to become integrated into the world and thing-like . . . to escape from the absolutely general and inevitable situation, which is that of being always open to a new future. The ideal is the ideal of simple, unambiguous *being*, such as can be completely described as essentially this or that. Men realise their ambiguous situation because they are always self-conscious, and therefore always aware that they are *not* either their future selves, their past selves, or the objects in their world. Does the inevitability of forming such an overriding project destroy the possibility of free choice in the particular projects which fall under it?

Now it might be thought that Sartre is propounding a very general truth about human nature, namely that people always desire to escape from their human predicament. If this were all that he was doing, then, though the status of this axiom would be ambiguous, at least the ambiguity would be philosophically familiar. For example, whatever philosophers may think of Mill's axiom that people desire only pleasure, they have not tended to think that to accept such an axiom destroys the possibility of asserting freedom of choice. There are, notoriously, different ways of interpreting Mill's axiom: he says that questions of ultimate ends are not susceptible of proof; but he also says that pleasure is the only thing which is desirable, and that this means that it is the only thing which people in fact desire. To some it has seemed that he is uttering a tautology, and is saying that whatever people desire, they desire under the heading of pleasure. It would be out of place to discuss the various interpretations here; but there is an analogy between Mill's axiom and Sartre's statement of the original project. For Sartre speaks of all particular projects as being undertaken, as it were, under the shadow of the original project; and it could be argued that, though a man might not be immediately aware that what he had decided to do was part of his hopeless passion to emancipate himself from his human predicament, yet he could be brought to view it in that light, if he had his eyes opened to what that predicament was. It is plain that Sartre thought that everyone *has* formed the initial project whether they know that they have or not; and that they could come to see how all their acts and all their feelings and attitudes stem from it, by means of Existential Psychoanalysis. Thus, for example, if a man felt vaguely horrified by pitch or treacle, he could have it explained to him that the horror of the viscous was inevitable, given his initial wish to be in complete control of his environment, and not threatened with extinction by the existence of things which, if they gained control of him, would reduce him to mindless and shapeless chaos. Thus the feeling of disgust at the stickiness of honey on one's fingers, or the horror of any sucking seething mud or marsh, could be interpreted as arising out of, or as reaffirming, the original project, to be something definite, hard and predictable, a thing, yet still in control of other things. Sartre thought that this kind of psychoanalysis of things could in principle be used to explain the particular likes and dislikes of an individual person. It would explain all his particular interpretations in the light of the original project. On this view of the matter, Sartre would seem to be saying not so much that an individual inevitably likes or dislikes, flees or pursues, the things he does, as that one can *understand* his likes and dislikes, his flights and pursuits, if one understands something more general which is true of all men.

This then would be like Mill's suggestion that one could understand all established rules of morality if one only understood that the principle from which they were derived and which they each of them reasserted was the Principle of Utility, to which we are supposedly committed by the axiom that we desire nothing except pleasure. The acceptance of the axiom does not enable people's choices to be predicted in other than very simple cases. But it does tend to enable us to *interpret* people's choice in a particular way.

If Sartre were asserting, in his assertion of the original project, merely a very well-established generalisation about people; or alternatively if he were propounding a way of describing human choices, of classifying human motives which he thought would prove illuminating, then we might dismiss the suggestion that the original project limited human freedom, and we might acquit Sartre of the charge of self-contradiction. But unfortunately it is not really possible to hold that this is all he is saying, though exactly what more he is saying is hard to make clear.

The fact is that Sartre has a metaphysical, and not merely an empirically psychological, theory on his hands. I take a metaphysical theory to be a theory which offers an account of the totality of what there is. Within such a theory, it may well be that the human being has a place, it may even be true, as I suspect it is for Sartre, that the human part of the account is the most interesting, or even forms the goal towards which all the rest of the account is directed. But it does not form the whole of the theory by itself, and the place of the human in the rest of being must essentially be derived, not from empirical considerations of what human beings are like, or of what generally goes on in the world, but from the more general consideration of being itself.

It would be absurd to think of Sartre's whole plan in *Being and Nothingness* as utterly different from Heidegger's, who was confessedly concerned with the *Dasein*, the Human Being in the World, only as a part of the totality of Being. Sartre, it is true, did not write into *Being and Nothingness* quite the grandiose claims that Heidegger made for *Being and Time*. Nevertheless, he is clearly concerned to divide the whole of existence into two and only two kinds, Beings-in-Themselves and Beings-for-Themselves or conscious beings. And this fact, that there is consciousness, as much for him as for Heidegger, constitutes the essence of the world, from which all explanations of it must flow. It is not a mere stylistic accident, therefore, that Sartre derives the idea of the original project from the nature of consciousness itself, consciousness which forms one of the unchangeable ultimate elements in the world. If consciousness as such is to be defined as that which necessarily undertakes the impossible task ascribed to it, then this is supposed to constitute a genuine overriding necessity. If such metaphysical theorising is possible at all, then it carries with it the necessity, above all others, of internal consistency. And it would be inconsistent to say that conscious beings could choose freely to go in whatever direction they liked. They are bound by their nature and the nature of the totality of things.

Now it may be said that the enemy of freedom is causation, and that Sartre nowhere suggests that the original project *causes* a man to choose in this way rather than that. And it is perfectly true that he does not. Not only so, but he insists over and over again that a man's situation does not *cause* him to act, and that no facts of any kind could cause him to act. Moreover his main criticism of Freud is based on the grounds that, according to Freud, a man is caused by his past to behave in a certain way in the future, and this Sartre holds to be nonsensical. It is because Sartre believed himself to have totally separated the concept of action from the concept of causation that he at times seems to have believed himself to have solved the problem of the freedom of the will, and to have *shown* that man is free.

But in fact Sartre could not really accommodate freedom with the different notion of total explicability, any more than Descartes or Spinoza could. Iris Murdoch justly described Sartre as a rationalist: his rationalism consisted not, obviously, in a belief in human reason, but in a belief that some *one total* account of the world was possible (and this in spite of his disclaiming the possibility, in another mood, of 'adopting the standpoint of the whole'). If the world is totally explicable, then it must work according to laws which can in principle be stated. The laws governing the world, in Sartre's early philosophy, were those laws which enabled him to distinguish Beings-in-Themselves from Beings-for-Themselves, unconscious from conscious beings.

He himself thought that to say that a man was not caused to act, but chose to act according to his own interpretation of his possibilities in a given situation, entitled him to say this man was free. For he could always claim, on any particular occasion, that another interpretation of the situation was possible. Thus if a man flung down his rucksack, saying that the road was too steep, and he was too tired to go on, Sartre could tell him that he himself had chosen to regard the road as steep, and had chosen to experience his exhaustion in a particular way, namely as unbearable. He *need not* have treated any of the phenomena in the particular way he did. Therefore he cannot evade responsibility for his failure to climb the hill. Whatever the situation, Sartre can always say that a man has no one but himself to blame. Even if he is complaining that he is ugly or that his legs are too short, Sartre will tell him that he was free to regard his appearance as an asset, or his legs as of the right length for the kind of person he had, or could have, decided to be. Sartre's man is quite certainly free, if freedom is to mean the shouldering of responsibility for what becomes of him. But nevertheless, the more his man comes to understand his own situation, the more he comes to realise why he has made the decisions he has, and why he feels as he does about particular aspects of his world; and the more he will realise that, being human, he cannot ultimately change the direction in which his desires and aspirations lead him.

It is very difficult, in the end, to distinguish Sartre's position from Spinoza's. The most freedom that a man can hope for is to realise what his position is. He can work through the stage of bad faith, and face the responsibilities he has, for what they are. But a further step in his understanding must lead him to the knowledge of necessity. He must realise that, being human, he is committed to the original human project, ineluctable, and, in the last resort, futile.

Hampshire on
freedom

John Watling

Hampshire on freedom

There are certain states, Stuart Hampshire argues in his book *Freedom of the Individual* (*F.I.*), which are peculiar to human beings and which distinguish them from other animals and from inanimate things. He seeks, on the one hand, to show that very many human states either are, or presuppose, states of this essentially human kind, and, on the other, to isolate one feature they all share in which lies their essentially human character. The feature he isolates is that of involving belief, or, as he puts it, being to a greater or a lesser degree saturated with belief. Belief must be understood to include, not only belief that certain things are true, but also belief that certain things are right. He investigates the explanation of beliefs and belief-saturated states, finding that it cannot always lie in their causes. Since, if such states always had causes, their explanation would always lie in those causes, determinism cannot be true. I want to examine this argument but, before I go on to take up the various steps separately, I must consider some rather puzzling remarks which Hampshire himself makes about the scope of its conclusion.

Hampshire does not fail to take note of the behaviourist objection to such arguments as this, that such concepts as belief, and hence all concepts of those states which he takes to be peculiar to human beings, are confused and unfit to enter into science, and should be discarded. If this behaviourist view were correct, it would discredit the premises of his argument. He claims, I think, to argue against the possibility of rejecting non-behaviourist concepts. 'For these reasons a thesis of determinism, which entails that the commonplace scheme of explanation of conduct is replaceable by a neutral vocabulary of natural law, seems to me unacceptable.' (*F.I.*, p. 111.) However, the arguments he refers to come very close to assuming their legitimacy. They tell against the possibility of causal explanation of states involving belief rather than against the possibility that there are no such states. It is true that some of the premises of these arguments concern language, asserting 'a normative element in first person present and future tense statements about some states of mind', not concepts, but it is not true that all the premises are of this kind. One concerns the explanation of desires. Even those of which it is true only doubtfully avoid assuming the legitimacy of non-behaviourist concepts, such as regret, with which the pieces of language under discussion are ordinarily taken to be concerned. In the light of this fact, that in general Hampshire's arguments assume the legitimacy of non-behaviourist concepts, using that basis to discuss their nature and their explanation, his next remark is a very puzzling one. 'But it is possible that some other thesis of determinism, which does not claim that a neutral vocabulary of natural law might "replace" the existing vocabulary, might be untouched by the arguments of these lectures.' (*Loc. cit.*) If this means that he has refuted behaviourism but may not have refuted a thesis of determinism which does not imply behaviourism, then it is puzzling, not only in the light of the actual nature of his arguments, but because of the suggestion that the refutation of a thesis which entails, but is not entailed by, determinism is a refutation of a form of determinism. If it were, the refutation of a form of determinism would be no difficult task. It would be sufficient to refute some proposition with which behaviourism might be conjoined. I do not think, therefore, that this straightforward interpretation can be what Hampshire intends. I think the form of determinism which he allows that he may not have refuted would be one which did imply behaviourism and did reject the concepts of belief and desire together with the scheme of explanation which they permit. What it would not do is reject the vocabulary of beliefs and desires; it would find some explanation, other than the legitimacy of the concepts of belief and desire, for the facts about language in its first person present uses to which Hampshire points. It would, in short, find another explanation of the functioning of the language in which we seem to speak of mental states. If this is his admission, then it is an admission of something to which I have pointed, that his argument from facts about language to the conclusion that the non-behaviourist concepts are legitimate is not completely cogent. It is, therefore, not an admission that his conclusion is limited in scope, but that his proof of it lacks rigour at one point. If it can be strengthened at that point, or if the justifiability of the non-behaviourist concepts can be assumed, then his arguments establish that determinism is false. If neither of these things can be done, then his arguments do not tell against any form of determinism at all.

Hampshire begins his book by arguing for a logical distinction between the powers of human beings and other animals, on the one hand, and the powers of inanimate things, on the other. The difference most relevant to his later argument lies in this: it may be true of a human being or animal that he had the power to do something but did not wish to do it, whereas this cannot be true of an inanimate thing. Someone who claims that *aqua regia* has the power to dissolve gold cannot excuse failure by claiming that it could have but on this occasion didn't want to. Hampshire would analyse the proposition that *aqua regia* has the power to dissolve gold as 'If gold is placed in *aqua regia*, then it dissolves'; he would not analyse the proposition that men have the power of locomotion as 'If a man is put in one place, then he will move to another'. I think Hampshire makes his case. Perhaps someone might claim that the powers are the same, but that *aqua regia* lacks the desire or the ability to inhibit its power. This claim would not be very plausible but, so far as Hampshire's case against determinism goes, there is no need to refute it. Hampshire holds that the fact that human beings have powers entails that they have wishes and desires, and even if it did not entail that it would certainly force it upon our attention.

Hampshire goes on to argue for a distinction between desires which he believes to have important consequences concerning their explanation and also to distinguish those which are peculiar to human beings from those which may exist in an animal. The distinction lies between those desires which are mediated by a description and those which are not. He says of those desires which are not mediated by a description that they terminate in their objects. I think that his discussion leaves considerable doubt about what distinction he intends. There are three possibilities, two of which cannot, I think, be his intention, while the third, which probably is what he intends, is not a distinction between desires at all. He introduces the distinction by means of an example concerning a man who 'wants to buy the most expensive picture in the gallery'. A man of whom this is true might want to buy whatever picture is most expensive or he might want a picture which happens to be the most expensive.

> In the second case, his desire to buy the picture is unmediated by this, or by any other, description of the picture: in the first case the desire to buy the picture is mediated by the description, which is essential to the desire, and specifies the exact nature of the desire. (*F.I.*, p. 46.)

Before distinguishing these two cases Hampshire declares that the original sentence is not ambiguous, although there are two or more states of affairs which it might represent. Certainly, the sentence is not ambiguous between the two cases Hampshire describes. In both these cases the man wants to buy a particular picture; the difference is that in one of them his reason for wanting to do so, if he has one, is not specified, while in the other it is. The sentence *is* ambiguous between an interpretation which implies that the man wants to buy any picture if it is the most expensive, but does not imply that there is a particular picture which he wants to buy, and one which implies that he wants to buy a particular picture, but does not imply that he has any reason for wanting to do so. Where Hampshire recognises two possibilities, there are in fact three. The sentence is ambiguous between two of them, but not between the two he recognises. There is no doubt that Hampshire would not regard the assertion that a man wants to do a particular thing as implying that he has a desire mediated by a description, but which of the other two possibilities exemplifies description-mediated desires? Are they desires in which a particular thing is desired for a reason, or are they desires, not for a particular thing, but for something of a certain kind?

Since what Hampshire says, for example on page 46, strongly suggests that he intends to distinguish between two types of desire, and since the distinction between desires for particular things and desires for something of a certain kind is a distinction between two types of desire, while that between desires for which a person has reasons and desires for which he has none is not, it might seem that by description-mediated desires he intends desires for something of a certain kind. However, that interpretation cannot survive the fact that Hampshire holds that description-mediated desires are peculiar to human beings. Now, if desires are to be attributed to animals at all, desires for things of a certain kind must be attributed to them. If horses have desires, then among them is the desire for grass. Perhaps someone might admit that horses have desires but doubt whether they ever desire particular fields of grass, or particular tufts of grass, but that they sometimes have the desire for anything if it is grass he could not doubt. Such a person would have to credit horses with the power to recognise something as being of the kind *grass*, although he might be able to do this without also crediting them with thoughts or beliefs. It is true that Hampshire says: 'When I am starving, my desire to eat does not depend for its existence on any particular conception that I have of this activity: it depends solely on my stomach', but I think that he must intend that when I desire to eat I do so, not for a reason, but because of the state of my stomach. He can hardly intend that the desire to eat is not a desire for something of a certain kind. Neither people nor horses normally cram things indiscriminately down their gullets and leave it to their stomachs to reject what is indigestible. Hampshire asserts that animals cannot have quixotic desires, which may be true, but a quixotic desire to perform an action is not characterised, as he says it is, by being one which depends upon a conception of that action: it is, rather, one which depends on certain special kinds of conception. The desire to perform an action which befits a gentleman, or to perform an action which befits some other ideal, is a quixotic desire.

Except for the fact that desires in which a particular thing is desired for a reason do not constitute a type – since the very same desire might have been entertained without a reason – such desires fit fairly well with what Hampshire requires of description-mediated desires. Obviously the description which mediates such a desire for a particular thing contains the person's reasons for desiring that thing. Again, such desires are dependent upon a thought or, better, upon a belief. The man who desires a particular picture because it is the most expensive would not want it if he did not believe it to be the most expensive. However, it is not quite obvious that a desire in which a particular thing is desired for a reason is belief-dependent. A person who held that a horse might want the grass in a particular field because it was grass, but who hesitated to attribute beliefs to horses, might argue that the horse's desire for that particular grass was dependent, not upon his belief that it was grass, but rather upon the fact that it was grass, or the fact that it resembled grass in being green and having slender blades. The horse's desire for the particular tuft of grass, like the man's for the particular picture, arises out of his desire for something of a certain kind. However, if this more mechanical view of the horse is correct, his desire for the tuft of grass would not be a belief-dependent desire. In this way, a desire might be one in which a particular thing was desired for a reason, without being a belief-dependent desire and without being peculiar to human beings.

Although I think that when he speaks of description-mediated desires Hampshire does intend desires in which particular things are desired for reasons, I think that he would not have held that they were peculiar to human beings, nor that they posed particular problems for determinism, unless he had confused them with desires of another kind, those which have the property of being belief-saturated. He defines this property later in the book, but the fact that he also uses the analogous term 'thought-impregnated' for those desires which are mediated by a description suggests that he held the two properties to be related. Hampshire argues that a person who does not believe an action of his to have been mistaken does not regret that action. I think he is right. This point could be put by saying that, if he had not believed the action to have been mistaken, he would not have regretted it. Put like this, the wish of the person with a regret seems to be belief-dependent in the same way as the desire of the person who wants a particular picture because it is the most expensive in the gallery: if the latter had not believed the picture to be the most expensive, he would not have wanted it. However, the similarity is illusory. In the case of regret, the wish entails the belief. In the case of the desire for the picture, the desire depends for its existence upon the belief in some non-logical fashion. The fact that a person desires any picture if it is of a certain kind has neither of these properties. It neither entails, nor is dependent upon, a belief. The fact that a particular picture was desired for a certain reason goes beyond the fact that it was desired. Perhaps that fact entails a belief, but the example of the horse wanting the grass in a particular field makes the entailment questionable.

Hampshire's case against determinism is brought out very clearly by the distinction between belief-dependent and belief-saturated states. A person may have a reason for a belief-dependent desire without having a reason for any belief which he holds. A person who has a reason for a belief-saturated desire has a reason for the belief which that desire involves. Now, perhaps a person who has a reason for a belief may have a reason for it in just the same way as he might have a reason for a state which is not, and does not involve, a belief. He might desire comfort and believe that in that belief he could find it. However, whether or not that is possible, he may have a reason of another kind. He may hold some proposition to be true and to imply the proposition he believes. Hampshire contends that a belief cannot both be held for such a reason and have a causal explanation. This is his case against determinism.

He argues for this contention from a number of observations concerning belief, many of them contrasts between a person's attitude towards his own present beliefs, on the one hand, and his attitude to his own past beliefs, or to the beliefs of other people, on the other. However, the explanations Hampshire offers of these contrasts do not seem to me to explain them, and their true explanation, although it does have the consequence that a person's reasons for his beliefs must be reasons for the truth of what he believes, does not have the consequence that the beliefs of such a person do not have a causal explanation. I will consider four of Hampshire's contrasts. They are linked with one another.

Hampshire's first observation is that a person's knowledge of his own present belief, or of the belief he is about to arrive at, cannot be what he calls inductive. That is, it cannot be that he infers what his beliefs are, or are about to become, from states of his environment, or from other states of himself, on the basis of scientific generalisations. Rather, his knowledge concerning his present beliefs lies in the fact that he adopts those beliefs. This is the distinction between two kinds of knowledge which Hampshire first introduces concerning a person's knowledge of his own intentions. This, he likewise holds, is not of the inductive kind. It is true that he is uncertain how closely the two kinds of knowledge resemble one another. On the one hand, he insists that both kinds of knowledge provide guides to the truth: someone who waits for me to decide what I will do waits for knowledge to be imparted to him. On the other hand, he holds that a person who formulates his intentions, or his beliefs, is not primarily, or principally, attempting to give the correct answer to the questions what will he do, or what does he believe, nor are his claims to knowledge of his own future conduct to be assessed as correct or incorrect by the test of correspondence with fact. This admits a very great distinction between the two kinds of knowledge. Indeed, it comes very close to admitting that non-inductive knowledge is not knowledge at all. If a claim to knowledge is not disallowed upon the discovery that what is claimed to be known is false, then it is not treated as a claim to knowledge. It is difficult to interpret Hampshire's contention that there is non-inductive knowledge when he admits that it is a kind of knowledge in which a person can know what is not true.

Hampshire's case for supposing, in the face of this fact, that non-inductive knowledge is a kind of knowledge, and for supposing it impossible that a person should have inductive knowledge of his own present beliefs and intentions, lies in his view that when a person comes to know, from a consideration of the matter, what he ought to believe and what he ought to do, then he comes to know what he does believe and what he will do.

'If I know that I can go, or not go, as I choose, and if I know that I have every reason for going and no reason not to go, and therefore that it would be an entire mistake not to go, then I know that I shall go.' This hypothetical proposition, which relates a belief about mistake in action to a belief about the future course of events, ought surely to be regarded as mysterious, as the meeting-place of the two kinds of knowledge. How can my belief about the future be grounded upon my belief about the mistakenness of a course of action? (*F.I.*, p. 73.)

Hampshire implies that it can be so grounded. Of course, this is a rather different kind of non-inductive knowledge from that which he distinguished at first. It is knowledge a person has in virtue of knowing what he ought to believe or do, not knowledge which he has merely in virtue of having formed a belief about what he ought to believe or do. Nevertheless, this is Hampshire's reason for holding that there is non-inductive knowledge and that it is incompatible with inductive knowledge. However, although, if a person could have non-inductive knowledge of this kind, he would have knowledge (whereas non-inductive knowledge as first described is dubiously knowledge at all), there is serious doubt about whether it exists. If this were the kind of non-inductive knowledge a person had of his own beliefs and actions, then it would be correct to argue: he didn't know what he believed, or what he would do, because he had formed a mistaken, although firm, opinion of what he ought to believe or do. This argument is obviously invalid.

Hampshire's second observation concerning belief would, if true, support the existence of non-inductive knowledge of the second, genuine, kind. It is that, for a person himself, the question 'What do I believe?' is identical with 'What ought I to believe?' and the question 'What shall I do?' almost identical with 'What ought I to do?' This is his contention that there is a normative element in first person present tense statements about states of mind such as belief. It is closely related to another of his contentions, that the sentence 'I believe that P' is used to assert that P, so that the question 'Do I believe that P?' is, for the person who asks it, identical to the question 'Is P true?' If these identities held, then when, in forming my beliefs and intentions, I address myself to the questions 'What ought I to believe?' and 'What ought I to do?', I would be addressing myself to the questions 'What do I believe?' and 'What shall I do?' It would follow that if I came to know the answer to the former questions, then I would come to know the answer to the latter. However, this observation offers no support to the existence of non-inductive knowledge of a genuine kind, since the identities do not hold. Although everyone supposes that he himself believes what he ought to believe, that he believes what is true, and, perhaps, that he is about to do what is the best thing for him to do, no one supposes it impossible that he himself believes what he ought not to believe, or believes what is not true, or is about to do what is not the best thing for him to do. Yet, if the identities held for him, he would regard these as impossibilities. This defence of the existence of non-inductive knowledge of a genuine kind, knowledge which would be incompatible with inductive knowledge, fails.

Of course, it is possible that non-inductive knowledge of the first kind, that which a person has if he has adopted a belief or decided on a course of action, is, even if none the less not knowledge, incompatible with inductive knowledge of what belief has been adopted, or what action will be taken. However, the truth seems to be that the search for non-inductive knowledge, which we make when we try to form an opinion, or decide on a course of action, is so different from the search for inductive knowledge, which we make when we try to discover what we believe, or what we will do, that it is impossible for anyone to carry on both of them at the same time. A person engaging in the former asks 'What ought I to believe?', 'Is P true?', 'What ought I to do?', 'Is X the best thing to do?' A person engaging in the latter asks 'What do I believe?', 'What will I do?' In deciding a question, or deciding upon a course of action, all information is welcome except the information that you will answer the question, or decide to act, in a particular way. I think it possible that these two purposes are incompatible, although I can think of no proof that they are. However, as I shall argue later, if the incompatibility between deciding and predicting arises only from the purpose a person must have in adopting a belief, then the existence of the incompatibility has consequences concerning the purpose a person has in forming a belief, but not concerning the explanation of that belief.

Hampshire's third observation is that, although a person may agree that his own past beliefs were imposed upon him, were 'formed, or changed, by factors other than evidence of truth', or that he was, in the past, 'saddled with a belief in the incredible', he cannot regard his own present beliefs in any of these ways. His fourth important observation is that a person must regard his beliefs as things which he is free to adopt or discard, but he cannot regard himself as able, or needing, to take steps to alter a belief, as he may do with any state of his which neither is, nor involves, a belief. It is because of this second feature that Hampshire calls belief and belief-saturated states active, in contrast to other states of himself which a person may set about modifying. The active states set a limit, although Hampshire does not explicitly say so, to what he calls the recessiveness of I. I may step back from a feeling that I have and try to remove it. I cannot do this to a belief.

Hampshire's explanation of both these observations is that a man could not count a state of his own which had been imposed upon him, or which was not formed by evidence of truth, or which he had tried to produce in himself, as a belief. 'If I now found myself discarding a so-called belief under some other influence than the appearance of falsehood, I would call in question my previous account of myself as having believed.' (*F.I.*, p. 85.) 'I must regard my own beliefs as formed in response to free enquiry, I could not otherwise count them as beliefs.' (*F.I.*, p. 87.) However, this cannot be an adequate explanation, since it makes no contrast between a person's attitudes to his past and to his present beliefs. (The former quotation, indeed, seems to suggest that there is no contrast and that the person would not even agree that he had held the belief. This runs quite counter to what Hampshire insists on elsewhere and must, I think, be a careless formulation.) If something formed other than by evidences of truth, or under causal influences, cannot be counted as a belief, then there cannot have been such beliefs of anyone at any time. If a person is prepared to agree that other people, and he himself at earlier times, held beliefs which were induced in them by subliminal suggestion, or influenced by their desires, then he cannot refuse to count his own present states as beliefs for that reason. It is not, in fact, clear that a person who comes to think that his belief has been induced in him, or is a symptom of paranoia, does come to doubt whether it is a belief. Rather, he calls in question the view he holds and perhaps abandons his belief in it. The examples by means of which Hampshire tries to show that people no longer count beliefs which they have come to suspect were induced in them as beliefs are loaded by the additional supposition that they no longer hold them. '. . . he still cannot say, "I believe that someone is following me", if he knows that this haunting thought is a symptom of paranoia and has no foundation in fact.' (*F.I.*, p. 76.)

The explanation of some of Hampshire's contrasts is so trivial that they cannot have important consequences concerning belief. 'He cannot find himself saddled with a belief in the incredible, as he may find himself saddled with an appetite for the unattainable, or with a fear of the harmless. He can only find that he *was* saddled with a belief in the incredible.' (*F.I.*, p. 76.) Surely this contrast arises only because it is a tautology that a person now believes what he now believes, while it is not a tautology that he now believes what he once believed. Of course a person cannot find himself saddled with a belief he finds incredible. Nor can he find himself saddled with an appetite for something he finds undesirable, or a fear of something he finds laughable. When, a little later, Hampshire moves beyond these tautological assertions he arrives at something which is not true. 'He cannot regard [a belief] as something that he happens to have, or as a fact about himself which he may deplore, but must accept.' (*F.I.*, p. 86.) This would be true only if a person could have no other reason for wishing that he did not hold a belief than the falsity of what he believed.

Not all of Hampshire's observations concerning belief require explanation. I want to make a suggestion which goes some way towards explaining those which do. I will approach it through a passage in which he expresses one of his contrasts.

> I may use some knowledge that I possess of entirely non-rational factors that influence beliefs in trying to change the beliefs of another man; but I cannot be in the position of trying to change my own beliefs in this way. I must regard my own beliefs as formed in response to free enquiry; I could not otherwise count them as beliefs. (*F.I.*, p. 87.)

I suggest that, in fact, a belief is necessarily the outcome of an enquiry, although not necessarily of a free enquiry, and that we recognise this both for our own beliefs and those of other people. This does not imply that in trying to change another person's beliefs by manipulating his hormone balance I am trying to do what it is logically impossible to do, for I may be trying to influence the results of his enquiry, not trying to prevent him making one. If, on the other hand, I tried to bring him to a belief in God by persuading him of the advantages of Pascal's wager, then I should be trying to do what is logically impossible. If he was persuaded, he would have turned away from an enquiry into whether God existed, so that nothing that resulted could be a belief. What I have suggested to be a necessary fact concerning beliefs does explain the contrast Hampshire makes, for a man who sets out to influence his own enquiry in a particular direction, perhaps towards a belief in the efficacy of a more belligerent policy by modifying his hormone balance, has abandoned enquiry. He has done so, not because his enquiry is under influence, but because he has *set out* to influence it in a particular direction. Of course, merely to set out to influence your enquiry by other means than the collection of and reflection upon evidence is not to abandon enquiry. A person may think that a change in some of his beliefs, he cannot quite see which, would clarify a whole problem. He may decide that a night's sleep, or a drink, will precipitate that change. To take such a step is not to abandon enquiry.

My suggestion explains, first, why a person cannot hold a belief for reasons other than reasons for the truth of the proposition in which it is a belief. Second, it explains the activity of belief, since it explains why a person can hold any belief he chooses to hold. This follows from the first point, since it could only appear to him that he could not hold a chosen belief if he could take causal steps to change his belief to that one, steps which might fail. But that would require that he had a purpose for changing it in that direction, and that purpose could only be one inconsistent with enquiry. If it were the only purpose consistent with enquiry, that of arriving at the truth, then he would already hold the belief. Third, it explains why, for the person asking them, the questions whether P is true and whether he should believe that P is true are identical. They are identical because the only reasons he can have for believing P are reasons for its truth. One person, however, may think, and try to bring it about, that another should believe what is not true. This identity is not the identity between 'Do I believe that P?' and 'Ought I to believe that P?' which Hampshire asserts, but that identity, I think, does not hold. My explanation recognises a normative element in enquiry, that is, in the formation of belief, but not in the description of it.

In this way those of Hampshire's observations about belief which are true can be explained. Since the explanation involves only that belief is the outcome of enquiry and that enquiry is an attempt to arrive at the truth, it has implications only concerning the reasons a person may have for holding his beliefs and none concerning the explanation of his holding the beliefs he does in terms of causal factors. Naturally, a person will hope, of certain factors, that his beliefs are not influenced by them, but he will scarcely suppose that none of his beliefs are influenced in this way. There seems to be an exact analogy between this situation and a person's attitude towards the truth of his beliefs. Naturally, he holds each one to be true, but, looking at them as a whole, he can scarcely doubt that there are some falsehoods among them. Hampshire's mistaken conclusion that his observations concerning beliefs tell against determinism arises, paradoxically enough, from a failure to separate the explanation a person gives of his beliefs when he gives his reasons for them and the explanation which can be given of them in terms of causes. Those observations do set limits to the reasons a person can have, but not on the type, or existence, of explanation.

There is one argument in favour of determinism which, if my explanation is correct, has no more force than these arguments against it. That is the argument from the premise that a person cannot hold any belief he wishes. If someone suggests to him that he should make a trial of a certain belief in order to see whether he is not happier in that state, he may truly reply that, much as he wishes to believe it, he cannot do so. The explanation is that although he can believe anything he chooses to believe, since only choices arising out of enquiry can be choices of beliefs, it is not true that he can believe anything he wishes, since he may wish to believe something for reasons other than the wish to arrive at the truth. In other words, he can get any belief he chooses because his choices are restricted; he cannot get any belief he wishes for, because his wishes are unrestricted. Since the explanation of this fact, that a person cannot believe anything he wishes to believe, lies in the fact that belief is, necessarily, the outcome of enquiry, it has no implications concerning the explanation of his holding the beliefs he holds. It does not imply that his beliefs are explained by causes.

My purpose in this paper has been a limited one. I have not tried to show that the fact that a person may hold a belief for reasons which are reasons for the truth of the proposition in which it is a belief is compatible with determinism. I have tried to show that some features of belief which seem to refute that compatibility do not refute it, and that one feature which seems to imply determinism does not imply it. However, this is a matter of some importance, for the features of belief which Hampshire stresses do indeed seem to constitute persuasive arguments against determinism. Equally, there is one other feature of belief which seems to constitute a persuasive argument in its favour. I have argued that the true explanation of these features shows that they yield no conclusions concerning the kind of explanation beliefs must have. If I am right, this issue must be decided on other grounds.

University College London

Towards a reasonable libertarianism

David Wiggins

Towards a
reasonable
libertarianism[1]

One of the many reasons, I believe, why philosophy falls short of a satisfying solution to the problem of freedom is that we still cannot refer to an unflawed statement of libertarianism. Perhaps libertarianism is in the last analysis untenable. But if we are to salvage its insights, we certainly need to know what is the least unreasonable statement the position could be given. Compatibilist resolutions to the problem of freedom[2] must wear an appearance of superficiality, however serious or deep the reflections from which they originate, until what they offer by way of freedom can be compared with something else, whether actual or possible or only seemingly imaginable, which is known to be the best that any indeterminist or libertarian could describe.

A sympathetic and serviceable statement of libertarianism cannot be contrived overnight, nor can it be put into two or three sentences, which is all that some utilitarian and compatibilist writers have been willing to spare for the position. If they were more anxious to destroy or supersede libertarianism than to understand and improve it, this was natural enough; but time or human obstinacy have shown that the issue is too complex for such summary treatment. What follows is offered as a small step in the direction of a more reasonable exposition. It concentrates on two or three points, where many need attention. If the treatment of these two or three points has the final effect of making the position even less credible, or of making me sacrificial scapegoat for oddities which persist, I still hope to have shown that the libertarian perceived something which was missed by all extant compatibilist resolutions of the problem of freedom; and that the point the libertarian was making must bear upon any future reconstruction of our notions and practices.

I What the libertarian means by 'He could have done otherwise'

The libertarian insists that a man is only responsible or free if sometimes he could do otherwise than he does do. It must be genuinely up to him what he chooses or decides to do. But what does this mean? Let us begin with three clarifications.

(i) It is characteristic of the libertarian to insist that for at least some of the things which the man with freedom does, or plans, or decides to do, he must have a genuine alternative open to him. That is, for some action A and some action B, where A ≠ B, he must be able to do A and he must be able to do B. But does the same apply to what the man with freedom thinks, what he believes, and what he infers?[3] In another place,[4] I have given an argument, whatever it may be worth, whose purpose was to show that the notions *open choice, decision, alternative, up to me, freedom* have a different point in the realm of belief, the state whose distinctive aspiration it is to match or represent the world *as it is*, from their point in the realm of action and volition. For of action and volition the proper province is not to match anything in the physical world but to affect or *act upon* the world. The world and its causal properties, whether or not these constitute it a deterministic world, are the unarguable framework within which action takes place; but for the libertarian it is typical and proper to insist that nothing in that world should completely determine the ends, objectives and ideals with which the free agent, if he is truly free, deliberates to change that world. There is no question of requiring of ends and ideals some correspondence with, some sentence-like satisfaction by, the things in the world. (If the onus were anywhere then, as Miss Anscombe has suggested, it would have to be the other way about.) The libertarian ought, on the other hand, to be content to allow the world, if it will only do so, to dictate to the free man how the world *is*.[5] Freedom does not consist in the exercise of the (colourable but irrelevant) right to go mad without interference or distraction by fact.[6] Alternatives of the kind which the libertarian defines and demands are alternatives in the realm not of theory but of practice.

(ii) To say that an agent is doing B or will do B and not A, and that there is something else, A, which he can do, is to say something ambiguous, even though (ignoring permissive and epistemic contexts) 'can' itself is most likely univocal (see (iii) below). A may be something the agent can generally do, for instance, or something he can for such and such a stretch of time do, *given the opportunity*. It is true and important that the latter claim is confirmed if the agent's wanting or trying to do A at an appropriate moment during that period is a sufficient condition of his producing a non-fluke performance of A. But read in this way *he can do otherwise* is irrelevant to what concerns the libertarian. What organises the whole dispute, and what holds the libertarian's position apart from his present day opponents' position, is rather his treatment of another question: if physical determinism is true, is there ever something different from what the agent will in fact do at some time t_1 such that the agent can at t_1 do that other thing at t_1 instead? If physical determinism is true, then the libertarian maintains that such an alternative is never really or truly available to the agent (see Section III). Sometimes earlier actions do completely determine successions of later events and actions. According to the libertarian, however, there can only be true alternatives if there are at least some movements or actions or mental events which, whether or not they completely determine their immediate successors, are not themselves entirely determined by some predecessor. (Of course, this is only a necessary condition of alternatives or freedom of action.) He readily allows that even if there were not such successions, we could, if we wished to ignore all sorts of relevant facts, mechanically continue to draw our conventional distinctions between different kinds of situations – between acting *voluntarily* and acting *reluctantly*, between *control* and *non-control*, between *freedom* and *constraint*. But determinism undermines their whole point, he says. It whittles away too much that is important from the notion of responsibility. It transforms it out of recognition. True freedom cannot be maintained by holding onto distinctions for which there is no factual backing or consistent rationale.

(iii) Though the sentence schemata *he could have done otherwise* and *he could have done A instead of B* may be used with varying truth conditions, one may hope to explain all these variations by differences of complementation with respect to (a) the time or period for which the ability subsists, (b) the particular fully specified value of the action variables, and (c) the time relevant for the acting itself. *Can* itself is, in my own provisional opinion, a unitary semantical element.[7] But those who have distinguished, e.g. a 'general' *can* from 'particular' *can* have performed an important service in forcing us to be clear about what exactly it is that a man could or could not have done. The (b)-place must be carefully and fully specified. The provision of two slots (a) and (c), for the times of the ability and the performance respectively, may seem questionable. But consider the fact that I may now, in Baker Street at 9.55 a.m., be able to catch the train from Paddington to Oxford at 10.15 a.m. Eight minutes later, however, at 10.03 a.m., if I have not progressed from Baker Street, then, given the state of the Inner Circle line and Marylebone Road, I shall certainly be unable to catch the train. What we have in this example is not a special case but a specially clear case. Both slots are always there – we cannot create them specially for the train case – but when they both take the same temporal specification (as they must in 'he could have done otherwise' in at least some important occurrences) then the ellipse of one of them is surely natural and intelligible enough.

So much for the sentence *he could have done otherwise* as it figures in the dispute. The other urgent need is for a clarification of the determinism which the libertarian finds incompatible with his understanding of the sentence.

II What determinism signifies

J. L. Austin once maintained that determinism was 'the name of nothing clear'.[8] But as a second-level non-scientific theory that the world admits of explanation by a certain kind of ground level scientific theory, it seems to me that the thesis can be made as plain as 'causality' and 'explanation' can. Whatever his other difficulties, I think the libertarian must find it depressingly easy to indicate what it is that he is afraid of.

I propose to say that a scientific theory for a subject-matter s is deterministic if and only if the theory possesses a store of predicates and relation-words for the characterisation of s-items (events, situations), and affirms lawlike general statements $L_1, L_2, \ldots L_n$, such that for every s-item s_j it can find a description D_j, and s-item s_i with description D_i which occurred some t seconds earlier, and a law L such that L implies (if a D_i event occurs, then a D_j event occurs t seconds later).[9]

A deterministic theory is *adequate* if its vocabulary of descriptions $D_1, D_2, \ldots D_n$ and its laws $L_1, L_2, \ldots L_n$ together yield explanations which are of universal correct applicability and the statements $L_1, L_2, \ldots$ are true.

As a first attempt then let us say that determinism is the theory that *for every event (situation, state of the world or whatever) there is a true description D_i and an adequate and deterministic theory T which explains that event under D_i*. I suppose our reason for thinking that this might hold is science's spectacular success in extending again and again the number and variety of events for which it can find theories with the title to be in my sense both adequate and deterministic.

Someone may comment that it is hardly surprising that we have discovered the regularities which were there to be discovered; that our success shows nothing about the residue; nor does the possibility of such success really guarantee the operational or empirical intelligibility of the thesis of determinism. Perhaps it is not intelligible, it may be said. The charge ignores falsification however; and those who persist in subscribing to determinism (in spite of, e.g. quantum phenomena) surely might reply to the whole objection with this question: 'How big then *is* the residue? Can there really be, what the objection purports to achieve, an *a priori* estimation of it?' At this point, however, we stumble upon the widespread idea, presumably shared by the objector, that every situation must be infinitely describable. If it were, then getting evidence for determinism would certainly be like filling a broken pitcher.

Those who claim to perceive this infinite describability in nature may try to support the objection in the following sort of terms. All we can do in a causal investigation is to pick out and test causal *strands* from a total physical background which is provisionally regarded as the 'normal' background;[10] there is no logical question of this procedure, the only operational procedure they say, either terminating or issuing in finished law-like generalisations which are closed and not subject to a never ending process of qualification.

Let us first answer the difficulty about generalisations and then return to infinite describability. Adequacy in our first formulation required the strict and universal truth of the laws employed in deterministic explanation. If one says all F's are G's then one means *all* F's; and if some restriction of the conditions under which all D_i events at t are followed by D_j events at t' is needed, then the restriction must, for purposes of this determinism, be made explicit. A body falling near the surface of the earth for t seconds will cover a distance of exactly $16t^2$ feet, for example, provided it is in a vacuum and provided it is falling freely. The hypothesis of determinism which we are considering precisely entails that in due course such qualifications can be everywhere spelled out and completed.

It is true, of course, that the objection is making an important point about the discovery of physical laws, and about the way in which everyday conceptions of causality lead into scientific ones. In deference to it, and in deference to Hart and Honoré's analysis of causality, we could meet the point in another way by saying that an explanation holds universally if *either* (1) there are no apparent exceptions to the predictions made by the use of the law or laws L which cover it; *or* (2) every such apparent exception can be explained in terms of an interference (a) describable by the vocabulary of the body of theory to which L belongs, and (b) for which there is *in its own turn* an explanation in terms of an adequate theory, this theory itself being compatible with L. Whatever one thinks of this strategy, it enables one to suppose that every causal generalisation starts life with a *ceteris paribus* clause, understood by means of (2) in such a way that the escape clause does not trivialise L. Then in the revised set of definitions, *deterministic* in terms of *adequate*, *adequate* in terms of *universal*, and then *universal* in terms of *adequate* again, there would of course be a circle. It may perhaps be seen as matching a similar circle in the beginnings of a science. It is not necessarily a vicious circle, however, because by conjoining a larger and larger set of good and consistent theories it will become possible, *if determinism is true*, to diminish the apparent exceptions to nil. We can then use the 'no exceptions' condition of clause (1) as a criterion of 'universality' and 'adequacy'.

If either of these replies is to carry the determinist the whole way against the objection, which has the virtue of bringing out just how exigent a thesis determinism is, then the idea that every situation is without redundancy infinitely describable must now be combated directly. About it I would simply ask, does the idea of infinite describability rest on an inductive argument? If so it cannot be in any better position than the deterministic argument which it challenges. If not, then what non-inductive or *a priori* support is there for the objection? I do not know the answer to this question, but for good will, and to free the discussion from deadlock, there is something the determinist may say at this point to meet any argument at all which might be produced. This riposte is best brought off by way of an important shortcoming in our first formulation of determinism. That formulation only undertook to find a theory to explain every item under *some* description or other. The flaw was this. What if the chosen descriptions were thin or uninformative (even as uninteresting as *something happened at* t)? Such a determinism might leave almost every significant feature of reality perfectly free of determination by physical law.

It is no good to try to stiffen the doctrine of determinism by requiring that for every description of every event there be an adequate deterministic theory T which explains the event under that description. How could every conceivable description, however arrived at, of anything, find its way into a law of nature or pull its weight in a serious theory?[11]

To amend the determinist thesis, and come to terms with any problem there may be of infinite or indefinite describability, I think we need instead the notion of a *saturated* description. A description D of item x is saturated, I shall say, if and only if (a) D is true of x and (b) there is no property P of x which can vary without variation in the property D stands for. On pain of relapse into the amendment of determinism just dismissed I emphasise that this idea has absolutely nothing to do with the *reduction* of all properties to saturated properties. If a picture is beautiful and serene and sad it cannot be modified in these respects without a modification in the chemical, structural, or physical properties which would enter into its saturated description. It does not follow at all from this tie between the aesthetic and scientific properties that we can find any complex description couched in the terms of physics or chemistry (or the Winsor and Newton trade list for that matter) which is satisfied by all and only pictures beautiful and serene and sad – or even by pictures which are these things to the very degree that x is. For what will make saturated descriptions important (and make important those descriptions which seem to promise that they might some day form a non-trivial component of some saturated description) has nothing to do with their reductive power. It has every-thing to do with their theoretical power and their claim to structure the rest of reality. It is, of course, the fact that so many of the scientific properties of things we have already discovered look as if they may be conjoined one day to achieve something approaching saturated description that reinforces the claims of physicalism as a candidate for serious intellectual consideration.

In its revised form the thesis of determinism can now be stated as follows. *For every event (situation . . .) there is a saturated description D_j and corresponding adequate and deterministic theory T which explains that event under D_j.* Saturated descriptions, if they exist, encode everything that is of any causal or scientific significance. Further refinements of this formulation might classify theories by the degree of computability of the functions they employ, by the degrees of solvability of the equations they invoke, or by other refinements into which there is no need to enter. The general character of the doctrine and the colour of its claims to be a factual doctrine[12] should by now have sufficiently emerged, as should the direction in which I for one should look for its verification or falsification – viz. the progress of the sciences of matter.

For this reason, and because it is germane to one objection to the anti-compatibilist argumentation of Section III below, it may be pertinent to express an attitude to the psychological, sociological or economic determinisms which attract some thinkers and have a powerful effect on the institutions, practice and methodology of the *social sciences*.

It is not unusual to find social scientists who believe that some day, somehow, their sciences will grow up and produce results comparable in their way with the splendid things which in its maturity physics has achieved. In its adolescence, we are to suppose, social science practises and rehearses the methods of dispassionate enquiry and conscientious and accurate measurement which are the *sine qua non* of the spirit of Science: but when the time comes, society will receive the instruments of stability and the dividend for which it has so presciently invested – namely applications of sociology, economics, psychology which will bear the same certain relation to the disciplines they apply as the products of modern technology do to chemistry, physics and the rest.

Unless what this really means is only that we shall in due course see some of the predictions of social scientists actually brought about by the trend-planning which is 'based' upon them, or that without the aid of any powerful theory or insight social science can already be used to safeguard our rulers against the dangers of too open a future, there is no very awesome reason to believe it.

In the absence of many hard results the only general argument I know for the likelihood of what social scientists hope (and libertarians fear) goes something like this. The physical sciences give quite good reason to believe that, at least on the macroscopic level, the world is a deterministic system. But every event economically described or sociologically described is also a physical event, so how could sociological events or economic events fail to make up a deterministic system themselves? They are physical events. So there must be universal laws and functional correlations out there awaiting the researcher who can make accurate enough measurements and can master (or hire enough brute computer force to master) the number of variables required to hit upon and solve the relevant equations.

This argument, which rests on a greater confidence than many people can muster in physical determinism itself, comprises an instructive and fundamental logical mistake. Economic events, say, or commercial events, could be part of a larger deterministic system without themselves (or as such) comprising a self-contained deterministic system. And it would not follow from the fact that any system they helped to make up was deterministic that the laws in virtue of which it was deterministic would be *laws of economics* or *laws of sociology*. Even if every state or event which is of sociological or economic interest is implied by some physical state or event X in virtue of some physical laws L, it does not follow that either X or L can be expressed in purely economic or sociological terms.[13] What the determinism of the sort earlier envisaged says (where e_i, e_j, . . . range over events, S ranges over all properties including sociological, economic, etc., ones and P is the property of being physical, i.e. satisfying a description of a science of matter) is this:

$$(e_i)(S(e_i) \to (\exists e_j)(P(e_j) \ \& \ (e_i = e_j))$$
For every economically or sociologically described event, there is a physical event identical with it.

Now, when K ranges over natural or scientifically significant kinds, K_s is an arbitrary kind including socially categorised kinds, and K_p is a category of physical events this no doubt entails

$$(e_i)((e_i \in K_s) \to (\exists e_j)(\exists K_p)[(e_j \in K_p) \ \& \ (e_i = e_j)])$$
For every event of sociological or economic kind there is an event of a natural kind recognised by a science of matter which is identical with it.

But it does not entail the statement the argument crucially needs

$$(K_s)(\exists K_p)(e_i)[(e_i \in K_s) \to (\exists e_j)(e_j = e_i \ \& \ e_j \in K_p)]$$
For every sociologically or economically characterised kind of event there is a natural kind of event recognised by a science of matter such that every event of the former kind belongs also to the latter kind.

And on the inherent unlikelihood of this proposition, where *kind* is construed narrowly, the class of all physical events is not a natural kind, and where *natural kind* is explained by reference to the notion of theory,[14] I am content (pending the production of a better argument or harder results) to rest my whole insistence that the determinism of physical science is the only determinism which need at the moment engage the concern of the libertarian – or of anybody.

III The logical character of the incompatibility of determinism and the ability to do otherwise

So much for serious determinism. It is a shaky hypothesis, and in its stricter forms open to disbelief. It is not a thesis to be disarmed by *a priori* arguments against its truth or significance; and it is not obviously equivalent to the *prima facie* weaker thesis that every event has some cause.[15] Its importance for freedom resides in the fact that if determinism is true and every action of every agent depends in its particular circumstances upon some specific physical condition being satisfied, then actions cannot be torn free from the nexus of physical effects and fully determining causes.[16] Here then we come to the problem of the incompatibility which the libertarian alleges between physical determinism and statements of the form 'he could at *t'* have done otherwise at *t''*.

Richard Taylor writes on page 54 of *Action and Purpose*, 'If however, existing conditions are causally sufficient for my moving my finger, then it follows that it is causally impossible for me not to move [it] . . . Since, however, it is true that . . . I can hold it still, it follows that [this] is not causally impossible.'[17] What is the underlying argument of the first sentence of this passage? For a moment one might suppose that the argument is this. (I) It's a law of nature or a consequence of a law of nature that under conditions C a man moves his finger. If this is a law of nature it is true for all time. *A fortiori* it is true for this time *t'* when the man, say, moves his finger. Hence it is causally impossible at *t'* that C should obtain and the man not move his finger at *t'*. But (II) from *t* onwards C did obtain. Therefore (III) it was causally impossible at *t'* that the man should not move his finger at *t'*. Therefore (IV) the man could not at *t'* keep his finger still at *t'*. But (V) he could at *t'* have kept his finger still at *t'*. Therefore (VI) some premiss must be false. So if we concede (II), the deterministic (I) is false. This can scarcely be the argument Taylor had in mind however. For its pattern at (I) (II) (III) follows that of the patently invalid argument:

(I) $\Box$ (p is known $\supset$ p is true)*
(II) I know q.
(III) $\Box$ (q)

And it is notorious that the necessity of the proposition q in (III) cannot be derived in this way. The only necessity which we can reach is

(10) $\Box[((I) \ \& \ (II)) \supset (III)]$

If Taylor's argument were similar and not some sort of enthymeme – I shall try later to see how it might go – then abbreviating the causal

---

* Editor's note: '$\Box$' may be read as 'it is necessary that . . . ', formulae of the form 'p $\supset$ q' as 'if p then q', and '$\Diamond$' as 'it is possible that . . .'.

or historical tensed modality as *inevitable at* t', and recording the physical movement the man made as R, it would have to proceed similarly as:

(I) inevitable at t' (C at $t \supset$ R at t')
(II) C at t
(III) inevitable at t' (R at t')

Nevertheless I feel convinced, with Taylor,[18] that there is some valid inference from (I) to (III). The problem is to discover another form for it and to formulate its additional premisses. If this much can be accomplished, then, it will become worthwhile to try to characterise and define the notion of historical inevitability which makes the argument work. The modal principles used in the argument will then need to be verified against the meaning discovered or stipulated for *inevitable at* t'. First then let us look for a candidate form for the inference.

Suppose that a law of nature assures us that in the conditions obtaining at a particular juncture t'

(1) Inevitable at t' (if C at t then R at t')

and suppose that we know that if R is true this causally or logically excludes some particular agent's doing A, so that

(2) Inevitable at t' (if R at t' then $\bar{A}$ at t').

Then, if 'Inevitable at t' (if . . . then —)' is transitive, it follows that

(3) Inevitable at t' (if C at t then $\bar{A}$ at t').

Suppose for instance that R records the movement of extending a finger and A says the man kept still. Suppose the man failed to keep still. The question will be: Could he have kept still even though, from the earlier moment t, C obtained? Propositions (1) and (2) are the contribution of determinism to the argument. For that thesis implies that there exists this sort of empirical truth. If the argument depends on (1) and (2) it will not be a fatalistic but a deterministic argument. The extra premiss which I believe the argument needs I do however derive from a fatalistic source (Diodorus Cronus – reading him as having said that the impossible does not follow from the possible):

(4) If p is possible and necessarily if p then q, then q is possible, i.e.

(4) $\Diamond p \supset ((\Box(p \supset q) \supset \Diamond q))$

This is an uncontroversial modal principle. If 'historically inevitable at

t'' which I shall write as $\Box t'$ is a modality, and if it has a dual 'histori-cally possible at t'' or '$\Diamond t'$', then we shall expect (and shall in due course verify) the corresponding truth

(4') $[\Diamond t'(\text{A at } t') \supset (\Box t'((\text{A at } t') \supset (\text{not C at } t)) \supset \Diamond t' \text{ not C at } t))]$

(Substitute 'A at t'' for 'p' and 'not-C at t' for 'q' in (4) and replace $\Diamond$ and $\Box$ with $\Diamond t'$ and $\Box t'$.) Now suppose that it is asserted that, in spite of the fact that (1) (2) (3) obtained, and in spite of the fact C, and in spite of the fact that the man made the movement and extended his finger (R was true) and did not keep still ($\bar{\text{A}}$ was true),

(5) *he could have kept still at* t′

I am not sure how to analyse 'he could have kept still at t'' in terms of possibility or necessity, but it seems plain that (5) must at least entail that it was not physically or historically impossible at t' that the man should keep still at t'. For surely

(6) X can φ at $t' \supset - \Box t' - (\varphi \text{ at } t')$

He who maintains (5) must by (6) admit

(7) $\Diamond t'$ (A at t')

But this is the antecedent of (4′) and so we can detach

(8) $(\Box t' ((\text{A at } t') \supset (\text{not C at } t)) \supset \Diamond t' (\text{not C at } t)$

But the antecedent of (8) is the contraposition of (3). So we have

(9) $\Diamond t'$ (not C at t)

or

(9′) $- \Box t' - (\text{not C at } t)$

But how could it be historically possible at t' for not C at t? t' is later than t. By t' there is nothing anybody or anything can do about C. But then, if (1) and (2) are true, the fault can only lie in (5).

(9) and (9′) are the consequence not of pure logic, or of (4) above, but of (4) with (1)–(3). That is to say that (9) is the consequence of empirical determinism. It is something in the nature of time which turns this into a refutation of (5). But if determinism is true then it does seem that no propositions of the form 'He could at t' have done otherwise at t'' are true. At any given moment a man has no real alter-native to what he does at that moment: in which case there is no way

for him to exploit the fact that he could if he were to do A now do B in the future, and could if he were to do not-A now do D in the future. For it is already *fixed* which of A and Ā will now come to pass. And the same argument will hamper the attempt to find his freedom at some earlier moment.

This anyway is a suggestion about the formal character of the inference which the libertarian wants to make. Nobody will feel comfortable about it without an expansion of the idea of historical inevitability at a time. But before coming to that something needs to be said about (1) (2) (3). They rest, amongst other things, on the lawlike generalisation which entails (1) and the analytic truth or lawlike generalisation (as the case may be) which entails (2). But laws of nature themselves will usually be much more general than (1) or (2), and will rarely or never bear much resemblance to (3). (3) especially is specific and may depend heavily upon the particular situation at t'. It does what no proper law by itself would normally do – it links very different kinds of description. That it is possible to conjoin laws of nature, which could not by themselves perform this task, with facts about particular situations in order to obtain particular statements like (3) is what makes it difficult to find human freedom in the fact that there are most likely no exceptionless empirical principles at all about the causal antecedents (or consequences) of actions classed by *action-kinds*. If a suitable notion of necessity can be defined to make a bridge from propositions like (1) to propositions like (3) then such exceptionless principles are not needed. An exceptionless principle about the connexion between the condition recorded in C and the physical movement recorded in R will suffice.

By 'it is historically inevitable at time t' that p' is intended something like this – whatever anybody or anything does at t' or thereafter it can make no difference to p, p being either a law of logic or a law of nature or already history or being the logical or physical consequence of what is already history. This definition already includes the notion of possibility, but this is no objection. The purpose of the enterprise is only to fix from within the circle of modal notions a sense of necessity which satisfies principle (4') and yields a strict implication which is transitive (for the passage from (1) and (2) to (3)). It is not necessary to break into the circle of modal notions from outside.

Briefly one might say p is historically necessary at t' if, and only if, p is true whatever may happen at t' or thereafter (consistently with laws of nature).* Or in the sort of language which many people have come to prefer, and which David Lewis uses in his forthcoming book *Counterfactuals* to characterise modal and counterfactual principles, one might stipulate $\square t'(p) \equiv p$ holds in every world whose history is indistinguishable from the history of the actual world up to (but not necessarily including) t'. Here we should have to understand its natural laws as comprising a part of the history of a world.[19]

It remains to verify 4'. If it is not historically necessary at t' that not-p then it is not the case that p holds in every world whose history is indistinguishable from our world's history up to t'. In that case there is a world W whose history is indistinguishable from our world's history up to t' and p does not hold in that world W. Now suppose that in every world indistinguishable from ours up to t' either p is false or q is true. W is one of these worlds and p is true in it. Then q must be true in W. Therefore if p is historically possible at t' and it is historically necessary at t' that if p then q, q must be historically possible at t'. Transitivity is equally obvious.

Many will share my own preference for an argument in a plainer if more confusing vernacular. Suppose (a) it is not the case that not-p is true whatever happens at t'. Suppose, in other words, it is not yet fixed at t' whether or not p. And suppose (b) that whatever happens at t' or thereafter, it is fixed that if p is true then q is true. Now suppose (c) that q is not possible at t'. Suppose, in other words, that it is (not not) the case that not-q is true whatever happens at or after t'. This is to suppose that not-q is already fixed at t. But (contraposing (b)) whatever happens at t' or after it is fixed that if not-q is true then not-p is true. So if not-q is already fixed then not-p is fixed too. But we said that it was not the case that it was fixed at t' that not-p. Therefore supposition (c) is false. Therefore q must be historically possible at t'.

The reaction of some to this whole exercise will be to say that it fortifies a dislike they had always had for natural necessity – even before it was relativised to a time. I reply that such scepticism must in consistency apply equally aptly to physical possibility, relativised or unrelativised, wherever it outruns actuality. And here we notice a curious thing. This scepticism, by reducing possibility to actuality, seems to undermine 'can do otherwise' *directly* – unless it treats animate possibility, the *can* of human ability, with some special indulgence. But that would be a strange concession to make, especially in the presence of libertarians. Its effect would be to mark off animate agents from the rest of nature in the sort of way which at least some libertarians have precisely wished to distinguish them.

IV Views of the self open to the libertarian

It may be said that the whole preceding demonstration turns on a confusion between what lies in the agent and what lies outside him.[20] It is perfectly absurd, it will be said, to lump together under conditions C things as diverse as the character of the agent, the present state of mind of the agent, the external causes of that state of mind, and the concrete particularities of the conditions under which he acts. It makes as much sense as saying that one of the circumstances under which an agent did a specific action was the circumstance that he was a man of a mean and murderous disposition. Nothing but confusion can come from such a way of speaking, it will be said; and the only possible philosophical outcome of speaking like this is a far fetched theory of the metaphysical, totally non-empirical, and characterless self whose difficulties match exactly the incoherences of the Lockean doctrine of substance – the thing with the property of having no properties, the substrate which explains the possibility of change by being both unchanged and identical with that which persists through change. Either the libertarian requires (cf. Section I (i)) that *nothing in the world outside the free agent himself* should determine for that agent how he will change or deliberate to change the world, or the libertarian simply requires that *nothing in the world* determine for the agent how he will change or deliberate to change the world. It will then be said that if the requirement is stated in the former way we can and must distinguish what lies within the agent from what lies without. If the requirement is stated in the latter way, however, then even the agent himself is excluded from determining anything – even *for himself* – unless the self is outside the world altogether. This is an unintelligible conception. Finally it may be said that the libertarian's expression 'determining for the agent' is pure rhetoric – the *man* deliberates and thus determines for himself what change he will import.

I hope this states the objection as dissolutionists or compatibilists want to see it stated. But without the discovery of a specific mistake in the argument above, the absurdities of the metaphysical self cannot themselves suffice to disprove the inference from determinism to *nobody can do otherwise than they do do*. How exactly the metaphysical self could be supposed to compensate for physical determinism is not at all clear.[21] But if determinism did really imply that if we were responsible then the doctrine of the metaphysical self would be true; and if the doctrine of the metaphysical self is absurd (as I for one am sure that it is), then either we are not responsible or the doctrine of determinism is not true. But then if determinism is true, the conclusion follows that we are *not* responsible. (At least in the sense of 'responsible' fixed by the question whether a man can do otherwise.) But that after all is exactly what the libertarian said. As for the confusion of character and circumstance, it is true that condition C groups them together. But why shouldn't it group them together without confusing them? Perhaps there is an important point to be made by comparing character and circumstance, by bringing out some similarity in them so far as historical inevitability is concerned. One can compare without confusing. In comparing for an important purpose one can also undermine the rationale of distinctions some people insist on making, if they are artificial or pointless distinctions.

It may also be objected to the compatibilist argument that it overrides and ignores the agent's point of view – his subjective but invincible experience of freedom. But this is overstated. The conviction of freedom is not by any means the only conviction human agents experience. Equally common is the feeling of unfreedom, the feeling that one is not really deciding a certain issue at all; or the fatalistic presentiment habitually experienced by men with the courage to recognise their standing incontinence in the face of certain temptations. These feelings or presentiments establish nothing either way. The objection seems in fact to rest on the idea that there can be two standpoints or perspectives, P(1) and P(2), upon some act of mine, my perspective and another's, such that P(1) is incompatible with P(2) and yet both are defensible. But what has this defensibility to do with truth? The law of non-contradiction assures us that one or other standpoint must be based on an illusion. If the supposition that real alternatives exist is an integral part of normal deliberation, and if determinism is true and shows that it was already fixed long beforehand which action the man would choose, then deliberation itself must involve some kind of illusion, however necessary an illusion.

There is another way for the compatibilist to move. If the conclusion of Section III is simply incredible – incredible regardless of the facts about scientific determinism – then perhaps this shows that *he could have done otherwise* never means what, in stating the doctrine of libertarianism in Sections I and II, we took such trouble to make it mean where it occurs in Section III. The step from (5) to (7) and the principle (6) are particularly relevant here. In the search for a compatibilist meaning for *can do otherwise* some philosophers have tried to gain favour for the analysis of *x can at* t' (*B at* t') as *if* (. . . *at* t) *then x does B at* t'; where . . . picks out some conditions distinguished from the rest of the circumstances of action by pertaining specially to what is *in* the agent. However bad analyses of this kind have proved so far, too little for my purpose is shown by that – except the undoubted inadequacy of most of our ideas about dispositions generally. And unfortunately I have no ready principle to collect, nor space to survey, all possible hypothetical analyses. But perhaps the most promising-looking hypothetical analysis may be approached by way of a consideration of the non-animate dispositions.

Carnap showed long ago the difficulties of trying to define such dispositions as brittleness or solubility in terms of conditionals like *if x is dropped then x breaks* or *if x is put in water then x melts*. Instead of these conditionals he proposed 'reductions sentences' which have the advantage of not verifying brittleness by the falsity of the antecedent. A typical reduction sentence would be *if x is dropped, then if x is brittle x breaks*. But even if a finite number of them could really fix the sense of 'brittle' – which is unclear or dubious – reduction-sentences are open to another difficulty. Brittle things may for various and divers reasons significantly frequently fail to break when dropped: and many things break when dropped even though they are not brittle. No satisfactory correction is obtained by converting the mood of the first or second sort of conditional into the subjunctive, but there is a remedy which suggests itself and has obvious relevance to the problem of animate abilities. Take 'is disposed' or 'tends' as *pro tempore* primitive (pending its further resolution into notions deriving from that of a *natural kind*) and analyse *x is fragile* (*during period* t) on something like these lines: *x is of a kind to be so disposed* (*during* t) *that* (*if x is dropped then x breaks*), where the hypothetical is now embedded within the characterisation of a categorically described disposition. The corresponding analysis of *x can at* t *A at* t might perhaps be *x is so disposed at* t (*that* (*if . . . then x does A at* t)), where . . . indicates some condition about something 'in' the agent. It could be trying or wanting or whatever.

Now this analysis may represent some kind of advance on previous attempts. The specification of the categorical state of ability requires an *if*, but not in the manner of the more usual hypothetical analyses. What is noteworthy, however, is that the improvement in the analysis does nothing at all to block the question of the possibility of . . . , the happening mentioned in the antecedent. Is it something *really* in the agent? The analysis seems powerless to trump the circumstantial demonstration of the physical impossibility, taking everything into account, of . . . coming to pass. Till this problem is faced no subtleties about *in the agent* or the agent's *will* or *will to will* can gain any purchase. It must however be admitted that the analysis of *can* is everybody's unfinished business. So it may be best to progress to what many will regard as a prior problem.

Maybe it is pointless to debate whether the sentence 'he could at t' have done otherwise at t''' does have the sense I have ascribed to it in the incompatibilist demonstration of Section III above until it has at least been shown that that sense is even a possible sense, or that it could do for the libertarian what he wanted. This is often taken to be equivalent to the following question: can the libertarian even specify a *possible* world, however different from the actual one, in which there are particular responsible actions which people can (in the libertarian's sense) do but do not do? Hume has been followed by a large number of philosophers in holding that not even a possible world of the required sort could be specified. If it were false that every event and every action were causally determined then the causally undetermined events and actions would surely, to that extent, be simply random. So the argument goes. That a man could have done x would mean no more than that it might have turned out that way – at random. It will be asked if it makes any better sense to hold a man responsible for actions which happen at random than for ones which arise from his character. Surely then, if it doesn't, we ought to prefer that our actions be caused?

Considered simply as an argument this objection is circular, and flagrantly so. One cannot prove that determinism is a precondition of free will by an argument which employs as a premiss *everything is either causally determined or random*. This is nothing other than a form of the conclusion, that whatever is undetermined is random. This is what had to be shown. But in the form of a challenge something in the objection can stand. If an event is undetermined, if an event of different specification might have taken its place, then what does it mean to deny that the event is simply random? What is it justifiably to ascribe the action identical with the event or comprised of the event to an agent whom one holds *responsible* for that action? In the unclaimed ground between the properly or determinatically caused and the random, what is there in fact to be found?[22]

Some philosophers have ventured the idea that what would make the difference, within the field of physically undetermined events, between the random and the non-random is the presence or absence of a prior mental event such as a *volition*. It was in this tradition (which goes back at least as far as the *clinamen* or *swerve* of Epicurus and Lucretius) that Russell and Eddington tried to deploy the phenomena of quantum-indeterminacy as having a bearing upon the free-will issue.[23]

If – as seems likely – there is an uninterrupted chain of purely physical causation throughout the process from sense-organ to muscle, it follows that human actions are determined in the degree to which physics is deterministic. Now physics is only deterministic as regards macroscopic occurrences, and even in regard to them it asserts only very high probability, not certainty. It might be that, without infringing the laws of physics, intelligence could make improbable things happen, as Maxwell's demon would have defeated the second law of thermo-dynamics by opening the trapdoor to fast-moving particles and closing it to slow-moving ones.

On these grounds it must be admitted that there is a bare possibility – not more – that, although occurrences in the brain do not infringe the laws of physics, nevertheless their outcome is not what it would be if no psychological factors were involved . . . So for those who are anxious to assert the power of mind over matter it is possible to find a loophole. It may be maintained that one characteristic of living matter is a condition of unstable equilibrium, and that this condition is most highly developed in the brains of human beings. A rock weighing many tons might be so delicately poised on the summit of a conical mountain that a child could, by a gentle push, send it thundering down into any of the valleys below; here a tiny difference in the initial impulse makes an enormous difference to the result. Perhaps in the brain the unstable equilibrium is so delicate that the difference between two possible occurrences in one atom suffices to produce macroscopic differences in the movements of muscles. And since, according to quantum physics, there are no physical laws to determine which of several possible transitions a given atom will undergo, we may imagine that, in a brain, the choice between possible transitions is determined by a psychological cause called 'volition'. All this is possible, but no more than possible.

Russell is not enthusiastic, and perhaps the idea is even less free of difficulty than he allows. (Could not the incidence of human acts of 'volition' upon quantum phenomena upset the probability distributions postulated by the quantum theory?) It is perplexing too that the theory bases action on occurrent mental events which it does not found in or relate to personality or character or even to purpose. Could it do this without seeming to threaten its own rationale in causal indeterminism? If the theory tried to find room for such components as these in the genesis of action, then would the whole idea of an as it were 'immaterial realisation' of the agent, the source of the volitions – paradoxical and absurd as it already sounds – be defenceless against the suggestion that there was no criterion by which the self or spiritual nucleus of an agent would qualify as a non-bodily thing not accountable to or determined by neurophysiological and physical laws? Nor, for the same sort of reason, is it clear that Russell's suggestion can give any very clear account of what would justify comparing the role of a volition to that of the child who gives the stone a gentle *push* in one or other of several possible directions.

But this is not the end of Eddington's and Russell's idea. They have simply given it a disastrously Cartesian expression. For indeterminism maybe all we really need to imagine or conceive is a world in which (a) there is some macroscopic indeterminacy founded in microscopic indeterminacy, and (b) an appreciable number of the free actions or policies or deliberations of individual agents, although they are not even in principle hypothetico-deductively derivable from antecedent conditions, can be such as to persuade us to fit them into meaningful sequences. We need not trace free actions back to volitions construed as little pushes aimed from outside the physical world. What we must find instead are patterns which are coherent and intelligible in the low level terms of practical deliberation, even though they are not amenable to the kind of generalisation or necessity which is the stuff of rigorous theory. On this conception the agent is conceived as an essentially and straightforwardly enmattered or embodied thing. His possible peculiarity as a natural thing among things in nature is that his biography unfolds not only non-deterministically but also intelligibly; non-deterministically in that personality and character are never something complete, and need not be the deterministic origin of action; intelligibly in that each new action or episode constitutes a comprehensible phase in the unfolding of the character, a further specification of what the man has by now *become*.

For help with such ideas, in spite of the physicalistic form in which I have couched them, we look naturally in the direction of J.-P. Sartre, and would best look not at the crazily optimistic positions of the early plays *Les Mouches* or *Huis Clos* or of *L'Etre et le Néant* but to what he now soberly tries to make of his position.[24] Here is Sartre's 1969 account of it.[25]

> For the idea which I have never ceased to develop is that in the end one is always responsible for what is made of one. Even if one can do nothing else besides assume this responsibility. For I believe that a man can always make something out of what is made of him. This is the limit I would today accord to freedom: the small movement which makes of a totally conditioned social being someone who does not render back completely what his conditioning has given him. Which makes of Genet a poet when he had been rigorously conditioned to be a thief.
>
> Perhaps the book where I have best explained what I mean by freedom is in fact, *Saint Genet*. For Genet was made a thief, he said 'I am a thief', and this tiny change was the start of a process whereby he became a poet, and then eventually a being no longer even on the margin of society, someone who no longer knows where he is, who falls silent. It cannot be a happy freedom, in a case like this. Freedom is not a triumph. For Genet, it simply marked out certain routes which were not initially given.

This is not of course the place to take up everything that is strange or interesting in the passage. Nor is the passage innocent of possible confusion where it employs the words *rigorously conditioned*, which belong with a view of the world which Sartre surely ought to see the life of Genet as refuting.[26] But the capital point is that it may not matter if the world *approximates* to a world which satisfies the principles of a neurophysiological determinism provided only that this fails in the last resort to characterise the world completely, and provided that there are actions which, for all that they are causally under-determined, are answerable to practical reason, or are at least *intelligible* in that dimension. These are not random.

V Conclusion: the prospects for a reasonable libertarianism

The free-will dispute has reached a point where real progress depends not only on the deeper research into necessity, possibility, disposition and causality which logic and philosophy are now edging into position to achieve but also, I claim, upon a more precise and much more sympathetic examination of what the libertarian wants, of why he wants it, and of how his conception of metaphysical freedom is connected with political or social freedom. Whether or not it is our world – that is another question – we must continue to press the question, 'What is the possible world which would afford the autonomy of thought and agency the libertarian craves in this one?' (A) Can *any* possible world really afford us that long sought autonomy? And (B), if none can, then what must we do with all the feelings and arguments which have led so many philosophers and men to reject compatibilism? Nothing, I think, will make them oblige philosophy and without vestige or trace disappear. I shall end by outlining some further problems in the specification of the libertarian's world, and then try to indicate what I think it would signify if these problems were simply insurmountable.

A. I have tried to describe an indeterministic world in which human beings rank as natural objects, as a set of natural objects amongst others, whose motions and capacities can nevertheless be appraised in a dimension defined by subtle and rather exacting standards of rationality. But in dropping the Cartesian conception of an extra-physical volitional origin of motion do I not exchange one mystery for another? How *is it* that just human beings, and other rational creatures if any, behave in the way they do, freely but practically rationally? Well, it might be said we have simply picked out the class of natural objects which do do so and we just happen ourselves to belong to it (which explains our interest in that category): to be puzzled about the question is like looking for some teleologically motivated agency which directed the course of evolution towards the emergence of some particular species and for its benefit wrote off countless others in the process – a search at once fruitless and prompted by a certain confinement of perspective, as if one were never allowed to see some thick and luxurious tree except from one angle in mid air just above it. (Compare the difficulty of believing that the earth is part of the Milky Way.) Again someone may ask, to what extent can a libertarian's 'developing or accumulating biography' view of persons and their characters supplant the cosmic *unfairness* of the determinist's view of these matters? If it is unfair to hold a man responsible for what through no fault of his own he is, is it not equally unfair to hold him responsible for his biography developing in one indeterministic fashion rather than another? If the reply were 'Well, it's him', would this do equally well for the compatibilist? Or wouldn't it? Is this simply to relapse into satisfaction with Hume's specious dilemma?

When we confront these and other questions it may be said by some libertarians and others, we shall come to see quantum phenomena not as the missing clue, not as the one piece we need to complete our theory of free action, but as the anomaly which points to the need for a whole conceptual revolution in our way of thinking about causality – particularly in its connexion with *generality, necessity* and *invariance*.[26]

B. But let me now finish with something about the other possibility – that such a conceptual revolution is an incoherent fantasy, even though the answers to the queries I have put could only be discovered within one. Let us face the idea that in the last resort the questions raised by the libertarian's world of freedom cannot be answered either piecemeal or by some new perspective upon causality. What would this show? *Not* I think that the libertarian has failed to explicate the notion of freedom which we and he began with. What he began with may have been both correctly identified and, in the last analysis, incoherent. It was not obviously incoherent. It was conceivable that this freedom was conceivable. But, in the end, the freedom itself turned out to be *not* conceivable – unless perhaps as a limiting case (and an impossible one) of absence of various kinds of causal determination. What then?

If we have the notion of freedom I have argued that we have, kept in place by *he could have done otherwise* understood in the sense I have ascribed to it; and if so understood this sentence may always be false and that notion is everywhere incoherent; then it can only darken counsel to pretend that our notion is another notion – some notion touted by utilitarians and dissolutionists, for instance – or to pretend that we never really had our deterministic notion. For all sorts of things in our social, judicial, and penal institutions, and all sorts of things in our relations with human beings, may be based (and are based I think) upon the supposition that men *can* do otherwise than they do do. Substitution of another notion of responsibility may be called for, but substitution is not the same as analysis. The practical and metaphysical import of substitution and analysis are completely different. If a dilemma exists here it should first be acknowledged and felt as such. Only barbarism and reaction can benefit by concealment. If the unreformed notion of responsibility, the notion which is our notion, is a sort of metaphysical joke must we not at the very least create some safe time or place in everyday life to laugh at it?[27] A reformed notion of responsibility need not rest on the simple causal

David Wiggins

efficacy of punishment – which is by no means the same thing as the efficacity working through consciousness of moral norms or ideals[28] – but it will *not* reconstruct what men at present feel by way of remorse at their own actions or by way of anger at those of others. Such looking backwards must be strictly senseless. Yet what happens if (except for instruction about the future) we try to ignore the past? What happens to moral consciousness itself as it arises from the generalisation of such affective attitudes?

In a British Academy lecture P. F. Strawson[29] once claimed that whatever we knew in favour of the hypothesis of total determinism, it could never be rational for us to opt out from all resentment or anger or gratitude or admiration or from the conceptual framework of responsibility in which these and like responses or attitudes have their meaning; no one who supposed that it would be rational had thought into what it would really signify for human life to attempt to abandon them. This was an important argument. Yet what it really told against, I think, was the utilitarian and substitutive resolution of the problem of freedom. It did not show the bankruptcy of libertarianism. How could a practical consideration – however all-embracing – prove the theoretical compatibility of freedom and determinism? But it does help the incompatibilist and the libertarian to improve his point about the range and variety of things which determinism puts in jeopardy, however 'panicky' or 'obscure' Strawson found libertarian metaphysics. What Strawson's lecture brings out is the character of the dilemma with which the problem of determinism confronts us – one set of considerations making an attitude rational, the other set undermining that attitude – and the complex conceptual constitution of the notion of rationality which figures in the argument. The dilemma, whatever else it does, demonstrates the bewildering variety of heterogeneous and incommensurable considerations – truth, consistency, diversity of experience, comfort, security, fellow feeling – between which rationality has in real life to hold sway. The theme can scarcely find its natural development here, but perhaps it is the most distinctive of all the marks of rational man to have reasoned himself to a point where he falls into barbarism if he takes the notion of autonomous agency, whether mythical or not, either too seriously – or too lightly.

Bedford College, London

Notes

1 This is an extended and revised version of one part of a paper read to the Oxford Philosophical Society in the summer of 1965. A version of another excerpt from that paper appeared as Part II of 'Freedom, Knowledge, Belief and Causality', p. 13, in *Knowledge and Necessity*, ed. G. Vesey (London: Macmillan, 1970). The conclusions of both parts of the latter paper will be referred to below. Both the nature and the limits of my debt to Richard Taylor's and Roderick Chisholm's respective efforts to refurbish the credentials of libertarianism will be evident to any reader of their works. See especially the latter's 'He could have done otherwise', *J. Phil.*, July 1967.

2 By *compatibilism* (or dissolutionism) I mean the position which says that freedom (the freedom of being able to do otherwise) and physical determinism can coexist. By *incompatibilism* the position that they cannot coexist. *Libertarianism* is a species of incompatibilism, one which saves freedom by denying physical determinism. In refurbishing libertarianism I do not myself mean to subscribe to *a priori* or introspective or extra-scientific arguments against physical determinism (or to take any kind of stand about its truth or falsity) but to subscribe to an interest in what the libertarian *wanted* by way of freedom, whether or not the world will allow of this freedom. Whether libertarianism is true or false, it is the only good source for the position which it entails (without being entailed by it), viz. incompatibilism. It is true that some classical determinists were incompatibilists of a sort, but for the most part libertarian writings are a better guide for the understanding of incompatibilism.

3 See, for instance, John Lucas in *Supplementary Proceedings of the Aristotelian Society*, 1967; Ted Honderich in *Punishment* (London, 1969) (recanted, *Supplementary Proceedings of the Aristotelian Society*, 1970).

4 Cf. my 'Freedom', pp. 145–8 (*op. cit.*, footnote 1).

5 Historically speaking and common-sensically speaking, the point of the demand for freedom of thought was not to conceive one's beliefs in a manner untrammelled or underdetermined by external reality, but to remove civil and clerical obstacles to that spirit of enquiry which allows only the way things are to determine belief. The contrast I am drawing here between theoretical and practical does *not* depend on a conception of knowledge or discovery which excludes or ignores intellectual fertility or active invention. It simply imposes conditions upon its working and possible outcomes. See, 'Freedom', p. 146.

6 It is worth adding that the causal determination by the world of a rational man's particular true belief P cannot in itself entail that the world would have lodged this belief with him *even if it had not been true* – the conditional is both subjunctive and contrary to fact – or that nobody could have told that P was not true if it had not been true.

7 I have discussed ambiguity and univocality in 'Sentence Sense, Word Sense, and Difference of Word Sense' in *Semantics: An Interdisciplinary Reader in Philosophy, Linguistics, and Psycholinguistics*, ed. Steinberg and

Jakobovits (Cambridge, 1971). The diversity of possible complementations is I think the best explanation of phenomena which writers have ascribed to an ambiguity in the word *can* itself. If the schema 'he can X' has to be unpacked – 'he (when?) can [(when?) (what?)]', then 'he can X if . . .' (contrast Austin's 'Ifs and Cans' discussion of this *if*, to which he gives a very peculiar treatment) has to be unpacked both in these ways and with respect to scope – '[he (when?) can (when?) (what?)] if (. . .)' and 'he (when?) can [(when?) (what?) if . . .]'. With ellipse also (which plays an important role in sentences about what can be performed *without*, e.g. *undue cost* or *harm* to persons or property, etc.) to help explain their apparent diversity of truth-conditions, I hope the ground is now cleared for the attempt to obtain a unified theory of *can* itself (where *can* ≠ *may*).

8 'Ifs and Cans', *Collected Papers* (Oxford, 1961), p. 179.

9 This still ignores place, which could not be omitted from a full treatment. It also leaves open the possibility that every event might be caused to happen sometime within a narrow interval, but not necessarily exactly when it does in fact happen. None of the ways in which determinism can be 'porous' can be dealt with here except in the following remark. It will make an important difference to the claims of a theory, however irreducibly statistical, to be a deterministic theory whether or not it can at very least specify stable and determinate probabilities for the events it describes.

10 I use here an idea of H. L. A. Hart and A. M. Honoré in *Causation in the Law* (Oxford, 1959), but there is no intention at all to ascribe to these authors any view at all about the import, sense, status or significance of the thesis of determinism.

11 On this point, and also more generally, Section II is indebted to the ideas of Davidson, now published in 'Mental Events', in Foster and Swanson (eds), *Experience and Theory* (University of Massachusetts Press, 1970).

12 On this point see the problem stated by B. A. W. Russell, 'On the Notion of Cause' in *Mysticism and Logic* (London, 1921) and C. G. Hempel in Sidney Hook (ed.), *Determinism and Freedom* (New York, 1958).

An objection parallel to the plea of infinite describability has found some circulation (see J. Passmore, *Philosophical Review*, Vol. 68 (1959), pp. 93–102, B. A. O. Williams's tentative exposition in D. F. Pears (ed.), *Freedom and the Will* (London, 1963)): that determinism is obliged to treat the universe as a sort of closed system or box, and to take seriously the idea of a total-state description of the world. It is certainly true that the classical Laplacean approach would characteristically have proceeded from outside to inside, from a total world state and total prediction to the prediction of constituent particular phenomena. (See La Place, Introduction to *Théorie Analytique des Probabilités*, Oeuvres Complètes VII, Paris, 1847.) But if the world satisfies the thesis of determinism as I have expounded it by means of the notions of saturated description, adequacy, and universality – *if* this logical possibility is exemplified – then it is as unnecessary to describe the whole world in order to explain a particular event as it is unnecessary to reckon with indefinite describability. The only difficulty is one of establishing, however tentatively, that determinism is true. But in testing this we proceed from inside to out, from smaller to larger tracts of the universe.

The exposition of determinism given here must be taken to supersede that in 'Freedom, Knowledge, Belief and Causality', and to vindicate its claim at para. 2, p. 151.

13 Cf. the situation in genetics. My parents' genotypes limit my genotype and hence my phenotype, but their phenotypes do not have anything like the same control over my phenotype. Not the only kind of comparison possible perhaps. It is not a comparison calculated to gladden those who would wish a more autonomous status for social science (or those who ignore the other kind of aspirations which transformational grammar can suggest to social science). But it is a comparison which might explain how it is that Dray's 'how possibly' pattern fits the explanations to be encountered in the practice of sociology, economics, anthropology, history, etc., better than the covering law pattern fits them.

14 See, e.g., W. V. Quine, 'Natural Kinds', in *Ontological Relativity and Other Essays* (New York, 1970).

15 Maybe all events have causes but there is nothing in a cause or its circumstances to fix absolutely everything about the character of its effect. On this and the problems of event reference and individuation of events which arise, see Milton Fisk, 'A Defence of the Principle of Event Causality', *British Journal of Philosophy of Science*, 1967 and cf. Donald Davidson, 'Causal Relations', *J. Phil.*, 1967.

16 If that is the character of the causal nexus we live within, then it makes no particular difference to this point whether or not actions are *identical* with movements of matter. Even if this were the wrong thing to say, actions still could not be constitutively independent of the arrangement of matter or of physical events. The undoubted problem of interpreting the physical movements of a man as actions scarcely amounts to *the availability to him at a given moment of alternative actions*. On the constriction of freedom which would result from the determinism of physics, whatever one thought of the identity view, see G. J. Warnock, *ab init.*, in *Freedom of the Will*, ed. Pears (London, 1963). It should be added that even if we adopted the mysterious view that mental events did not occur in the physical world, still if physical determinism were true then bodily movements would fall within its ambit and the autonomy of the mental would be limited to mental events with no proximate physical cause and no practical (acted) outcome. Autonomy would be something utterly inert.

17 Prentice-Hall, New York, 1966.

18 And amongst many others Hobbes. His suggestive but equally incomplete formulation in the *De Corpore* runs as follows: 'Every act which is not impossible is possible. Every act therefore which is possible shall at some time be produced; for if it shall never be produced then those things shall never concur which are requisite for the production of it; wherefore that act is impossible by the definition; which is contrary to what was supposed.' Cf. Broad's candid but again equally incomplete statement in 'Determinism, Indeterminism and Libertarianism', in *Ethics and the History of Philosophy* (London, 1952), p. 207.

19 It should be noted that none of these definitions makes 'Theaetetus sits at *t*' historically necessary at *t* even though Theaetetus sits at *t*. The sentence is

not true *whatever* Theaetetus does at *t*. And, unless determinism happens to be true, there is a possible world historically indistinguishable from ours up to *t* in which Theaetetus stands and does not sit at *t*. The proof of (9) does not therefore depend on the fatalistic type of puzzle revived at *Analysis*, Vol. 25 (no. 4, 1965), or on a special view of truth, but on the absurdity of its being *now* possible for something *in the past* to have been different. I should not deny that the definition might be slightly improved by amending it to read 'indistinguishable from the history of the actual world *appreciably* before *t*'. This abandons the precision of the Dedekind section in favour of a serviceable and perhaps indispensable vagueness. Two equally intelligible worlds can scarcely resemble one another up to *t* and differ in that in one Theaetetus sits promptly at *t*, and in the other he promptly stands at *t*. One or other world would involve a discontinuity.

20 Cf. Aristotle's distinction between what is and is not *en tō prattonti* in Book III of *Nicomachean Ethics*.

21 See note 16 and contrast the situation with the partially indeterminist option of Russell shortly to be mentioned.

22 See note 15 and associated sentence of text. If 'every event has a cause' is weaker than the determinism defined in Section II, then the simply caused may comprise part of what stands between the random and the deterministically caused. To be certain of this would be to simplify the answer to the question posed to libertarians by Hume, Bradley, Hobart and others of dissolutionist persuasion.

23 B. A. W. Russell, *Human Knowledge: Its Scope and Limits*, Chapter V: 'The Physiology of Sensation and Volition', p. 54.

24 He is now prepared to be 'scandalised' by his previous assertion (of Resistance times) that 'whatever the circumstances and wherever the site, a man is always free to choose to be a traitor or not . . .'. 'When I read this', he goes on, 'I said to myself: it's incredible, I actually believed that!' See *New Left Review*, no. 58, reproduced in *New York Review of Books*, 26 March 1970, p. 22.

25 In *New Left Review*.

26 See here G. E. M. Anscombe, 'Causality and Determination', Inaugural Lecture in the University of Cambridge (Cambridge University Press, 1971). To vindicate the libertarian's possible world would, of course, involve consideration of the *because* of explanations of human policies, deliberations, and actions. Some philosophers have been exercised by the question, *Can reasons be caused?* I think they have been fully answered by Ayer, Davidson and Pears, who believe, roughly, *Reasons are causes*. The question about the libertarian's possible world is not this, however, but, *Must reasons be (totally deterministic) causes?*

27 Even if we do not laugh in the same way at admiration or gratitude or loving feelings? There was perhaps something absurd in the Greek city-states taking the Olympic games so seriously that they provided their own victors with free public meals for the rest of their lives. But one *can*, I suppose, take a game that seriously, while recognising it all the time as a game. With games, in fact, one does sense the possibility of an asymmetry between admiration and its reverse. When the Toltecs played

the game of tennis, and when they made their Maya subjects play it, the losing team was ritually beheaded. For as long as there are men, the ruins of Chichenitza will chill the onlooker with a horror and awe reserved for the totally alien. This was no game. It passes outside the framework by which games and diversions must of their essence be contained. But between commitment to a game and commitment to an attitude to other men, there is at best a weak analogy. The practices and beliefs which the libertarian has to scrutinise are not part of any *game*. All the same, even outside the game context, an asymmetrical indulgence in gratitude and in blame is not as patently or obviously irrational as most thinkers seem to have supposed.

28 A distinction over and over again ignored by those who continue to see the solution to the dilemma of freedom and determinism in the efficacy of punishment. Bradley's comment is still apt: 'I was once told of a West Country sportsman who, on starting for the field before the day's work was begun, used regularly to tie up his dogs to a gate and thrash them, and, at intervals during the day, repeat the nouthetesis. Whether it was wise to correct for no fault is a question for the dog breaker, but surely no man in his senses would call it punishment. And yet it was good utilitarian punishment.' (*Ethical Studies*, Oxford, 1927, p. 32.) To reduce the problem to the efficacy of *treatment*, notwithstanding the civilised intentions of those who would cut the Gordian knot and 'eliminate' responsibility, poses in practice an even more insidious threat to human existence. As Hart has pointed out, it is constitutive of freedom itself for a distinction to be made between acts which do and acts which do not lay citizens open to the attentions or treatment of the State, however reformative, remedial, therapeutic or benevolent. It is not, however, clear that we could finally explain why this distinction is so important except by reference to the notion of a fully autonomous agent in the libertarian's sense. Could we really explain and vindicate the need for this distinction, the distinction between that for which we are held responsible and that for which we are not held responsible, in terms of what is only the 'necessary illusion' of being able to help what one does? Less rhetorically, if one cannot do otherwise, can there be such a thing as a slight upon one's autonomy to decide for oneself?

29 'Freedom and Resentment', *Proceedings of the British Academy*, Vol. XLVIII (1962). See especially pp. 204, 209, 211.

  * We are not defining a purely technical notion here. If we were it would be all too easy for someone to go back to premiss (6) and question that. We are characterising an existing everyday notion whose dual, historical possibility figures in such contexts as this one. 'It's too late now. H.M.S. *Hermes* can't now intercept the *Bismarck* before *Bismarck* rounds the cape. It's not now possible for her to get there in time.' Certainly, if the definition does help explicate this sort of 'possible', then he who denies (6) leaves himself desperately little room for manœuvre when he comes to deal with our actual notion of responsibility and its rationale.

Coercion and moral responsibility

Harry G. Frankfurt

Coercion
and moral
responsibility

On some actions praise indeed is not bestowed, but pardon is,
when one does what he ought not under pressure which
overstrains human nature . . .

Aristotle, *Nicomachean Ethics* III, 1, 1110a

I

The courts may refuse to admit in evidence, on the grounds that it was
coerced, a confession which the police have obtained from a prisoner by
threatening to beat him. But the prisoner's accomplices, who are com-
promised by his confession, are less likely to agree that he was genuinely
coerced into confessing. They may feel, perhaps justifiably, that he
made a reprehensible choice and that he acted badly: he ought to have
accepted the beating rather than to have betrayed them. Thus sometimes, though not always, the use of the term 'coercion' conveys an exclusion of moral responsibility. A person who acts 'under coercion' is for
that reason regarded as not having acted freely, or of his own free will.
It may be established that a person is not to be credited or blamed for
what he has done, then, by showing that he was 'coerced' into doing it.

A person is sometimes said to have been coerced even when he has
performed no action at all. Suppose that one man applies intense
pressure to another man's wrist, forcing him to drop the knife in his
hand. In this case, which involves what may be called 'physical
coercion', the victim is not made to act; what happens is that his fingers
are made to open by the pressure applied to his wrist. It may in certain
situations be difficult, or even impossible, to know whether or not an
action has been performed. Perhaps it will be unclear whether the man
dropped the knife because his fingers were forced open or because he
wished to avoid a continuation of the pressure on his wrist. Or suppose
that a man is being severely tortured in order to compel him to reveal a
password, and that at a certain point he utters the word. There may be
no way of discovering whether he spoke the word in submission to the
threat of further pain, or whether – his will having been overcome by

the agony which he had already suffered – the word passed involuntarily through his lips.

I propose to consider those cases of coercion in which the victim is made to perform an action, by being provided with a certain kind of motive for doing so, but which resemble cases of physical coercion in that the victim is not to be regarded as morally responsible for what he has been coerced into doing. We might say that in instances of physical coercion the victim's body is used as an instrument, whose movements are made subject to another person's will. In those instances of coercion that concern me, on the other hand, it is the victim's will which is subjected to the will of another. How, in those cases, does coercion affect its victim's freedom? What basis does it provide for the judgment that he is not morally responsible for doing what he is made to do?

There are various ways in which one person may attempt to motivate another to perform a certain action. I shall confine my attention to only two of them: issuing a conditional threat and making a conditional offer. In each of these, the one person (P) proposes to bring about a certain state of affairs (C) if the other person (Q) performs a certain action (A). Whether a person who makes a proposal of this sort is actually making either a threat or an offer depends in part on his motives, intentions and beliefs. Considerations of the same kinds are also relevant in interpreting the subsequent response of the person to whom the threat or offer is made. But, to simplify my discussion, I shall generally ignore these factors. When I speak of someone as making a threat or an offer, it is to be assumed that he satisfies all the necessary conditions for doing so that pertain to his motives, intentions, and beliefs; and similarly when I speak of someone as submitting to or defying a threat or as accepting or declining an offer. It is also to be assumed that all threats and offers are credibly firm: everyone involved has sufficient reason to believe that the proposals in question will be carried out if their conditions are fulfilled.

The proposals in which conditional threats and offers are formulated are, in fact, often implicitly or explicitly *bi*conditional. When P proposes to bring about C if Q does A, he often also states or implies that he will not bring C about if Q does not do A. This need not be so. P may leave it open that he will do what he threatens or offers to do even if Q performs some action other than the one with which P's proposal is concerned. But when a highwayman tells a traveller that it's his money or his life, biconditionality is presumably intended: the highwayman will kill the traveller if the traveller refuses to hand over his money, while he will spare his life otherwise. And when an employer offers to pay someone a certain salary for doing a certain job, it will often be clear to the prospective employee that the salary will not be paid to him if he declines the offer. [1]

It may seem reasonable to construe every biconditional proposal that makes either a threat or an offer as necessarily making both. When the highwayman threatens to kill the traveller, he may seem by the same token to be offering the traveller his life in exchange for his money; and the employer, when he offers someone a position, may seem thereby to be implicitly threatening to withhold money from that person unless he takes the job in question. I agree with Nozick, however, in rejecting the view that any biconditional proposal making a threat or an offer is also making a corresponding offer or threat.[2] Surely a merchant is not ordinarily to be regarded as threatening his customers, even by implication, when he offers his goods for sale, although his offer to sell is naturally combined with a proposal to withhold the goods if the customer declines to pay his price.

Threats and offers differ in a number of ways. A person who fulfils the condition of an offer often has the option of declining to accept what he has been offered in return, while this option is characteristically not available to someone who fulfils the condition of a threat. It may be sensible for a person who has received an offer to shop around for a better one, but someone to whom a threat has been made has no such correspondingly sensible alternative. Threatening a person is generally thought to require justification, while there is no similar presumption against the legitimacy of making someone an offer.

The most fundamental difference between threats and offers, however, is this: a threat holds out to its recipient the danger of incurring a penalty, while an offer holds out to him the possibility of gaining a benefit. Given that one half of a biconditional proposal is a threat, then, the other half is an offer if and only if withholding the threatened penalty would be tantamount to conferring a benefit; and given that one half of a biconditional is an offer, the proposal joined with it is a threat if and only if withholding the offered benefit would be tantamount to imposing a penalty. But what are the characteristics of penalties and benefits, and under what conditions is withholding the one equivalent to imposing or conferring the other? What determines whether P's proposal to bring about C if and only if Q does A includes only an offer, or only a threat, or both at once?

Nozick suggests the following criterion for distinguishing threats and offers. If C 'makes the consequences of Q's action worse than they would have been in the normal and expected course of events', then P's proposal is a threat; if C makes the consequences better, the proposal is an offer. He adds in explication that 'the term "expected" is meant to shift or straddle *predicted* and *morally required*'.[3] Now this criterion requires the course of events when Q does A and P brings about C to be compared with another course of events in which Q does A. But it is not entirely clear how to identify this second course of events, which provides the baseline for evaluating the import of P's proposal. What are the 'normal and expected' consequences when Q does A, with which the consequences when P brings about C are to be compared?

Nozick's criterion permits a variety of interpretations. Let us consider the interpretation he himself gives it when he applies it in his examination of the following two situations:[4]

(1) P is Q's usual supplier of drugs, and today when he comes to Q he says that he will not sell them to Q, as he normally does, for twenty dollars, but rather will give them to Q if and only if Q beats up a certain person.

(2) P is a stranger who has been observing Q, and knows that Q is a drug addict. Both know that Q's usual supplier of drugs was arrested this morning and that P had nothing to do with his arrest. P approaches Q and says that he will give Q drugs if and only if Q beats up a certain person.

Nozick believes that the second of these situations involves no threat but only an offer. 'In the normal course of events', he explains, P2 'does not supply Q with drugs at all, nor is he expected to do so'. If P2 does not give Q drugs 'he is not *withholding* drugs from Q nor is he *depriving* Q of drugs'. He is merely 'offering Q drugs', therefore, 'as an inducement to beat up the person'. On the other hand, Nozick maintains that the first situation involves both an offer and a threat. Since 'the normal course of events is one in which [P1] supplies Q with drugs for money', the terms of his proposal mean that he will make things worse than normal for Q in the event that Q does not beat up the person. Therefore, P1 is threatening Q. He is also, of course, making him an offer: since Q does not normally get drugs from P1 for beating up the person, the desirability to Q of performing this action is enhanced by P1's proposal.[5]

In my opinion, what Nozick says about these two situations is mistaken. P1's proposal does indeed, as he maintains, include both a threat and an offer. But the criterion he employs for identifying threats and offers leads him to give an incorrect account of why the proposal has this dual character. Moreover, when this criterion is replaced with a more satisfactory one, it becomes apparent that Nozick is also mistaken in regarding P2's proposal as only an offer. The fact is that P2's proposal includes not only an offer but a threat as well. And it does so in virtue of the same features that make part of P1's proposal a threat.

If P1's proposal were to be construed for the reason Nozick cites as threatening Q with a penalty, then a butcher would be threatening his customers with a penalty whenever he raised his price for meat. What P1 does when he substitutes his new proposal for his old one is, after all, simply to raise his price for the drug. Instead of requiring Q to give him twenty dollars for it, as before, he now requires Q to do something in order to get the drug which (we are to suppose) Q likes doing less than he likes giving P1 twenty dollars. Now surely the butcher is not proposing to penalise his customers just because he tells them that he is changing his price to their disadvantage. The likelihood is that when he does this he is still making only an offer, though a less attractive one than before.[6] Thus the fact that P1 makes the addict's situation worse than it had been by changing the terms on which he proposes to sell him drugs cannot be, as Nozick claims, what accounts for the fact that P1's proposal is a threat. Nozick's criterion, as he himself interprets it, is not acceptable: it fails to preserve the distinction between threatening to penalise someone and worsening his options by making him a poorer offer than before.

To decide whether P1 and the butcher are making threats or offers it is not essential to consider, as Nozick recommends, how what they propose to do compares with what they *used* to do. Rather, it is necessary to consider how the courses of events their current proposals envisage compare with what would *now* happen but for their proposed interventions. And the question of what would now happen without these interventions is not to be answered by citing the terms of the butcher's and P1's earlier proposals. For those terms are entirely cancelled by the terms which have replaced them. When they make their new proposals, P1 and the butcher actually do two things: they wipe out their earlier proposals, and they set new terms. Since the terms of the old proposals are withdrawn and a fresh start made, there is no basis for the supposition, which alone would justify Nozick's procedure, that the earlier proposals serve to define what would now happen if the terms of the current proposals should not be carried out.

I am not suggesting that the terms on which people have had dealings in the past can have no bearing whatever on the evaluation of the terms governing their current dealings. Those earlier terms may, as I will explain later, have a certain current relevance. Moreover, I am not suggesting that the terms of a prior proposal never define the appropriate baseline against which the course of events envisaged by a current proposal is to be measured. Imagine that a prosecutor says he will ask for the death penalty if the defendant pleads innocent, and that he later proposes to ask for a lesser penalty if the defendant pleads innocent *if* the defendant gives him useful evidence against another person. Here the prosecutor's earlier proposal does define the baseline for evaluating his later one; it remains decisively relevant to the question of what will happen if the defendant should reject the later proposal. But this is because, unlike what occurs in the situations involving the addict and the butcher's customer, the prosecutor's second proposal does not entirely cancel the terms of his first.

In order to evaluate a proposal by P to intervene in the course of events that is initiated when Q does A, we need to know whether this intervention by P will leave Q better off or worse off than he would be without it. Measuring the impact of the proposal just requires, therefore, that we compare the course of events when P intervenes according to the terms of his proposal with what will happen if this intervention is subtracted from that course of events. This comparison leaves out of account the terms of any proposal which is cancelled by P's current proposal, and it takes into account the terms of any proposal which is left still intact.[7]

Proceeding in this way avoids Nozick's error, and it is correct so far as it goes. But it does not take us to the end of the matter, for it does not enable us to deal satisfactorily with situations in which what P proposes is that he will *not* intervene in a certain way in the course of events initiated by Q's action. Beating up someone and getting drugs from P1 is more desirable, from the addict's point of view, than doing the same thing without getting drugs from P1. So P1's proposal to give the addict drugs if and only if he beats up the person includes an offer, albeit not so good an offer as the one in terms of which P1 and the addict used to do business. The butcher's proposal to his customer similarly includes an offer: it is better for the customer to get meat for his money, even though it is less meat than he formerly got for the same money, than to give the butcher money and get no meat. But suppose that the addict declines to beat up anyone, and that the customer declines to pay the butcher.

The course of events then envisaged by the two proposals are: P1 gives the addict no drugs, and the butcher gives the customer no meat. In the eventualities in question, P1 and the butcher propose not to intervene at all. They will neither add to nor subtract from the courses of events that would occur if they were entirely unaware of what the addict and the customer were doing or not doing, and if they made no response whatever to their actions. It would none the less be a mistake to conclude that their proposals – to give the addict no drugs and to give the customer no meat – are of the same nature. On the contrary, P1 threatens the addict when he proposes not to give him drugs if the addict declines to beat up the person, while the butcher makes no corresponding threat. How are we to account for the fact that a proposal to refrain from conferring a certain benefit is in the one case a threat and in the other case not?

It will be helpful to approach this problem by focusing attention on certain things which we are inclined to take quietly for granted when we think about the situations in which P1 and the butcher are involved. Thus consider how differently P1's biconditional proposal to the addict will strike us if we suppose that there is an enormous over-supply of drugs in the market and that the addict has convenient access to numerous sellers whose prices are quite a bit lower than P1's. Consider also how differently the butcher's proposal will strike us if we suppose both that his customer will starve if the butcher does not give him meat and that the butcher's price is outrageously high. Changing our assumptions concerning the two situations in these ways would, it seems to me, lead us to alter our evaluations. We would no longer regard P1 as threatening the addict but only as making him a rather unattractive offer. And we would construe the butcher's proposal to his customer as including not only an offer but a substantial threat as well.

We find no element of threat in the butcher's proposal to raise his price as long as we suppose that he is not, in making this proposal, taking improper advantage of a situation in which he has the customer in his power. His proposal acquires the character of a threat, on the other hand, when three conditions are satisfied. First, the customer is *dependent* on the butcher for meat: he cannot readily obtain it from another source. Second, the customer *needs* meat: it is essential either for preventing what he would regard as a significant deterioration of his welfare or for preventing his continuation in what he would regard as an undesirable condition. Third, the butcher *exploits* the customer's dependency and need: he demands for his meat an unfair or improper price. When the first two of these conditions are satisfied, the butcher has the customer in his power. If he then offers meat at an exploitative price, his proposal to refrain from giving the customer meat if the customer does not pay what he asks is a threat.

It is hardly plausible to regard P's proposal to refuse Q a certain benefit as tantamount to a threat – even a weak or ineffective threat – to penalise him, unless Q cannot easily obtain an equivalent benefit elsewhere. For only in that case does Q have any reason to be interested in whether he gets the benefit from P or not, and a penalty to which it is reasonable to be entirely indifferent is not a penalty at all.[8] As for the second of the three conditions I have specified, suppose that P proposes to give Q a million dollars if and only if Q performs a certain action, that Q has no other chance of acquiring so much money, and that P's offer is in some way unfair or improper. The proposal still does not include a threat because (let us presume) the maintenance of Q's welfare above a level he regards as undesirable is not contingent upon his having a million dollars. While he may come to want the money badly once P's proposal makes it seem within his grasp, he does not need it. The point of the third condition is that without it someone with monopolistic control over a necessity would be issuing a threat if he asked any price whatever for the benefit he controls. But it would be unreasonable to construe the suppliers of electricity as threatening the public, despite their monopolistic control over a necessity, even when they proposed to sell electricity at a philanthropic price – a price far below their own cost, let us say, and well within everyone's ability to pay.

When considering whether the price asked for a benefit is exploitative, it may be appropriate to take into account the price at which similar benefits have been conferred in the past. Further, the history of the relationship between two people may shed light on the question of whether one of them is dependent for some necessity on the other. Moreover, the fact that one person has customarily been willing to transact with another at a given price may, under certain conditions, create an obligation for him to continue to maintain that price even when it would be fair and proper for someone else to set a higher price. Perhaps there are also other ways in which the past may have a significant bearing on the question of whether the obverse of a current offer is a threat. But none of these considerations justifies Nozick's claim that while P1's proposal to the addict is both a threat and an offer, the proposal P2 makes to the addict is an offer only.

P1's proposal does not include a threat unless we suppose that the addict is dependent on him for drugs, that the addict needs drugs, and that the price P1 asks is exploitative. It seems as reasonable to make these suppositions concerning the second of Nozick's two situations as to make them concerning the first. P2's proposal is plainly an offer, since it envisages a beneficial intervention by P2 in a course of events which would be less attractive to the addict if it were not to include this intervention. But the proposal also includes a threat, for the very same reason that there is a threat in P1's proposal.

With his regular supplier in the hands of the police, the addict will recognise that he is dependent on P2 for drugs as soon as P2 reveals his readiness to supply them. The fact that P2 has not in the past given the addict drugs is not pertinent to the question of whether P2 is making a threat or an offer.[9] What counts is that P2 gets the addict in his power by making him understand that he must choose between doing what P2 asks and going without the drugs he needs. Moreover, there is no reason to think the price in question fairer or more proper when P2 sets it on the drugs than when P1 does so. What makes this price unfair or improper when P1 demands it is not that it is higher than his usual price for drugs – price increases are not inherently exploitative – but that it requires the addict to perform a wrongful and risky action. The action has these same characteristics, of course, when it is required by P2. Assuming that P1 exploits the addict when he raises his price, then, P2 also exploits him when he sets that higher price for their initial transaction.

Withholding a benefit is, under the conditions I have sketched, tantamount to imposing a penalty. Under what conditions does withholding a penalty confer a benefit? Suppose that someone has stolen five thousand dollars, that he has already spent all but one hundred of it, that he has been convicted of his crime, and that the judge proposes to send him to prison for ten years if and only if he refuses to pay a fine of fifty dollars. Here the judge is threatening to penalise the criminal by imprisoning him if he does not pay the fine, but he is also offering the criminal a benefit – his freedom – if he does pay it. The judge's proposal offers a benefit because the price it sets for withholding the penalty it threatens is a very good one. The proposal gives the criminal an opportunity to get a bargain – this being the contrary of exploitation (there is evidently no antonym of 'exploited') – since the price it asks for his freedom is below the price that might fairly and properly have been asked for it. Generally: P's proposal to withhold a threatened penalty amounts to the offer of a benefit if P has Q in his power so far as the penalty is concerned – i.e. Q has no ready means of avoiding the penalty except on P's terms, and the penalty would deprive him of something he needs – and if P's price for withholding the penalty is lower than the price it would be fair and proper for P to demand. Just as P exploits Q when he takes unfair advantage of the fact that he has Q in his power, so P benefits Q when he takes less advantage of his power over him than it would be fair or proper for him to take.

There are three ways in which P may penalise Q for doing A. First, P may intervene in the course of events initiated when Q does A by adding to it something which it would not have included but for his intervention, and which makes the resulting course of events less desirable to Q than it would have been without this intervention by P.

Second, he may intervene in the course of events initiated when Q does A by subtracting from it something which it would have included but for his intervention, and whose absence makes the resulting course of events less desirable to Q than it would have been without this intervention by P. This rather unwelcomely implies that P is threatening to penalise Q for speaking when he proposes to turn off his hearing aid if Q says another word. The example is Nozick's, and we might attempt to cope with it by adapting a suggestion of his: P's intervention imposes a penalty on Q only if it leaves Q worse off, having done A, than Q would have been if he had not done A and P had not intervened.[10] But invoking this criterion would mean that whenever P threatens to penalise Q for doing A, it is necessarily better for Q to refrain from doing A than to do it and incur the penalty. It seems undesirable to build this into the notion of a penalty; clearly, some penalties are ineffective. I am willing to accept the implication that, in the hearing aid example, P penalises Q by turning off his hearing aid. After all, 'I stopped talking because he threatened to turn off his hearing aid' seems at least marginally acceptable.

Third, P may, without adding or subtracting from the course of events initiated by Q's doing A, unfairly or improperly make it a consequence of Q's action that Q does not get something he needs. We cannot, without intolerable artificiality, say that the addict gets drugs from P2 when he declines to beat up the person unless P2 intervenes to subtract his getting them from the course of events which follows. It is not by an 'intervention' of this sort that P2 penalises the addict for not beating up the person. Rather, it is by making it a consequence of the addict's refusal to beat up the person that the addict gets no drugs. This is equivalent to setting on drugs the exploitative price that the addict beats up the person. Having to do without drugs would not be a *consequence* of the addict's refusal to beat up the person (though it might be a *sequel* to it) if P2 did not make it such. It is possible, accordingly, to construe P's withholding a benefit or penalty from Q as a particular sort of intervention by him – one which has, as it were, low visibility – in the course of events initiated when Q does A.

There are also three ways, corresponding to these in a manner which should be clear, in which P may confer a benefit on Q for doing A.

Offering someone a benefit for performing a certain action enhances the desirability to him of performing it, while threatening to penalise him for performing it reduces its desirability to him. An offer (threat) will be *superfluous* if it enhances (reduces) the desirability of an action which is already more (less) desirable than its alternative. It will be *ineffective* if it enhances (reduces) the desirability of an action without succeeding in making it more (less) desirable than its alternative. Superfluous and ineffective offers and threats are, of course, threats or offers none the less.

II

But what is coercion? Coercing someone into performing a certain action cannot be, if it is to imply his freedom from moral responsibility, merely a matter of getting him to perform the action by means of a threat. A person who is coerced is *compelled* to do what he does. He has *no choice* but to do it. This is at least part of what is essential if coercion is to relieve its victim of moral responsibility – if it is to make it inappropriate either to praise him or to blame him for having done what he was coerced into doing. Now it is not necessarily true of a person who decides to avoid a penalty with which he has been threatened that he is compelled to do so or that he has no other choice. Nor is it true that a person bears no moral responsibility for what he has done just because he does it in submission to a threat. Such a person may be described as acting 'under duress'; but not all duress is coercion.

It might be suggested that someone is coerced if, in addition to his acting in order to avoid a threatened penalty, two further conditions are satisfied: (1) the penalty with which he is threatened renders the action against which the threat is issued *substantially* less attractive to him than it would have been otherwise; and (2) he believes that he would be left worse off by defying the threat than by submitting to it.[11] Adding these conditions does not, however, serve adequately to identify instances of coercion.

Suppose that P threatens to step on Q's toe unless Q sets fire to a crowded hospital, and that Q sets the fire in order to keep P off his toe. This does not satisfy the first condition, which excludes trivial threats: the penalty Q seeks to avoid by submitting to P's demand is not a substantial one. Suppose instead, then, that P threatens to break Q's thumb unless Q sets fire to the hospital, and that Q submits to this threat. Here the penalty with which P threatens Q is substantial: any course of action is rendered substantially less attractive to a person if it leads him to a broken thumb than it would if it did not involve this consequence. Thus the first condition is now satisfied. It may be, moreover, that the second condition is satisfied too. Suppose that Q thinks he will not be apprehended or punished for setting fire to the hospital, and that he does not expect to be troubled very greatly by his conscience for doing so. Then he may well believe that he would be left worse off by defying P's threat and having his thumb broken than by doing what P demands of him. Even if both conditions are satisfied in this way, however, it does not seem appropriate to describe Q as being coerced into setting the fire.

Why are we disinclined to regard Q as being coerced even when we suppose that he believes he will suffer substantially more by defying P's threat than by submitting to it? One suggestion would be that it is because we think that since Q must realise that it is better to suffer even a broken thumb than to set fire to a hospital, he cannot believe that his submission to P's threat is justifiable or reasonable. We might, accordingly, consider revising the second condition to make it require that Q believes it would be unreasonable for him to defy P's threat, or believes that he is justified in submitting to it.

Now the satisfaction of this revised condition would ensure that a person who has been coerced into performing a certain action *believes* that he cannot properly be *blamed* for having performed it. But the criterion of coercion for which we are looking must do more than this. It must ensure that a coerced person cannot properly be held *morally responsible at all* for what he has been coerced into doing. And this would not be accomplished even by strengthening (2) still further so that it required Q to believe *correctly* that he is justified in submitting to P's threat, or that it would be unreasonable for him to defy it. In fact the satisfaction of the second condition in any plausible version is neither necessary for coercion nor, even in conjunction with the satisfaction of the first condition, sufficient for it.

Suppose P threatens to take from Q something worth one hundred dollars to Q unless Q gives him something which Q values at fifty dollars. The penalty of losing something worth one hundred dollars is a substantial one. Moreover, we may plausibly suppose, Q both believes that he will be left worse off by defying P's threat than by submitting to it, and is correct in thinking that it would be quite justifiable for him to submit. But while Q may well choose to submit to this threat, nothing *compels* him to do so. The choice between the alternatives with which P's threat confronts him is entirely up to him. He must, of course, choose between them; he must decide whether to do what P demands and escape the penalty, or whether to refuse to do it and incur the penalty. He is free, however, to make either decision. And while he may decide that it is both in his best interests and entirely reasonable for him to do what P demands of him, he could have decided to do otherwise. The choice is his own, and there is no basis for claiming that he bears anything less than full moral responsibility for whichever decision he makes.

We do sometimes describe a person as having had no choice when the alternative he chose was plainly superior to his other alternatives. What we mean then is that he had no *reasonable* choice – that no other choice than the one he made would have been reasonable. But to have no choice in this sense does not imply that a person deserves neither credit nor blame for what he does. Indeed, a person may well be praiseworthy for having made a plainly reasonable choice. Now coercion requires something more special than this. It requires that the victim of a threat should have no alternative to submission, in a sense in which this implies not merely that the person would act reasonably in submitting and therefore is not to be blamed for submitting, but rather that he is not morally responsible for his submissive action.

This requirement can only be satisfied when the threat appeals to desires or motives which are beyond the victim's ability to control, or when the victim is convinced that this is the case.[12] If the victim's desire or motive to avoid the penalty with which he is threatened is – or is taken by him to be – so powerful that he cannot prevent it from leading him to submit to the threat, then he really has no alternative other than to submit. He cannot effectively choose to do otherwise. It is only then that it *may* be proper to regard him as bearing no moral responsibility for his submission. Whether or not it *is* in fact proper to regard him so –

i.e. as being genuinely coerced – depends upon whether a still further condition, which I shall discuss later, is also satisfied.

A person may be quite incapable of defying a threat which he knows it would be more reasonable for him to defy. Suppose that someone is pathologically terrified of being stung by a bee. He may be coerced into performing some action by the threat that he will otherwise be stung, even though he himself recognises that it would be more reasonable for him to suffer the sting than to perform the action. I am not maintaining that coercion occurs only when the victim of a threat is driven headlong into submission by a wave of panic. He may be coerced into doing what is demanded of him when he judges quite calmly that the penalty he faces is one which he could not bring himself to accept.

Nor am I suggesting that a person is susceptible to coercion only because he has, as it were, a repertoire of fears so imperious that he can be made to do anything you like by a threat which arouses one of them. The extent to which a person is in command of himself varies considerably from one situation to another. A man who is easily coerced by a threat of death into giving his money to a thief, for example, may unhesitatingly defy the same threat of death when it is not his money but the life of his child that is at stake. It does not follow from the fact that this man was capable of resistance in the latter situation that he was not coerced in the former.

It should not be assumed that the difference between these two situations is simply that the man judged it reasonable to avoid the penalty of death in the one, and that he judged it reasonable to accept that penalty in the other. He may well have made these judgments. But what is essential so far as the question of coercion is concerned is the difference in the extents to which he was able in the two situations to mobilise his potential strength. Realising that the cost of pursuing a certain course of action exceeds the gain will lead a person to think that pursuing the course of action would be unreasonable. But it may also tend to block his access to all his energies, and to make it actually impossible for him to pursue it. Knowing that what would be lost is too precious to lose, on the other hand, may enable him to find resources within himself upon which he is incapable of drawing in less portentous contexts. A person's evaluations may not only affect his judgments concerning what it is reasonable for him to do. They may also have an effect upon what he is capable of doing.

Faced with a coercive threat, the victim has no choice but to submit:

he cannot prevent his desire to avoid the penalty in question from determining his response. When he decides that it is reasonable for him to submit to a threat which is not coercive, his submission is not in this way made inescapable by forces within himself which he is unable to overcome. Sometimes we speak of threats as coercive even when we have no particular evidence that their victims are incapable of defying them. This is because there are certain penalties which we do not expect anyone to be able to choose to incur. A person who surpasses this expectation thereby performs not merely rightly or wrongly but with a certain heroic quality.

We do on some occasions find it appropriate to make an adverse judgment concerning a person's submission to a threat, even though we recognise that he has genuinely been coerced and that he is therefore not properly to be held morally responsible for his submission. This is because we think that the person, although he was in fact quite unable to control a certain desire, ought to have been able to control it. There are two considerations which may underlie and account for an opinion of this kind. We may believe that the person is morally responsible for his own inability to defy the threat; it may seem to us that it is because of something he himself has done, and which he is morally responsible for having done, that he is now unable to defy the threat. The other consideration is only in a rather special sense a matter of moral judgment. It is fundamentally a matter of our lack of respect for the person who has been coerced. It may be that we have a low opinion of someone who is incapable of defying a threat of the kind in question; and our judgment that he ought to have been able to defy it may express this feeling that he is not much of a man. This has nothing to do with judging him as deserving blame – if he should feel anything, it is not guilt but shame – and it is entirely compatible with the belief that he had actually no choice but to do what he did. Indeed it depends upon this belief. It is just because we recognise that we cannot expect better from him that we hold him in a certain contempt.

A coercive threat arouses in its victim a desire – i.e. to avoid the penalty – so powerful that it will move him to perform the required action regardless of whether he wants to perform it or considers that it would be reasonable for him to do so. Now an offer may also arouse in the person who receives it a desire – i.e. to acquire the benefit – which is similarly irresistible. This suggests that a person may be coerced by an offer as well as by a threat. It would be too hasty, however, to conclude that an offer is coercive whenever its recipient is incapable of declining the benefit it enables him to acquire. For it is only a *necessary* condition of coercion that a person should have or be convinced that he has no choice but to submit. Even if someone is unable to withstand the motivating force of his desire for a benefit which he is offered, accordingly, the offer may not be coercive.

Suppose that a person receives an offer inviting him to perform an action which he already wanted and intended to perform; suppose further that the benefit the offer holds out to him is something which he has long hoped for but never been able to obtain, and which he thinks it would be entirely reasonable for him to have; and suppose, still further, that what actually moves him to perform the action in question is his desire for that benefit. This desire may well be too strong for him to withstand. But our supposition is not only that the action is one which he himself wants to perform. We are also supposing that the desire which finally motivates him when he performs the action is one by which he in no way resents being motivated. He has no desire or inclination to resist the desire which moves him into compliance with the terms of the offer, nor does he in any way regret being motivated by it.

Surely this person is not coerced. For coercion must involve a violation of its victim's autonomy. The victim of coercion is necessarily either moved in some way against his will or his will is in some way circumvented, and this condition is not satisfied in the situation at hand. Neither in what he does nor in the motive with which he does it is the autonomy of the person in this situation impaired because of the offer to which he responds. The fact that the desire which moves him is irresistible is also consistent with his autonomy, since he identifies himself wholeheartedly with this desire. Its thrust – though in fact beyond his capacity to control – in no way diverts him from the pursuit of his own aims.

An offer is coercive, on the other hand, when the person who receives it is moved into compliance by a desire which is not only irresistible but which he would overcome if he could.[13] In that case the desire which drives the person is a desire by which he does not want to be driven. When he loses the conflict within himself, the result is that he is motivated against his own will to do what he does. Thus a man who prefers fame to obscurity but who does not want to be motivated by this preference may none the less find that he cannot bring himself to decline an offer to make him famous, despite his best efforts to overcome his desire to seek fame. This man is coerced into doing whatever he does to comply with the terms of the offer, regardless of whether or not it is something which he already wanted and intended to do. For his will when he acts is a will he does not want to be his own. He acts under a compulsion which violates his own desires.[14]

The irresistibility of the desire that a *threat* arouses is similarly, of course, insufficient in itself to make the threat coercive. A coercive threat, like a coercive offer, is only coercive because it also violates its victim's autonomy. Now a person's autonomy may be violated by a threat in the same way in which this violation is accomplished by a coercive offer. Thus the man who is uncontrollably terrified of being stung by a bee may be threatened with this penalty and succumb to his fear despite his best efforts to overcome it. In that case he is moved against his own will to submit to the threat, and this entails that he is coerced regardless of his attitude towards the action he performs in submission to it.

Irresistible threats are coercive, however, even when they do not lead their victims to this kind of inner defeat. Indeed, the condition that coercion must involve a violation of its victim's autonomy is satisfied by *every* effective threat. Although a person is coerced into acting as he does only when he is motivated to act by an irresistible desire, he acts in some way against his own will when he submits to *any* threat. In submitting to a threat, a person invariably does something which he does not really want to do. Hence irresistible threats, unlike irresistible offers, are necessarily coercive.

How are we to account for this? What is it about an effective threat which entails a violation of its victim's autonomy? The answer may seem obvious when the victim is made by the threat to perform an action which he would otherwise have preferred not to perform. But sometimes a threat will coincide with its victim's own desires and move him in just the same direction in which they would otherwise have moved him. Consider a man who, in an expansively benevolent frame of mind, decides to go for a walk and to give the money in his pocket to the first person he meets on the road. The first person he meets points a pistol at his head and threatens to kill him unless he hands over his money. The man is terrified, he loses touch with his original intention in the midst of his fear, and he hands over his money in order to escape death.

Here the action performed is one which the agent wanted and intended to perform; if he had not been coerced, he would have performed the action on his own. Moreover, he would not have defied the threat even if he had been capable of doing so; on the contrary, since he really does prefer to give up his money than to die, he would doubtless have fought against any impulse towards defiance which might have arisen in him. In what, then, does the coercion consist? Wherein is the man's autonomy impaired?

It is true that the man genuinely prefers being moved by the desire to save his life than by the desire to keep his money; he prefers to submit to the threat rather than to defy it. These are not, however, his only alternatives: submission and defiance are not the only possible responses to a threat. It is also possible that a person who receives a threat should be unmoved by it, and that he should abstain from taking it into account. In the present case, the man might thus have handed over his money with his original benevolent intention rather than with the intention of saving his life. He would then have *complied* with the threat, but he would not have been coerced into doing so. His motive in acting would have been just the motive from which he wanted to act, and there would have been no violation of his autonomy at all.

It seems that a threat is only coercive, then, when the motive from which it causes its victim to act is a motive from which he would prefer not to act. But actually, this formulation of the condition is not quite correct. Suppose that P threatens to penalise Q for doing A, that Q all along wanted and intended to refrain from doing A, but that the threat so infuriates Q that he is moved irresistibly – despite his best efforts to overcome his spiteful rage – to *defy* the threat and hence to do A. In this case the threat seems to cause Q to act from a motive by which he would prefer not to be moved. But, while his autonomy is indeed violated by the fury which overwhelms him, he is surely not coerced by P into doing A. Evidently a threat is only coercive when it causes its victim to perform, from a motive by which he would prefer not to be moved, an action which *complies* with the threat.

Now why is it invariably true that a person's motive when he submits to a threat is one by which he would prefer not to be moved?[15] It is not an adequate answer, or at least not an adequately precise one, that he is always in such cases moved by fear. For a person's motive in acting to acquire a benefit may be altogether his own, and it is difficult to specify whatever differences there may be between a desire to acquire a benefit and a fear of missing it. A somewhat better answer is that a person who submits to (and who does not merely comply with) a threat necessarily does so in order to avoid a penalty. That is, his motive is not to improve his condition but to keep it from becoming worse.

This seems sufficient to account for the fact that he would prefer to have a different motive for acting.[16] It also suggests why there is a *prima facie* case against threatening people and why threats, unlike offers, are generally thought to require justification. Someone to whom a threat is made has nothing to gain from it and everything to lose. A threat, unlike an offer, exposes a person to the risk of an additional penalty without providing him with any opportunity to acquire a benefit which would otherwise not have been available to him.

When P coerces Q into doing A, then Q does not do A freely or of his own free will. It is also true in a sense that P subjects Q to his will, or that he replaces Q's will with his own: Q's motive is not one which Q wants, but one which P causes him to have. Now we do not speak of coercion except when one person imposes his will in this way upon another. We have good reasons for especially noticing the roles played in our lives by the actions of other men and for distinguishing them from the roles played by circumstances of other kinds. Our ways of coping with and of regulating these two sorts of conditions are very different. But the effect of coercion on its victim, in virtue of which the victim's autonomy or freedom is undermined, is not essentially due to the fact that he is subjected to the will of another.

Consider the following two situations. Suppose first that a man comes to a fork in the road, that someone on a hillside adjoining the left-hand fork threatens to start an avalanche which will crush him if he goes that way, and that the man takes the fork to the right in order to satisfy a commanding desire to preserve his own life. Next, suppose that when the man comes to the fork he finds no one issuing threats but instead notices that on account of the natural condition of things he will be crushed by an avalanche if he takes the left-hand fork, and that he is moved irresistibly by his desire to live to proceed by the fork to the right. There are interesting differences between these situations, to be sure, but there is no basis for regarding the man as acting more or less freely or of his own free will in the one case than in the other. Whether he is morally responsible for his decision or action in each case depends not on the source of the injury he is motivated to avoid but on the way in which his desire to avoid it operates within him.[17]

We do tend, of course, to be more resentful when another person places obstacles in our way than when the environment does so. What accounts for this greater resentment is not, however, the love of liberty. It is pride; or, what is closely related to pride, a sense of injustice. Only another person can *coerce* us, or interfere with our *social*

Harry G. Frankfurt

or *political* freedom, but this is no more than a matter of useful terminology. When a person chooses to act in order to acquire a benefit or in order to escape an injury, the degree to which his choice is autonomous and the degree to which he acts freely do not depend on the origin of the conditions which lead him to choose and to act as he does. A man's will may not be his own even when he is not moved by the will of another.[18]

The Rockefeller University and All Souls College, Oxford

Notes

1 I shall not discuss complex proposals, in which P proposes to bring about a certain consequence if Q does A and to do something other than merely refrain from bringing about that consequence if Q does not do A.

2 Robert Nozick, 'Coercion', in S. Morgenbesser, P. Suppes, and M. White (eds), *Philosophy, Science, and Method: Essays in Honor of Ernest Nagel* (New York: St. Martin's Press, 1969), p. 447. I am very greatly indebted to this splendid essay, which has provided an indispensable basis for my own examination of some of the topics with which it deals. Although I am critical of several of Nozick's views, my essay follows his in a number of ways which will readily be apparent to anyone who is familiar with both.

3 *Op. cit.*, p. 447. Nozick does not comment on the distinction between 'normal' and 'predicted'.

4 *Ibid.*

5 *Ibid.*, pp. 447–8.

6 It may be objected that, despite my desire to leave such considerations to one side, the butcher's motives must be taken into account. But even if we suppose that part of the butcher's reason for raising his price is that he wants to make things worse for his customers (cf. Nozick's condition 3', *op. cit.*, p. 442), it does not follow that his proposal is a threat. The proposal may still be just an offer, despite the fact that it is (intended to be) so unattractive as to dissuade the butcher's customers from doing business with him. Of course, the butcher's proposal *may* be a threat. But if it is, it is not because it is (intended to be) less favourable to the customers than an earlier proposal. It is because of other circumstances, which I will discuss below.

7 Suppose that P offers to pay Q a certain amount of money for coming to work for him. Nozick's criterion would have us compare this with the 'normal and expected' consequences of Q's coming to work for P. But what is 'normal' or 'to be expected' when Q comes to work for P? Perhaps the best answer is that P pays Q a fair wage for his work. Clearly, however, the appropriate comparison is not between what P says he will pay Q and what it would be fair for him to pay Q (or what people normally get for such work, or what Q normally gets, or what Q normally gets from P, or what P normally pays, or what P normally pays Q). It is

84

between P's giving Q what he says he will give him, and P's giving Q nothing for his work.

8 Suppose that the customer could in fact get comparable meat from other nearby butchers, but only at the same unreasonably high price or at even higher prices. In that case too the butcher would be making a threat when he raised his price, whether or not he did so in collusion with the others, because the customer would actually have no useful option apart from the ones which the butcher's proposal defines. His dependency on the butcher is therefore not significantly relieved by the fact that he has other alternatives. But perhaps it ought to be said that, in virtue of those other alternatives, the butcher does not have him so closely in *his* power.

9 This fact may none the less mean that P2 acts less reprehensibly than P1.

10 *Op. cit.*, p. 443.

11 These two conditions are based on Nozick's conditions 2' and 7 (*op. cit.*, pp. 442, 443), which are the only items in his list of the necessary and sufficient conditions for coercion which bear on the distinction between coercive threats and threats which are effective but not coercive. It must be noted, however, that Nozick does not purport to define conditions for the exclusion of moral responsibility. His use of the term 'coercion' differs, therefore, from mine.

12 I shall not consider whether, or in what ways, the victim's conviction here must be justifiable. In what follows I shall in any case, for the sake of convenience, refer simply to the victim's ability to control his desires or motives rather than to the full disjunctive condition formulated above, assuming that the bearing of the missing disjunct will be apparent.

13 Nozick denies that offers may be coercive – indeed, he defines coercion in terms of threats – but he does not take into account the kinds of considerations which lead me to construe some offers as coercive. He limits his discussion at crucial points to what he calls 'the Rational Man': someone who is 'able to resist those temptations which he thinks he should resist' (*op. cit.*, p. 460). This keeps him, of course, from even considering the kinds of threats and the kinds of offers which I regard as peculiarly coercive. His use of the term 'temptation', incidentally, strikes me as somewhat imprecise. Presumably his Rational Man is capable not only of resisting temptation but also of subduing those desires and impulses which, while he is not at all *tempted* to give in to them, none the less threaten to overwhelm his efforts to direct his behaviour entirely in accordance with the dictates of his reason.

14 For further adumbration of some of the concepts employed here and below, see my 'Freedom of the Will and the Concept of a Person', *Journal of Philosophy*, LXVIII (1971), pp. 5–20. That essay develops a conception of the freedom of the will in terms of which coercion, as here understood, may be said to deprive its victim of free will.

15 Nozick points out (*op. cit.*, pp. 46ff.) that it is in the nature of threats that a person will not think it in his interest to be threatened (he explains plausibly how apparent counter examples to this may be handled). The use to which he thinks this point can be put, however, is not altogether clear to me. The mere fact that a person is in a situation in which he would prefer not to be certainly does not, in itself, entail that he is less than fully autonomous in

whatever choice he makes among the alternatives with which the situation provides him. For a person may defy a threat or, in the manner described above, comply with it without submitting to it; and in those events his autonomy is not impaired at all, despite the fact that he would not have chosen to be threatened. The focus of Nozick's discussion is somewhat blurred, I think, by the example he discusses. It is not an example of a threat at all, but concerns someone whose leg has been broken and who is choosing between having a decorated cast or an undecorated one put on the broken leg. This choice is unlike the choices often available to people who have been threatened, for it may be open to them to act as though the threat had not been made.

16 For a suggestive discussion of this and related points, see Gerald Dworkin, 'Acting Freely', *Nous*, IV (1970), pp. 367–83.

17 The argument might be made that it is always to some extent desirable that a threat should be defied, regardless of its terms, and that there is no corresponding *prima facie* desirability to defying the natural environment. If an argument of this kind should be sound, it would be more difficult to justify an action performed in order to avoid a threatened penalty than to justify one performed in order to escape being comparably injured by the natural environment. But it would not mean that a person's moral responsibility for what he does is affected differently depending on whether his motives are motives another person has caused him to have or whether they arise from his encounter with natural conditions in which no other person has intervened.

18 This essay would be less defective than it is if I had known better how to accommodate the valuable comments concerning an earlier version of it which were made to me by Peter Hacker, Anthony Kenny, Sidney Morgenbesser, and Joseph Raz.

Freedom, spontaneity and indifference

Anthony Kenny

Freedom,
spontaneity
and indifference

'The problem of freewill', said Tolstoy, 'from earliest times has occupied the best intellects of mankind and has from earliest times appeared in all its colossal significance. The problem lies in the fact that if we regard man as a subject for observation from whatever point of view – theological, historical, ethical or philosophic – we find the universal law of necessity to which he (like everything else that exists) is subject. But looking upon man from within ourselves – man as the object of our own inner consciousness of self – we feel ourselves to be free.' The existence of freedom, Tolstoy thought, was incompatible with the existence of scientific laws. Reason teaches us the laws of necessity: the consciousness of freedom must at best be the expression of ignorance of laws. 'It is necessary' – these are the last words of *War and Peace* – 'to renounce a freedom that does not exist and to recognise a dependence of which we are not personally conscious.'

Like Tolstoy, Dr Johnson regarded freedom and determinism as incompatible; because of the incompatibility, he rejected determinism. 'We know our will is free and there is an end on it', he said. Tolstoy and Johnson present, in effect, two parallel and conflicting arguments.

(1) Freedom and determinism are incompatible
   We know determinism is true
   Therefore, freedom is illusory

(2) Freedom and determinism are incompatible
   We know we are free
   Therefore, determinism is false.

Philosophers as distinguished as Hobbes, Hume and Kant have considered the possibility of rejecting the major premiss which is common to both Johnson and Tolstoy. In this paper I would like to explore afresh the possibility that indeterminism is not essential for the freedom which constitutes the autonomy of which human beings are conscious.

Philosophers who have rejected the incompatibility of freedom and determinism have commonly made a distinction between various senses of freedom. They have admitted that there are senses in which freedom is incompatible with determinism but have denied that we know that we are in these senses free. The sense in which we know we are free, they have claimed, is one in which freedom leaves room for determinism.

An early and influential distinction of this kind was the distinction between liberty of indifference and liberty of spontaneity. It began as a theological distinction and was used by those who – like Jonathan Edwards – were committed to determinism by their admiration for Calvin.[1] It was used also by those who – like David Hume – were committed to determinism out of admiration for Newton.[2] The concept of liberty of spontaneity approaches free will through the notion of desire or wanting: it sees the exercise of free will essentially as the execution of one's wants; to act freely is to act because one wants to. The concept of liberty of indifference approaches free will through the notion of ability or power: it sees free will as essentially a capacity for alternative action; to act freely is to act in possession of the power to act otherwise. Only liberty of indifference presents an obvious contrast with determinism; the contradictory of spontaneity is not determinism but compulsion. The two types of liberty appear to be distinct and in theory separable. If Descartes is right, a man with a clear and distinct perception of what he should do enjoys liberty of spontaneity without liberty of indifference; if Heisenberg is right some elementary particles are free from determinism without enjoying liberty of spontaneity.

Once the distinction has been drawn it seems easy enough for the defender of determinism to reply to Dr Johnson's argument. The freedom which is incompatible with determinism, he may say, is liberty of indifference; the freedom which we know we have is liberty of spontaneity. Whether or not we enjoy liberty of indifference cannot be a matter of bluff common-sense experience. For how could experience show us that there is no sufficient antecedent condition for our actions? Whether there are such conditions depends on the nature of the totality of physical laws governing life in our universe; and how could the introspection even of a Dr Johnson be sufficient to establish the nature of these? How could one feel within oneself the lack of a law correlating one's present action with one's previous history? 'All theory', Dr Johnson said, in another pronouncement, 'is against the freedom of the will; all experience for it.' What theory was against was liberty of indifference, what experience was for was liberty of spontaneity.

So far I have presented a simple version of compatibilism, the theory that freedom and determinism are compatible with each other.[3] The difficulty with the compatibilist theory as put forward by a writer such as Hobbes is that it involves a naïve conception of mental causation. The determinism which is put forward is a psychological determinism. It is observed that the fact that we can do what we want does not mean that we can want what we want. If all our wants are determined, the theory goes, then it may be true that we can do whatever we want and yet all our actions will still be determined.

This theory has not lacked defenders in the present century; but nowadays, I think, most philosophers would regard it as incorrect to think of wants as mental events which determine action. To say that someone did an act because he wanted to is not to postulate a mental event as causing the action through some mental mechanism whose operation is as yet imperfectly understood. Some wants, of course, *are* mental events: pangs of hunger, pricks of lust or sudden impulses to pluck a flower. None the less, the wanting which makes an act voluntary, the wanting which makes the difference between voluntariness and non-voluntariness, is not a mental event. The sentence I have just uttered I uttered voluntarily; I chose each word of it; yet there was no mental event of desiring to utter the word, no act of will distinguishable from the utterance of the word itself. And if some voluntary events – such as saying 'difference' – do not demand a specific event to cause them, why should any?

Certainly, when one says that a man brought about a certain result because he *wanted* to one is saying something about the causation of that result. But what one is saying is not that the act was caused by a certain mental event but that the agent was in a certain state in relation to causes when he did it. Following a tradition which is as old as Aristotle, but as recent as Austin and Ryle, I think that it is a statement about the *absence* of certain causes or causal circumstances. Aristotle thought to say that an act was voluntary was to say that it was not done under constraint or by mistake.[4] I think that Aristotle's list of the conditions which must be absent is almost certainly too short, and I must confess that I do not know how it should be completed. But one may criticise Aristotle on this point without agreeing with the proponents of liberty of indifference that in order to be voluntary an act must be totally uncaused.

The proponents of liberty of spontaneity are right to say that A's doing x because he wants to is compatible with the causal predetermination of the event which is his doing x. However, this is not because his wanting to do x is a cause that is itself causally determined, but rather because the types of causal determinism that are ruled out by saying that he acted voluntarily do not necessarily exhaust the types of causal determinism that there are. Pre-eminent among the types of causal determinism that *are* ruled out are psychological determinisms, by which I mean determinisms in virtue of laws in the statement of which mental predicates must occur non-vacuously. Among determinisms so defined, there are obviously included economic and sociological determinisms. Physiological determinism, however, is neither entailed nor excluded by liberty of spontaneity. It seems to me that there is no incompatibility between explanation by neurophysiological states and explanation in terms of wants and intentions; and this is so even if the laws of neurophysiology should turn out in the end to be fundamentally deterministic.

In order to defend this view, most contemporary compatibilists invoke a difference between levels of explanation. The compatibilism of Hobbes and Hume does not involve any differentiation of levels: the level at which the determinism operates is the same as the level at which freedom is experienced, namely that of introspectionist psychology. The contemporary compatibilist, instead of distinguishing between liberty of spontaneity and liberty of indifference, replies to Dr Johnson's modern counterpart by introducing a distinction between levels of description and explanation. He can agree that freedom and indeterminism are incompatible at a single level, while denying that there need be any incompatibility at a different level. He can agree that we know that at the psychological level we are free and therefore at the psychological level undetermined. But he can deny that we know anything about determinism at the physiological level. Let us follow the debate between compatibilist and incompatibilist on this new terrain.

The differentiation of levels is sometimes made by talking of language strata. There are an innumerable number of things, it may be argued, to say about a single tract of a single human life. Consider ten minutes during the reading of a philosophy paper. On an everyday level several things could be said about the philosopher: he is reading a paper, criticising determinist arguments, speaking English, earning his supper. Further to this a more detailed description might be given of the sounds issuing from his mouth, of the movements of his muscles, of neurophysiological events in his nervous system and in various areas of his cortex, and of the history of the jostling molecules making up his lips and tongue and mouth and throat. To give a full description of even a minute portion of a single human activity seems a super-human task.

Nor is the difficulty merely a practical one. It may be only a practical impossibility to give a complete record of what happens in terms of all the relevant disciplines, but it is more than practically impossible that the perfecting of one type of description might make the others unnecessary. The Vienna Circle once sought, as an ideal, a complete description in terms of a single science, namely physics. It seems that a description in terms of physics, even complete, could never substitute for a description in terms of everyday human activities; not because there has to be some sphere of human activity, or some component of human activity, which does not obey the laws of physics; but because a description in terms of physics is in an important sense irrelevant to a description in terms of human actions. However detailed, however accurate a description is given in terms of physics, it will never approximate to, or substitute for, the description in human terms. For irrelevant data do not become relevant data merely by being multiplied and refined. No element of the pattern of human behaviour will be left out in the complete physical description; but the pattern itself will not be given by the description.

To see this, consider the following simple case which involves no reference to physics but only the comparatively minor shift of level from the level of human-action description to the level of bodily movement. There are many ways in which one may obey the order 'Come here' uttered by someone standing a few feet away from one. One may move one's right foot first, or one's left foot first; one may take three steps or four; one may take up any of a large number of different positions and stances. If one were to begin to give a mechanistic description of what happened, one would have to specify all these details. None of them need to be specified for the action to be described in terms of human conduct whether as 'he stepped towards the table' or as 'he obeyed instantly'.

It must not be thought that the description in terms of human behaviour merely describes in a slipshod manner what the description in terms of bodily movements describes in precise detail. The imprecision in question is not a regrettable inadequacy of language, but a valuable asset in communication and prediction. For how difficult it would be to ask someone to pass the bread if one could do so only by specifying the Cartesian co-ordinates of the path which his hand had to travel, and the chemical composition of the substance desired. *The Merchant of Venice* is an imaginative portrayal of the terrors of living in such a universe. Shylock, like the rest of us, uses words in a broad and humane sense, where $15\frac{3}{4}$ ounces will do for a pound, and where flesh is none the worse for a bit of blood attached. Portia, *Tractatus*-like, insists that everything that can be asked for can be asked for accurately, and what one cannot specify precisely, that one cannot have.

And even if imprecision is an asset, imprecision is not the only characteristic which distinguishes descriptions in terms of human behaviour from descriptions in terms of bodily movements. If in one sense human-behaviour descriptions say less, in another sense they say more. To describe what a man did by saying 'he obeyed instantly' is to say more than 'he stepped three paces forward smartly' even if that was what his obedience consisted in. For what made his three paces forward a case of obedience was, among other things, that they had been preceded by a word of command from somebody else. So that one might describe the difference between human-behaviour descriptions and bodily movement descriptions very broadly by saying that the latter may tell us more about what is taking place at a particular moment, while the former tell us more about what preceded and followed the moment.

The reference to what goes before which may be contained in an intentional description of a human action is a reference to what goes before described in the same terms. In this way, descriptions in terms of command and obedience differ from descriptions in terms of stimulus and response. A stimulus, which can be described in mechanistic terms, causes a response, which can be described likewise. Whereas to say that a certain action was an act of obedience is not to say that it was preceded by an event conforming to a specified mechanistic description. For one and the same order might have been given in speech or writing, in many different languages, or by signs and gestures – events which would need very different phonological or physiological descriptions. So, too, phonetically identical stimuli may produce very different responses: e.g. the words 'go and do your good deed for today' spoken by a scoutmaster to a group of boy-scouts.

The relevance of this to the issue between free-will and determinism is as follows. It is only actions described in terms of human behaviour that libertarians claim to be free. Even one hundred per cent certain predictability at the level of physiology need not by itself involve any increase in predictability at the human level. For physiological laws will enable us to predict only physiological effects from physiological causes; and we shall need in addition at least translation-rules from the language of physiology into the language of human behaviour. On the other hand, from an action described in human terms a further action described in the same terms may well be predicted; as in certain circumstances from the making of an appointment one may predict the keeping of the appointment. But it would be impossible for prediction in these terms to achieve one hundred per cent certainty, since the everyday language of intention and motive, praise and blame, reward and reprimand presupposes a structure of freedom and limited unpredictability.

This sort of freedom, it seems, is possible without the violation of any physiological laws; just as it is possible to say that a given sequence of coin-tossings is a random sequence without claiming that the laws of motion were suspended for any particular toss.[5] However, it does not seem to be compatible with the existence of sociological or economic laws, since the expression of any such laws would have to make reference to precisely such features of intention and motive as presuppose the structure of freedom and limited unpredictability.

Physiology, however, is in a different position and the crucial question raised by the argument so far is whether there can be translation rules between the language of physiology and the language of human behaviour. If there can, then it seems that human behaviour is as predictable as any physiological event; and physiological determinism will be incompatible with human freedom.

It is clear that the mere existence of different language strata does not establish compatibility between determinism and freedom. One sometimes hears arguments such as the following. A paradigm case of predictability is the motion of billiards balls on a billiards table, once they have left the cue. But the rules of the game of billiards leave out of account as irrelevant many details such as the velocity of the balls, the exact point on their circumference at which two balls may collide, the order in which one ball hits another.[6] They count as relevant only a certain selection of the physical data about the billiards balls during any given portion of the given game: such as which collisions take place, the colour of the balls, the position of the balls in the pockets and so on. Hence, a complete knowledge of the physical data of a future game of billiards would not enable one to predict its course as a game since even the most complete mastery of physics would not enable one to know which of the physical data were relevant to billiards considered as a game. Similarly, it is argued, the rules of the language-games for describing free human conduct leave out of account as irrelevant many details about the colour of people's hair, the blood-groups to which they belong, the chemistry of their bone-tissue. Further discoveries in these fields, therefore, can no more prevent us from saying that human actions are free than the discovery of the Newtonian laws of motion compelled us to say that billiards was not truly a game.

The analogy is misleading and the argument is inadequate. The analogy is misleading because the account of billiards masks the facts that the motion of the cue is not predictable from Newtonian mechanics alone but depends upon human agency. The argument is inadequate because if it were the case that human-behaviour descriptions subsumed under themselves many physiological descriptions in the way in which billiards-situations subsume under themselves many physical situations, then the defender of free will would merely have put off the evil day by this argument. For given the physical data about the billiards balls, one can translate this into an account of a game merely by applying the rules of the game. Admittedly, these rules are not to be found out by research into physics; but the libertarian cannot appeal to the fact that they arise from free human convention under pain of importing into his analogy the very problem which it was designed to clarify. Applying his analogy strictly, we should have to say that given the predictability of a human being's behaviour under a purely physiological description, one would need to know merely the appropriate translation-rule in order to be able to predict what he will do in ordinary human terms. Thus, one could not claim that a particular murder was free and undetermined solely on the grounds that 'murder' was a term which subsumed under itself many different activities such as stabbing and poisoning which would need different physiological descriptions. For in order to predict the murder all one would need to do would be to predict the activity in physiological terms and then classify it in accordance with the translation rules.

The conclusion this suggests is that physiological determinism is compatible with liberty only if there is no possibility of systematic translation from one level of language to another. There seems to be good reason – though I will not argue the matter here – for doubting whether any systematic correlation could ever be established between physical events and human behaviour. The impossibility of the prediction of murder, it might be argued, lies not so much in the fact that many different physical movements might constitute murder as in the fact that one and the same physical movement in different circumstances may or may not be murder (was the agent a soldier? a surgeon? insane?); and that the relevant circumstances cannot be specified merely by giving an ever more detailed physiological description of what occurred at the moment of the action.

This does not, however, settle the question in favour of compatibilism. The problem of overlap occurs between natural languages too (one French word may correspond to many English words, and one English word to many French words) and yet translation is not impossible. And surely, if every movement of a man's hands, every twitch of every muscle was predictable; then surely his whole observable life would be predictable, no matter in what terms it was described.[7] The untidy nature of the translation from physiological into intentional terms does not really count against this. The situation might be compared to a jigsaw puzzle. A man's life, told in the terms which would appear in his biography, might be compared with the picture on the completed puzzle; the physiological events which make up his life might be compared to the pieces of the puzzle. There is no systematic correlation between pieces of the puzzle and details of the picture, neither one-one, many-one, nor one-many. For all that, once the pieces are fitted together, there you have the picture; and anyone who knows how to put the pieces together can *eo ipso* lay down the picture.

Here there is no longer any real ground for talking of 'translation' at all; but if the compatibilist seizes on this fact the defender of the incompatibility between freedom and determinism is likely to protest. 'My actions are mostly physical movements', says one incompatibilist, 'if these physical movements are physically predetermined by processes which I do not control, then my freedom is illusory. The truth of physical indeterminism is then indispensable if we are to make anything of the claim to freedom.'[8]

It is open to the defender of compatibilism to attack this protest on purely logical grounds. The argument appeals to the principle, sometimes known as Leibniz's law, that if x is identical with y then whatever is true of x is also true of y. My actions are identical with certain physical movements, so the argument goes, these physical movements are determined, therefore my actions are determined. However, it is well known that Leibniz's law cannot be relied on in modal contexts, that is to say, in contexts where the predicates true of x and y involve the notions of necessity and possibility. The number of members in the Common Market is identical with the number six; the number six is necessarily smaller than seven; but the number of members of the Common Market is not necessarily smaller than seven, only contingently so at this time. But the predicate 'determined' is a modal predicate: to say that an event was determined is to say that there was no possibility of things turning out otherwise.

This reply to the incompatibilist is suggested by recent work of Davidson.[9] Davidson's own solution to the question of the relationship between freedom and determinism is to say that while being caused is a relationship which links events in themselves, being determined is a property which attaches to events under certain descriptions. For an event to be determined is for the event to fall under a description such that there exists a law from which with certain antecedent conditions it could be deduced that an event of that description would occur. For Davidson events are part of the furniture of the world in a way in which laws are not; according to his theory, laws are essentially linguistic.

The Davidsonian answer to the incompatibilist does not seem to me conclusive. Laws may perhaps be linguistic, but natural possibilities and impossibilities are surely not. To take an instance of a natural impossibility, I cannot fly; this is not a property which belongs to me only under some descriptions and not under others, it is true of me, however I am described, that I cannot fly. The necessity and possibility which is formalised by standard modal logics is essentially logical necessity – the necessity which attaches to logical truths. Many philosophers have believed that logical necessity is essentially linguistic necessity: if they are right, then the failure of Leibniz's law in modal contexts may be ultimately a linguistic phenomenon from which no lesson can be drawn about non-linguistic necessities and possibilities.

I do not myself believe that logical necessity is essentially a matter of language. Logical truths can, if you like, be regarded as truths about all possible languages, but that very formulation shows the hopelessness of dealing with possibility as an entirely intra-linguistic notion.

Quite apart from this, however, there are good reasons for thinking that the 'cans' and 'musts' of natural necessity and possibility are not adequately captured by any of the standard modal logics. I shall list some of these in a moment, but first I wish to draw attention to the significance of these considerations for our overall purpose. The expression of deterministic theory demands the use of the notions of natural necessity and possibility. The reporting of free actions demands the use of the notion of rational or mind-guided possibility. Whatever relation the latter type of possibility may have to the former necessity, we clearly need a formal logic for natural necessity and possibility. If we have not yet a logic adequate to formalise these notions it seems that we are not yet in a position to know how to set about constructing a computer programme to simulate the activity of an autonomous agent.

The basis of contemporary developments in formal logic is the first-order predicate calculus, the part of logic which deals with predicates of objects and the quantifiers which correspond to the words 'all' and 'some'. This is a system of considerable power whose properties are extremely well known. Among the things which are known about it is that it is inadequate for the description of human mental states and activities. For human mental states such as belief and desire have a certain property known as intentionality. When we say that beliefs and desires are intentional we mean that various principles of reasoning which are valid in the lower predicate calculus will lead from true premises to false conclusions if they are applied to the thoughts and wants of human beings. The best known of such principles is once again Leibniz's law: this fails in intentional contexts no less than in modal contexts. If the detective knows that Mr Hyde is a murderer, and if Dr Jekyll is identical with Mr Hyde, it does not follow that the detective knows that Dr Jekyll is a murderer.

Since Leibniz's law fails in modal contexts as well as in intentional contexts it might be thought that modal logics would be adequate for the description of human activities and capacities. However, a number of arguments make it clear that standard modal logics do not suffice to formalise even the simplest statements about human abilities. In most standard modal logics the following three laws appear either as axioms or as theorems: (a) If p, then possibly p. (b) It is possible that either p or q if and only if either it is possible that p or it is possible that q. (c) If it is possible that it is possible that p then it is possible that p.[10] Now if modal logic is to be able to formalise statements about human abilities and skills it is necessary to translate a sentence of the form, 'I can do x' into the form, 'It is possible that I am doing x' and vice versa. But once we allow this transformation it is obvious that the three laws I have just stated can very easily be falsified.

Consider first the law 'if p, then possibly p'. I cannot spell the word 'seize'; I can never remember whether or not it is an exception to the rule about i before e. Yet on a particular occasion I may spell it correctly, assuming that I toss a coin each time to decide the order of the vowels. On such an occasion, 'I am spelling "seize"' is true and yet, 'I can spell "seize"' is false.

For an example of the second law consider the case in which I know two identical twins whom I cannot tell apart. When I meet both of them I can point to either Tweedledum or Tweedledee but it isn't true either that I can point to Tweedledum or that I can point to Tweedledee.

It is hard to translate the third law at all into 'can' sentences because it is not clear what is meant by 'I can can do x'. The only plausible sense seems to be 'I can acquire the ability to do x'. If it is so interpreted then the law that if possibly possibly p, then possibly p, is false. I would hardly be justified in answering 'yes' to a questionnaire which asked 'Can you speak Russian?' simply on the grounds that I can acquire the ability to speak Russian, e.g. by attending night school for two years. For these reasons, and for several others which it would take too long to detail, it seems clear that modal logic of the classical kind is inadequate to deal with the capacities of human beings.

Let us return to the incompatibilist argument that if our actions are identical with physical movements which are determined then our actions are themselves determined. Whether this argument is valid depends on whether the predicates involved in the statement of determinism and freedom are predicates to which Leibniz's law applies. If my recent argument is correct we cannot argue from the analogy of modal contexts that the law does not apply, for the 'cans' and 'musts' of determinism and freedom are not those formalised by modal logics. However, there are independent reasons for thinking that these 'cans' and 'musts' are not subject to Leibniz's law, as they must be if the incompatibilist argument is to work.

There is something wrong with the pattern of argument

> I can (cannot) do x
> Doing x is doing y
> Therefore I can (cannot) do y.

The argument works, of course, if the identity between doing x and doing y is a logically necessary one; but it does not work if what is meant by the second premiss is simply that a particular instance of doing x is the same as a particular instance of doing y.[11] I may be able to hit the dartboard; on a particular occasion I may hit the dartboard by hitting the centre of the bull, but it by no means follows that I am capable of hitting the centre of the bull. Any particular exercise of power and skill will have other descriptions besides the one which occurs in the specification of the power; and the possession of the power specified in no way involves the possession of the power to perform acts answering to those other descriptions. The example concerns a human skill; but similar considerations apply to natural possibilities and necessities.

Notice that the argument makes no appeal to a difference of levels between the two descriptions of the act performed; indeed in the example just given both descriptions were at an everyday level of common language. But obviously the same types of consideration apply also in those cases where there is a crossing of levels. The difficulty of giving illuminating examples here is that once one alters the level of description, then what is the agent at one level becomes an inappropriate subject for the attribution of powers at the other level. When we want to consider the validity of the argument that if the molecules composing my mouth can move only in one way then I cannot say anything other than I do, we have to consider a conclusion which differs from the premiss not only in its predicate but also in its subject. This is not of course an unimportant point, nor one irrelevant to the whole issue we have been discussing. But if the argument does not hold in the case where it would be most likely to hold, namely where the subject of the verb in the conclusion is the same as the subject of the verb in the predicate, and where both verbs belong to the same vocabulary, there seems little reason to believe that the argument will work elsewhere.

The considerations I have just advanced have been abstract. I should reinforce my case against the incompatibilist argument by quoting a vivid illustration from the lecture from which I drew its formulation. To show that statistical laws at a microscopic level are compatible with rational patterns at macroscopic level Professor Anscombe imagines a glass box full of minute coloured particles whose motions, though governed by statistical laws, always have the effect that the words Coca-Cola are clearly legible in the box. It is by no means clear, she says, that this supposition would involve any violation of statistical laws at the microscopic level. To this it seems open to reply that if the mere imaginability of the phenomenon is to prove anything at all it proves too much for the incompatibilist. For it is equally unclear that there is any contradiction in the supposition that the words remain legible even though the laws governing the behaviour of the particles are deterministic.

To argue for compatibilism is in effect to say that liberty of spontaneity does not involve liberty of indifference, at least if liberty of indifference is interpreted in any way which entails indeterminism. It has sometimes been argued that liberty of indifference is presupposed as a condition of the significance of ordinary language and of the rationality of human social institutions. Unless there is liberty of indifference, the argument goes, then we have all been talking nonsense for much of our lives. The argument fails. It is true that when, in ordinary life, we ask whether an agent could have done otherwise – for instance, when we are wondering whether to hold him responsible, and punish him for some misdeed – we are using the language of liberty of indifference. But it might well be that we can make the distinctions we make, and serve the purposes we have in making these distinctions, without accepting the theoretical account on which they are putatively based. We could continue to accept the same criteria for the appropriateness of the attribution of responsibility, while denying that they were criteria for the absence of sufficient antecedent conditions. The distinctions now made between determined and free actions would reappear as distinctions between different patterns of causation of actions. Indeed it is arguable that this is already beginning to be the case: that many people have ceased to believe in liberty of indifference but continue to use the expressions implying it, just as the distinction between natural and violent death has long outlived the Aristotelian physics from which the terms of the distinction were drawn.[12]

It may well be, however, that liberty of indifference and liberty of spontaneity are connected in a subtle way. There may be some truth in the Aristotelian contention that it is only to agents who are of a kind to be able both to do x and not do x that one can attribute wants or desires to do x, as opposed to tendencies to do x. It does not follow from this that when somebody does x this cannot be explained by saying that he wanted to do x, unless it was on that occasion in his power not to do x. Moreover the notion of power involved does not seem to me to be one which is incompatible with predictability, much less incompatible with determinism. On occasion it may well be true that I can do x even if it is predictable that I will not do x.[13] There is nothing contradictory in saying that I can, but will not, do x any more than there is anything contradictory in saying that I could have done x but did not do x. Thirty seconds ago I did not lift my left leg; but I could have lifted my left leg and my not having done so did not take away the power that I then had.

When we have an adequate logic for the description of this type of power, it may well turn out that even liberty of indifference is compatible with determinism. If that is so, then it will be possible to answer the arguments of Tolstoy and Johnson from which we started without appealing either to the distinction between spontaneity and indifference, or to a distinction between levels of explanation. It would be rash to anticipate the form of such a logic; but if our recent argument has been correct, the only reason for supposing that it would show determinism incompatible with liberty of indifference rests on a misapplication of Leibniz's law.

I have been arguing that it is unproven that determinism and freedom are incompatible. I should make clear in conclusion that my motive in doing so has not been a belief that determinism is true. I have merely been criticising one argument purporting to show it to be false.

Whether determinism is true or false seems to me something which cannot be settled on *a priori* grounds, if it can ever be settled at all. It is not altogether easy to account for the popularity of determinism in philosophical circles, given its unfashionableness in physics. No one, I think, suggests that determinism might be a datum of experience or introspection as some have suggested that freedom might be. The main sources of belief in determinism among philosophers seem to be a philosophical confusion and an extrapolation from the history of science.

In the passage from Tolstoy from which I started there can be detected a confusion between the notion of a set of laws being *exceptionless* and its being *complete*. 'If one man only out of millions once in a thousand years had the power of acting freely, i.e. as he chose, it is obvious that one single free act of that man in violation of the laws would be enough to prove that laws governing all human action cannot possibly exist.' Tolstoy thinks that an action must be either determined by laws or be a violation of laws. But laws may be exceptionless (apply to all items of a certain kind) without being complete in the sense of determining each item of that kind: as the laws of chess are exceptionless (they apply to every move in the game) without determining every move in the game (as the rules of, e.g. beggar-my-neighbour do, so that every move can be predicted from the initial hands dealt). Philosophers more professional than Tolstoy have not escaped this confusion.

Others seem to have based their determinism on a certain view of the history of the progress of science. All the natural sciences, we may be told, have made progress to the extent that they have sought sufficient antecedent conditions for phenomena and have refused to be content with the suggestion that different phenomena might arise in identical antecedent conditions. Does it not therefore seem reasonable to suppose that the way to success for the sciences of human behaviour must also lie in the uncovering of the determinants of the phenomena which constitute such behaviour?

In answer to this one may query whether we have any reason to believe that there can be a successful science of human behaviour; but this response will no doubt appear unhelpful and pessimistic. It may be more productive to inquire from what features of the history of scientific progress one is supposed to extrapolate. Is one to point to the success of deterministic explanation in Newtonian mechanics, or to its lack of success in stimulus-response psychology? It is impossible not to be impressed by the present availability of mechanistic explanations for many physical phenomena which were explained teleologically until the time of Descartes. But perhaps one should be no less impressed by the continuing impossibility of explaining, in terms of sufficient antecedent conditions, any psychological phenomenon which would have been regarded as voluntary in the time of Aristotle.[14]

Balliol College, Oxford

Notes

1 J. Edwards, *Freedom of the Will*, Part II, Section VII.
2 D. Hume, *A Treatise of Human Nature*, Book II, Part III, Section II.
3 Cf. Hobbes, *The Questions Concerning Liberty, Necessity and Chance*, and A. J. Ayer, *Philosophical Essays*, p. 278.
4 *Nicomachean Ethics*, 1111a22.
5 B. Lonergan, *Insight*, 61.
6 Cf. Lonergan, *Insight*, 355.
7 Cf. P. T. Geach, *God and the Soul*, p. 97.
8 G. E. M. Anscombe, *Causation and Determination*, p. 26. For a similar argument, see J. R. Lucas, *The Freedom of the Will*, p. 18.
9 'Causal Relations', *Journal of Philosophy*, LXIV, 21, 9 November 1967, p. 691.
10 Cf. G. H. von Wright, *An Essay on Modal Logic*, 1951.
11 The incompatibilist argument also depends on the possibility that there can be identity between events under different descriptions, which is a matter of dispute. See A. Goldman, *A Theory of Human Action*, Chapter 1.
12 Cf. C. Taylor, *The Explanation of Behaviour*, p. 25.
13 See M. Ayers, *The Refutation of Determinism*, passim.
14 Parts of pp. 90–2 and 97–102 of this paper were delivered in a Gifford Lecture in the University of Edinburgh in 1971.

Rational explanation of actions and psychological determinism

David Pears

HEF

Rational explanation of actions and psychological determinism

I

Determinism in psychology is often treated as an inappropriate import from classical mechanics. I shall argue that it is related to rational explanations of actions (i.e. explanations which give the agent's reasons) in much the same way that it is related to ordinary causal explanations of physical events. It is not presupposed by either of the two types of explanation, but it serves both as the focal point which fixes the direction of a certain line of improvement. This rough statement of the thesis for which I shall argue leaves many questions open. Are there not differences underlying the general similarity of the relations between the two types of explanation and determinism? Is it realistic to expect the improvement in psychology? Is our ignorance the only obstacle, or is there some kind of insuperable conceptual barrier? I shall try to answer these questions as I go, thus making my thesis more precise as I argue for it.

First, the field of discussion must be limited. There are two points at which the impact of psychological determinism is usually felt. When a person deliberates and acts, it may seem that, given his desires, he could not have chosen to act in any other way; and it may seem that his desires at that moment could not have been other than they were, given his endowment as an infant and subsequent history. These are the views of one side and they are imprecisely stated, but they may serve to locate two different areas of controversy. I shall be concerned almost exclusively with the first area.

Is the view that, given his desires, the agent could not have chosen to act in any other way than he did, simply an inappropriate import from classical mechanics? An affirmative answer to this question evidently implies that rational explanations of actions do not presuppose psychological determinism. But it also implies that they do not even point in the direction of psychological determinism. I accept the first of these two implicates, but reject the second. My rejection of the second now has to be made into something more than a vague gesture.

If rational explanations of actions point in the direction of psychological determinism, they must have a structure which is something like the structure of ordinary causal explanations of physical events, and it must be possible to imagine ways in which their structure could be improved by being made less loose and more closely articulated. So the development of my thesis falls into two parts. First, the actual structure of rational explanations of actions must be established, and then the possibility of the improvement needs to be examined.

I shall start by establishing one important fact about the structure of rational explanations of actions: that they are open to a kind of falsification by negative instances which has the same form as the falsification of ordinary causal explanations of physical events. This common form of falsifiability clearly indicates a common structure, and I shall argue that it is their common structure which gives the two types of explanation their similar relations to determinism.

There are many vague ways of giving a rational explanation of an action. In order to get to the heart of the matter quickly, I shall take two comparatively precise kinds of statement. An agent may say 'I did A only in order to achieve B' or he may say 'I would not have done A unless I had wanted to achieve B'. The first of these two statements implies that the desire mentioned was sufficient to lead to the action without any other desires, while the second implies that it was necessary. Since the procedures for falsifying an implication of sufficiency and an implication of necessity are related to one another in a familiar way, it will not be necessary to describe them both. The one that I shall select for description is the implication of sufficiency, because it has raised more controversy than the other.

The statement 'I did A only in order to achieve B' entails its counter-factual contrapositive 'If I had not done A, I would not have wanted to achieve B'. But this hypothetical is not directly testable, and so, if we want to test the sufficiency-implication of the agent's original statement we shall have to look further afield and see what happens at other similar points in his history. Here much depends on the way in which he specified his motivating desire. He will have specified it through its object, but the description of its object may have been so highly particularised that it would be difficult to find another occasion on which the same desire occurred again. In fact, some specifications of objects make recurrences impossible. However, even in these extreme cases, a slight generalisation will usually yield a criterion of identity which allows recurrences of the same desire. And often we do not encounter this difficulty, because the agent himself specified his desire in a way that was sufficiently general to allow recurrences.

But this is not the only difficulty that we encounter when we look for similar points in the agent's history. No doubt, his statement that he did A only in order to achieve B does imply that at similar points in his history he will perform a similar action. But this general implicate is, as it stands, too vague to yield a usable test. The first step towards making it precise is to stipulate that the desires, which, according to his own statement, were engaged on the first occasion, have not decreased in number or in strength in the interim.

We cannot assume that if any of those desires are not engaged on the second occasion, or are engaged in a weaker form, the explanation must be that there is some difference in the opportunities offered. For this part of the general pattern of his desires might simply have changed. So, in order to set up a valid test, we need to establish that it has not changed. If the agent's statement implied that this aspect of his character was constant, as Ryle claimed in the *Concept of Mind*, we would not need to bother about this difficult point. We would merely observe the agent on a second occasion which offered the same opportunities, and, if he did not perform a similar action, we would conclude that he had not given a full account of his motivation on the first occasion. But in fact a rational explanation of an action does not carry any such implication of constancy, and so we do need to establish the difficult point.

There is also another, more familiar way in which the scope of the general implicate is restricted. The test is valid only if a negative instance, if it occurs, is not attributable to anything that would explain non-performance in spite of the general sufficiency of the desire mentioned on the first occasion. For example, a new feature of the situation must not bring in new opposition from old desires. Also the occasion must offer a genuine opportunity, and the agent must be aware that it does: otherwise the desire will remain unengaged. Furthermore, he must have, and must know that he has, the capacity to exploit the opportunity. Moreover, if the instance is negative, it must not be attributable to bad luck, or to any defect of character which operates neither by making performance psychologically impossible nor by generating an opposed desire.

Here then are two kinds of restriction on the scope of the general implicate. It is not implied that the desires mentioned by the agent are sufficient to lead to a similar action whenever an opportunity is presented, but only when they have not decreased in number or in strength in the interim, and only when there is no new opposition either from desires or from factors other than desires. If these two conditions are met on another occasion, we can test the agent's statement, that he did A only in order to achieve B, by observing what he then does. If he does not perform a similar action, we may infer that his statement of his reason on the first occasion was deficient, and this inference will be confirmed if we can find a second, auxiliary desire which influenced him on the first occasion. Of course, if his action on the first occasion was over-determined, because it issued from two desires, each sufficient by itself, and if he only mentions one of them, this test will not reveal the deficiency in his statement.

If this account of the structure of rational explanations of actions is correct, it is easy to see how it is related to psychological determinism. If the structure is to become deterministic, it only needs to be improved in a few obvious ways. But, of course, it is one thing to dream of a deterministic system, and quite another thing to find one that actually works. So the interesting question is, what kinds of obstacle stand in the way of this improvement. But that question can wait. First, the account given of the actual structure of rational explanations of actions must be defended against objections.

Is the account correct? As far as it goes, it seems to be an accurate and almost platitudinous description of our actual method of assessing the truth of such explanations. Admittedly, the method is often unusable, because we are often unable to find a point in the agent's history which really does meet the conditions laid down. Now it is by no means clear how this inability ought to be interpreted, and this problem is connected with the speculation about the improvement. But that does not cast any doubt on the accuracy of the description given, nor does it suggest that there is another entirely different description which we might substitute for it.

II

There are, however, objections which, if they were valid, would show that the description of the method of falsification which has been given is not even nothing but the truth. There are also objections of a milder kind which are designed to show that it is not the whole truth. I shall take the fiercer objections first.

The first one that I shall examine is familiar. It is often objected that the account given of rational explanation represents a desire as the contingently sufficient condition of the action which would issue from it if there were no opposition from factors other than desires, whereas really it is logically sufficient.

If this objection were valid, there would be no truth whatsoever in the apparently platitudinous description that has been given of the structure of rational explanations. For if the general implicate of an agent's statement of his reason were true by definition, it would be a simple error to treat it as empirically falsifiable. Now the objection is commonly directed against the thesis that, if the agent wants to do A all things considered, his desire is a contingently sufficient condition of his doing A, given that there is no opposition from factors other than desires. I do not believe that the objection is valid even against this thesis. For it seems to me to be possible to drive a wedge of contingency between the behavioural criterion of the desire to do A all things considered and the criterion based on the agent's say so. However, I shall not argue that point here. Instead, I shall argue on the assumption that the objection is valid against this thesis, because I want to show that even so it is not valid against the thesis that has been put forward here.

Can there really be such a crucial difference between the two theses? I think so. Suppose that the agent wants to do A all things considered, says so, and does it. Then he will have given a non-analytical description of his desire. But if we want to know why he did A, we shall ask him to break his desire down into its components and to give an analytical description of it. For example, he may then tell us that he wanted to do A only in order to achieve B and C. Suppose that this is true (and that the action was not over-determined). Then it is a contingent fact that his desire to do A all things considered consisted of these two components (and that there was nothing to spare).

Now suppose that we wonder whether his statement of his reason really was true. Then we may test it by testing the contingent general implicate that the same two desires – to achieve B and to achieve C – provided that their strength remains the same, are sufficient to lead him to do A on another occasion when there is no new opposition either from his desires or from other factors. Of course, when the original action was over-determined, the test might give a positive result in spite of the fact that a third auxiliary desire, not mentioned by him, was operating on the first occasion. But that is a detail which does not affect my present argument.

My argument concedes one point, but insists on another. It concedes (without conviction) that the agent's desire to do A all things considered is a logically sufficient condition of his doing A, unless there is some opposition from factors other than desires. But it insists that both on the original occasion and on the later, testing occasion, it is a contingent fact, if it is a fact, that the two component desires amount to the desire to do A all things considered.

The crucial point is that the agent's desire on each occasion may be described analytically or non-analytically. The difference between these two kinds of description is a difference in the claim made by the agent, which does not necessarily involve any difference in the predicates incorporated in the descriptions (though it may do). For example, the agent might begin by describing his desire non-analytically as 'the desire to do A all things considered', and then, when he is asked for his reason for doing A, he might describe his desire analytically in the very same way, merely omitting the words 'all things considered'. This would be the limiting case in which he did A for its own sake, so that his desire to do A all things considered had only one component, the desire to do A for its own sake. But usually the analytical description of his desire will incorporate different predicates from the non-analytical description of it, as it did in the earlier example. However, the important point is that there need not be this difference, but that what must differ is the claim made by the agent. If he offers an analytical description, he makes a claim about his reason for doing what he did: if he offers a non-analytical description, he makes no such claim.

It is worth noticing that even in the earlier example it would be possible to describe the action in a way that would connect it logically with the agent's desire analytically described (given my concession): it could be described as 'achieving B and C'. But the fact, if it is a fact, that on both occasions the component desires mentioned in the agent's analytical description amounted to the desire to do A all things considered, cannot be purged of its contingency in this way or in any other way.

III

The next objection that I shall consider is also a fierce one, which would deny that there is any truth whatsoever in the account given of rational explanations. The argument is not that the suggested general implicate of the agent's statement of his reason is of the wrong kind to be tested empirically, but simply that it is not logically implied. This objection is seldom stated explicitly, although it is a corollary of the fairly common thesis that the agent's statement is immune from error. But a parallel objection to the Humean account of causal statements about physical events has recently been developed by Professor Anscombe,[1] and it might be instructive to transfer some of her arguments from that area to the area of rational explanations of actions, where Hume's theory may seem more precarious.

One of her arguments against the Humean account of physical causation is that it simply is not true to say that the only available evidence is the constant conjunction of cause and effect. Sometimes we also observe the effect issuing from the cause. Hume denies this only because he assumes that, if efficacy is observable, the observation of it must be exactly like that of colours. No doubt, the claim that the white ball made the red ball move does entail a general proposition. But we also see it making it move, and we have a word for what we see it doing – 'pushing'. The concept of 'pushing' is a typical causal concept. It is not based on observation in the same way as the concepts of 'white' and 'red', but it is based in its own way on the observation of the particular event. There are, then, two possible bases for causal concepts, constant conjunction and direct observation. It follows that it is not necessary that all singular causal propositions about physical events should entail or be supported by general propositions. It is an open question which do and which do not, and the only way to settle it is to examine them individually.

A second argument is that, when a general proposition is entailed by an ordinary singular causal statement about a physical event, it will always be an incomplete general proposition. Theories may contain complete general propositions, but theories are abstract, and in the hurly-burly of actual events it is a fraud to pretend that we can write in all the possible interferences which must keep away if the theory is going to be perfectly exemplified. So when a general proposition is entailed, it will be incomplete and perhaps uncompletable.

These two arguments have different aims. The first is designed to open the door of Humean dogmatism and to allow the possibility that there may be no entailed general proposition; while the second tries to prove that in an actual situation, if there is an entailed general proposition, it will have to carry an unlimited load of detail.

Both arguments may be applied to rational explanations of actions.

The second argument is persuasive when it is transferred to this area. For it does seem to be impossible that we should ever be absolutely certain that we have made a complete list of all the kinds of factor other than desires which must be absent on the second occasion when we require that the desire mentioned by the agent on the first occasion should lead to a similar action. Here much depends on the specificity of our descriptions of the factors. The descriptions used in the list that was given earlier were so general that we are extremely unlikely to discover a new opposing factor which would not fall under any of them. But if we try to make our descriptions more specific – if, for example, we start to list the various kinds of things which might make the action impossible – we shall be far from sure of completeness. So, if the instance is negative, our inference, that the agent's statement of his reason was deficient, may only be probable.

It is worth adding that, even if we could be sure that our list of possible specific interfering factors was complete, we often cannot tell in a negative instance that all of them really were absent. This consideration tends to reduce the probability of the inference by a larger amount than the previous one.

However, there are two points to be remembered on the other side. First, the inference can often be confirmed by the discovery of a second auxiliary desire which was operating on the first occasion. Second, when this confirmation is not available, we shall be balancing one probability against another, and this is a situation which we are used to accepting.

The other argument is more ambitious, and its success more dubious in both areas. If a singular causal statement had no general implicate, what would be the difference between a case in which X produced Y and a case in which X was merely followed by Y? The parallel question about desire and action may look easier to answer, but nobody has yet found an answer to it.

It is important to keep this question clearly distinguished from other related questions. Hume himself often put his own answer to it in needless jeopardy when he tied it to a theory about the way in which we tell the difference between production and mere temporal succession. We may well reject the theory that this ability always requires previous experience of the conjunction of Xs and Ys. For we can sometimes tell the difference the first time that we are confronted by an X and a Y. But this leaves Hume's account of the difference itself untouched. It would not be upset even by the discovery that our ability to tell the difference was innate. For there might still be a general implicate through which the ability would be tested.

But, someone might say, if we had this innate ability, there would be no need for the test. If this is true, it is a step towards an answer to a different question. The question asked was about our concept of causation, and it must not be confused with a question about possible alternative concepts of causation. This confusion is easily made, especially if we put the original question in this form: if a singular causal statement about a physical event had no general implicate, how could there be general agreement that it was a case of production and not a case of mere temporal succession? The obvious Humean answer to this is that there could be no such general agreement without some change in our abilities.

Although this answer is entirely adequate, it is unduly restrained. For the defence of Hume's theory need not be restricted to our actual predicament. It can be extended to an imagined world in which our abilities have been increased, provided that it is clear that this raises a separate question. Now there are differences in nature which we can establish only through differences in our immediate reactions, relying on nothing more than general agreement in judgments. So though the difference between production and mere temporal succession is not of this character, it may seem that we can imagine an improvement in our abilities which would give it this character. But this would be an illusion caused by concentration on the question, how do we establish causal statements, and by neglect of the question, what we do with them after we have established them. If in the imagined world we made no inferences based on the principle, 'Same cause, same effect', the concept that we were applying would be so far removed from our concept of causation that we could not even regard it as a possible alternative concept of causation.

If we confine ourselves to our actual predicament, without any imagined improvement in our abilities, there is a further question which needs to be answered. This question can be introduced in the following way. It is undeniable that many singular causal statements about physical events, like the one about the billiards balls, have general implicates which, at some degree of specificity and involvement in the details of the particular case, become uncompletable. A parallel thesis about rational explanations of actions is being defended in this paper. Now one reaction to these two theses is to allow that there are general implicates in both cases, but to deny that they are criterial, and to give them some weaker form of connection with the singular statements. If this were right, it would follow that each of the two types of statement must have some other criterion which is logically independent of the truth of its general implicate. Then in each case the other criterion will provide the statement with a basis, to which it would be possible to attach more weight than to the truth of the general implicate. Now I do not wish to take up the question whether this possibility is in fact realised. I am interested only in the prior question, whether it exists.

Does the possibility exist, as things are with us? Is there in fact in either of the two cases a basis which might be sufficient in itself to support a workable distinction between 'because' and 'and then', and which is logically independent of the truth of any general implicate?

There is a complication concealed in this question. We can often formulate a reasonably complete general implicate, which we then use as a test of the original singular statement. But sometimes we are less fortunate, and can hardly begin to formulate the general implicate. In the most baffling cases of all the only general implicate that we can produce is the proposition that there is some true general hypothetical covering the particular case. In these rare cases, instead of putting forward a theory, we put forward the theory that there is a theory.

Now we are all familiar with the direct observation of causes, and so we may suppose that it would be easy to describe cases in which our causal statements might be adequately supported by a basis that was logically independent of any specific general implicate, and even of the proposition that there is some true general hypothetical covering the particular case. But the requirement of independence is not so easily met. What is required is that the directly observed basis should support the singular statement and yet be logically independent of any general implicate. It may well be that the kind of basis which would meet this requirement is a kind with no instances in our experience. Certainly, I have never seen such a basis convincingly described either for singular causal statements or for rational explanations of actions. The type of case which makes the best show of meeting the requirements of adequacy and independence is one in which the observer is enormously impressed by his direct observation of the operation of the cause, but utterly unable to formulate any specific general hypothetical: for example, a child watches vitriol burn paper for the first time. But, though the theory that there is a theory cannot be used to test the singular causal statement 'It burned it', it does play an indispensable role. It commits the speaker to the favourable result of an undiscovered test of a familiar form. If he were freed from this commitment, he might just as well have said that the combustion was spontaneous and coincidental.

It might be objected that a Humean would not be convinced by any attempt to meet the requirements of adequacy and independence because he could not be convinced, and that he could not be convinced only because he has swallowed some suitably qualified form of the principle 'Same cause, same effect'. But this would be no more than a half truth. The truth is that he accepts the principle because we have no other way of making the distinction between 'because' and 'and then'; and because if the imagined improvement in our abilities put the distinction exclusively on another basis, that would change the meaning of the word 'because'.

IV

I now turn to some milder objections designed to show that the account given of rational explanations of actions is not the whole truth. The first one that I shall examine claims that it does not adequately cover the concept of the operativeness of a desire or a physical cause. My answer to this will be that, though this is true, what needs to be added is not that these concepts have a basis that is logically independent of any general implicate. The necessary supplement can be developed within the limits set by Humean theory. If this is right, it will reinforce the answer given to the previous objection.

Consider the following example.[2] Someone is selecting people for a certain kind of job, using a short list of requirements. He accepts a particular candidate only because he meets the requirements (so he says). Then on a later occasion another candidate, who meets the same requirements, is rejected by him because (so he says) he has a defect which the first candidate did not have. Now is it not absurd to conclude that, if the desires, which, according to his own statement, were engaged on the first occasion, had not decreased in number or in strength in the interim, and if there was no new opposition from factors other than desires on the second occasion, then his statement of his reason on the first occasion must have been deficient? Anyone who drew this conclusion would have to allow that that statement lay open to supplementation by the mention of the absence of a number of features on the first occasion – a number limited only by the number of the agent's desires which would have been engaged against acceptance if the features had not been absent. Yet much of this extra material would not have occurred to him at the time, and so the associated desires would not have been operative.

The short answer to this objection is that my theory is forearmed against it by the proviso that the testing occasion must not have any feature which engages new opposition from old desires. But it would be more interesting to remove this proviso and to explore the effect of this new kind of negative instance. For presumably, if we want to assess an agent's statement of his reason for an action, we would make some use of a situation which engaged an opposed desire that was not engaged on the first occasion, provided that it existed at that time. So the interesting question is, what use we would make of it.

If we make any use of this kind of situation, we need some way of distinguishing between those desires that were operative on the first occasion and those that were not operative. This is the point of the objector's argument. It does not exploit the possibility that there might be some undetected change in the number or strength of the desires which, according to the agent's own statement, were engaged on the first occasion, or the possibility that there might be new and un-detected opposition from some other kind of factor on the second occasion. It is conceded that the test is properly set up, as far as those two points go. It is also assumed that new opposition from old desires on the testing occasion is in order. The problem then is how to interpret the result. For although the result supports the conclusion that the selector would not have accepted the candidate if he too had had the defect, it does not follow that the fact that he did not have the defect was part of his reason for accepting him.

It is always illuminating to compare the structure of rational explanations of actions with the structure of causal explanations of physical events. At this particular point there is an important similarity between the two structures. For when the billiards player says that the red ball moved because his white ball struck it, we do not regard his statement as deficient on the ground that it would not have moved if the other player had held it fast. But what exactly is the similarity? It cannot simply be that a full account of a physical cause need not mention the absence of a factor which would have interfered if it had been present, or that a full statement of a reason for an action need not mention the absence of a feature which would have engaged an opposed desire if it had been present. For it is impossible to draw a general line between the presence of a feature and the absence of the correlative negative feature: and in any case, it simply is not true that, when it is more natural to describe a situation in the second way, the absence of the feature will always play a part that is so minor that it need not be mentioned in the agent's statement of his reason or in the causal explanation of a physical event. The absence of the defect might have been rare, and so it might have been part of the selector's reason for accepting the first candidate. Similarly, the absence of the other player's intervention might have been an unusual feature of a game of billiards played by children, and so it might be necessary to include it in a full causal explanation of the red ball's movement. So the similarity is not that absent opposition need not be mentioned, but rather that it need not be mentioned when its presence is rare; and, symmetrically, that present support need not be mentioned when its absence is rare. There are, of course, other principles of discrimination between what one should mention and what one need not mention in explanations. Another is that we tend to mention a particular kind of positive factor – the event which tips the scales.

There is, however, a difference masked by this similarity. In the game of billiards the absent factor makes its contribution simply by being absent. But in the other case the absence of the defect may make a more complex contribution than this. Naturally, it must do at least what the absent factor does in the game of billiards: for it must at least be true that, if the first candidate had had the defect (we need not add 'and if it had been noticed', because this is included in the general restrictions), then he would not have been selected. But if the absence of the defect was part of the agent's reason for selecting him, a further condition must be met: the desire to select a candidate without the defect must have been operative. So, if it is a question of rarity, it is not merely that the absence of the defect must be rare enough to be worth mentioning: it must also be rare enough to have influenced the agent at the time. The criterion of 'influencing' is, of course, problematical, and it will be discussed later, but it is clear that we must have a way of distinguishing between the two contributions which might be made by the absence of the defect.

This difference between the two structures is connected with another, more striking difference. When an agent gives his reason for an action, he makes a selection from a set of desires. If he offers a full statement of his reason ('only because'), he must mention every operative desire.

But, whatever the principle of selection, the set from which the selection is made will always be a set of positive desires. In the example, if the man choosing people for a certain kind of job does not want a candidate with the defect, he must want one without the defect. Of course, the inference from 'he does not want X' to 'he wants not-X' is invalid. But in this kind of example *ex hypothesi* the agent wanted to fill a vacancy on the first occasion, and so he must have wanted a candidate without the defect, and then the only remaining question is whether that desire was operative. If we took a different kind of case, in which the agent might want to do nothing – say, because the vacancies did not have to be filled – the positive desire which might have been operative on the first occasion will be the desire to take a candidate only if he lacks the defect. So, in general, when an agent offers a full statement of his reason for an action, he always selects from a set of positive desires. But the set of factors from which we select when we offer a causal explanation of a physical event will often include members which it would be unnatural to regard as positive. This is a striking difference between the structures of the two kinds of explanation.

What is the importance of this difference between the two structures, and of the similarity mentioned earlier? I shall now argue that the similarity explains the part of the concept of 'operativeness' which is not adequately covered by the Humean theory, and that the explanation keeps within the limits set by that theory. I shall also argue that the difference between the two structures is important, because it provides part of the explanation of the widespread feeling that the residual element is larger in the concept of the operativeness of a desire than it is in the concept of the operativeness of a physical cause.

First, it is evident that the best cases of so-called 'direct observation of causation' are cases in which the observed event is conspicuous and even dramatic. We see the white ball making the red ball move. This is the positive factor which visibly makes the difference, and we do not need to mention the absence of interfering factors when their presence is rare. Similarly, an agent feels a particular desire influencing him to perform a certain action, and this is the main positive feature which he will mention if he is simply asked for his reason. He need not put in any additions or qualifications unless he is asked for a full account of his motivation. This principle of selection is deeply rooted in our experience of causation and we put great trust in it, especially when the event is dramatic and isolated (cf. the child and the vitriol).

Second, this account of the residual element in the concept of 'operativeness', though it adds something to the Humean analysis, does not add anything that is logically independent of that analysis. What it adds is a principle of selection which connects the factor selected with a familiar basis in experience. But this basis cannot support an explanation of either of the two kinds without entailing a general proposition.

Third, the difference between the two structures provides part of the explanation of the feeling that the extra element is larger in the concept of the operativeness of a desire. For desires may always be regarded as positive factors, but it is not always possible to regard physical causal factors in this way.

However, this is not the whole explanation of the feeling that the extra element is larger in the concept of the operativeness of a desire. There is also the fact that the agent's awareness of the operativeness of one of his own desires is so intimate that it has been credited with immunity from error. It is evident that this peculiar intimacy gives the concept of the operativeness of a desire an especially firm basis in direct experience. Now if the agent really did enjoy total immunity from error, I would be faced with a dilemma: either my account of the way in which we test the agent's statement of his reason would have to be abandoned, or else negative results would always have to be taken as establishing that he had been untruthful. I would reject the first of these alternatives on the ground that my account is platitudinous, and the second is unacceptable because it attributes to the agent a quite unbelievable amount of general knowledge about himself. I shall, therefore, argue that the agent does not enjoy immunity from error on such matters. This will allow me to defend my thesis that the direct basis in his experience is not independent of any general implicate, without attributing to him an incredible amount of general self-knowledge. So my strategy will be to try to do full justice to the peculiar intimacy of the agent's awareness of the operation of his desires while avoiding the exaggerated thesis that he is immune from error.

When we describe the agent's awareness of the operation of the desire to achieve B as 'intimate', that is a metaphor. A plain description of it would include three points. He feels the desire influencing him; he knows that it is *as the desire to achieve B* that it influences him; and, more generally, if he has to add other desires in order to get a full account of his motivation, he knows that he will be selecting from a set with most of whose members he is acquainted.

The first of these three points is matched on the billiards table. But the second is not generally true of physical causes, and the fact, that it is not, is important, because it is connected with my argument for the thesis that the direct experimental basis of the concept of operativeness could not give that concept any support if it were logically independent of any general implicate. I argued that it simply is not sufficient in itself to support a workable distinction between production and mere temporal succession. Now in the case of the billiards balls the implicate would be a fairly fully formulated, but presumably not completely formulated, general proposition. But in a totally unfamiliar case of physical causation all that would be implied is that there is some true, but probably incomplete, general proposition covering the particular case. If this were the only general implicate that we could produce, we would be unable to test for the difference between production and mere temporal succession. Nevertheless, we would still believe that there was a test which we could use if we could discover it. The second point about desires is that the agent is never restricted to this *pis aller*. He knows the description under which his desire influenced him.

The third point is important when the agent is asked to give a full account of his motivation. Since he will be selecting from a set of desires with most of whose members he is acquainted, he will have a better chance of producing a full account. In fact, we do not have any definite idea of the fullness of a causal explanation in the hurly-burly of physical events, and so we always have to apply some sort of restriction to the field. But we have a much more definite idea of what we mean by a full account of an agent's reason for his action; we mean an account which mentions all the desires which influenced him. Careful introspection may be needed before the agent can produce such an account, and even then he may not succeed. But the situation is not nearly so open as it is when we are seeking a physical cause, because the agent starts with the advantage of acquaintance with most of the desires which might have influenced him. This contrast can be drawn in a way that connects it with the main thesis of this paper: a full account of an agent's reason for his action will imply a general proposition which is complete as far as desires are concerned, but an equally full, and therefore usually unattainable, account of the cause of a physical event would imply a general proposition which was complete as far as any kind of factor is concerned.

But is an agent's statement of his reason for an action immune from error? Much depends on the kind of statement that he makes. If he only makes the minimal claim that the desire to achieve B was among those that influenced him, it may seem that he can hardly be mistaken. For he will remember that it occurred to him at the time that he wanted to achieve B, and that he would achieve B if he did A: and he will not be offering a complete analytical description of his motivation, so that he will not be specifying any set of desires to which the desire to achieve B needs to be added, and when added is sufficient to lead him to perform a similar action. So this looks like a case in which the direct experience of operativeness is sufficient in itself to support the agent's statement, independently of any general implicate. He is like the child watching the drops of vitriol except that he knows that it is *as the desire to achieve B* that his desire to achieve B influenced him.

But even this minimal claim cannot be based on a direct experience of operativeness which is independent of any general implicate. For if the agent does want to achieve B, there will be some situation in which that desire will lead him to perform whatever action he believes to be necessary and sufficient to achieve B: and it is possible that we might become so doubtful of the truth of this multiple general proposition that we would reject the claim that he does want to achieve B. Now it seems to me that, when we did this, we would not necessarily accuse him of untruthfulness. However, if anyone disagrees with this, and maintains that untruthfulness would be the only possible explanation, that will not upset my general thesis. For I am trying to establish that, if the direct experience of operativeness is independent of any general implicate, it cannot support any kind of agent's statement of his reason for an action. Now this particular kind of statement makes a minimal claim and has a general implicate with very little content. So if anyone maintains that an agent could not make a false statement of this kind unless he was being untruthful, I need only point out that this is easily compatible with my thesis, because it does not credit the agent with an implausible amount of general self-knowledge.

However, I cannot argue in this way about the statements, 'My main reason was that I wanted to achieve B' and, 'My only reason was that I wanted to achieve B'. For if an agent could not make a false statement of either of these two kinds unless he was being untruthful, my thesis would collapse. For it would involve the attribution of far too much general self-knowledge to agents.

The question whether error is possible is raised in its clearest form by the statement, 'My only reason was that I wanted to achieve B'. Anyone who answers it in the negative will have to maintain that, whenever a desire influences an agent, he will be aware of its influence at the time. But if this is meant as a factual proposition, it is vulnerable to two kinds of counter-example. First, we are all familiar with cases of pre-conscious motivation. Second, the main source of an action may be a desire which is working itself out in a devious way: in such a case the agent may be unconscious of the operation of the desire, and perhaps even of its existence. Now counter-examples of the second kind do not come into head-on collision with the idea of immunity from error. This is partly because unconscious desires often operate through conscious desires, and partly because it seems excessive to apply to the agent's statement of his reason a standard of fullness which requires him to select from a set of desires some of whose members are not known by him to exist. Also, even when he is aware of their existence it may seem excessive to require him to include desires which operate in a devious, symbolical way. After all, the standard of fullness which we apply to agents' statements of their reasons was devised for ordinary cases, and, though it may be raised, there are natural resistances to this process. It is, therefore, an important fact that no such doubts and difficulties affect counter-examples of the other kind – cases of pre-conscious motivation.

However, the proposition that, whenever a desire influences an agent, he will be aware of its influence, may be regarded as an imprecisely stated conceptual truth. A more precise way of expressing it would be to say that it is a feature of the concept of an agent's reason that, if a desire influences him without his being aware of its influence, then that desire cannot be part of his reason. In support of this it might be argued that the agent's awareness of the operation of his desire has to be part of the mechanism of its operation, if it is to be brought under the concept.

The short answer to this is that it simply is not true of our concept of an agent's reason. The best evidence for this answer is provided by the way in which we describe cases of pre-conscious motivation. It is reasonable to exclude a desire on the ground that it operates in such a devious way that the agent is unconscious of its operation and perhaps even of its existence. But it is not reasonable to exclude a desire which operates in a straightforward way on the ground that he happens to be unaware of its operation. Why should the standard of fullness make allowances for ignorance which cannot be attributed to any general difficulty?

The argument used brings in no real reinforcement. It is quite true that awareness of the operation of a desire is often part of the mechanism of its operation. For there may be a pre-conscious inoperative desire which would have operated if the agent had been aware of its tendency: and, conversely, there may be a pre-conscious operative desire which would not have operated if he had been aware of its operation. These possibilities force us to distinguish between various ways in which a desire may operate. First, it may operate in a way which may or may not be accompanied by awareness of its operation. Second, if the agent becomes aware that it is operating in this generic way, and if his awareness becomes part of the mechanism of its operation, it will then be operating in another, more specific way. There is also the other species in the genus, the third mode of operation, of which the agent is unaware. But none of these considerations provide any support for the thesis that it is a feature of the concept of an agent's reason that it only includes desires which influence him through his awareness of their influence. For we can distinguish between the three ways in which a desire may operate without regarding the second way as necessary for a desire that is brought under the concept of a reason.

I conclude that an adequate account of the operativeness of a desire can be given within the limits set by Humean theory: and that, since the agent does not enjoy immunity from error when he states his reason for an action, the Humean treatment of the concept does not commit us to crediting him with an unbelievable amount of general self-knowledge.

V

The last objection that I shall examine is also a mild one, designed to show that the account given of rational explanations of actions is still less than the whole truth. I shall try to deal with it in the same way as the previous objection, by arguing that, though something more needs to be added to the account so far given, the addition is not independent of the truth of any general implicate.

The objection, in its most general form, is that we are able to assess the truth of agents' statements of their reasons for their actions far more often than we are able to use the method of falsification that has been described, and that this shows that we must have another method of assessing their truth. If the objection were left in this general form, it would not be very impressive. The other method might merely be collecting indirect evidence of the agent's truthfulness. But his truthfulness would be independent of the truth of any general implicate only because he might be mistaken. If there were further methods of assessing the truth of such statements, it would still be an open question whether they really were independent of the truth of any general implicate. So when the objection is presented in its most general form, it achieves very little.

However, it can be made more powerful by being made more specific. The objector may describe other methods of assessing the truth of agents' statements of their reasons, and he may try to demonstrate that they are independent of the truth of any general implicates. Or he may offer explanations of the fact that we are not so often in a position to use the test that has been described.

One obvious explanation is that it is seldom possible to ascertain that the desires, which, according to the agent's statement, were engaged on the first occasion, remain the same in number and strength on the second, testing occasion. How can we be sure that one of these desires has not ceased to exist or become weaker in the interim?

There is also another explanation of the frequent unavailability of the test – an explanation which is connected with the way in which I answered the previous objection. Suppose that we lift one of the restrictions that were originally placed on the testing situation, and allow that a negative instance is relevant even when there is new opposition from the agent's old desires. Then we shall face two difficulties. First, we shall not often be able to tell in advance which of the agent's desires would produce a negative instance if they were engaged on the opposite side, and so we shall have to wait for observation to show us how to construct this list, item by item. Second, when we do put an item on the list, it will be an open question whether we ought to add something to the agent's statement of the reason for his action on the first occasion. In the example discussed, it was an open question whether the reason that the selector gave for accepting the first candidate ought to be supplemented in the light of the negative instance. Was it or was it not part of his reason that he wanted a candidate without the defect? Both these difficulties would help to explain the fact that we are often uncertain how to apply the test that has been described, and yet this uncertainty does not seem to affect our ability to judge agents' statements of their reasons for their actions.

These two difficulties are interesting and worth elaborating. The objector could present them by saying that we do not always know which way of identifying the agent's desires on the first occasion will yield the most probable psychological theory about him. The obvious way to identify them is the way in which he himself identifies them, and it is natural to assume that the most probable psychological theory is that if the conditions laid down are met, then his desires, identified in that way, will lead to a similar action. But if these conditions no longer include the stipulation that there must be no new opposition from his desires on later occasions, the general hypothetical which seemed at first to be the most probable psychological theory will have to be modified. Now it might be thought that this complication comes in only because we have taken on the unnecessary task of formulating a theory which will cover all partially similar instances. But this is not really so. For sometimes, when we get a negative instance produced by new opposition from the agent's desires, we shall add something to the agent's statement of his reasons on the first occasion, and in such cases our identification of the desires that were operative on that occasion will differ from his identification of them. This shows that we cannot evade the task of formulating the most probable psychological theory on the ground that it is not relevant to the question of the agent's motivation on the particular occasion with which we were originally concerned.

But if we do undertake this task, how can we ever complete it? If we have to add one qualification to the psychological theory, may we then not have to add another, and so on, to no definite terminus? How, then, can we tell when we have discovered the identifications of the agent's desires which yield the most probable psychological theory about him? Nor is this the end of our problems. For, whenever we do add a qualification to the theory, we shall have to answer the question whether we must make a consequential addition to the agent's state-ment of his reason on the first occasion. But there does not seem to be any firm way of answering this question. It is all very well to point out that there may have been pre-conscious motivation. But how are we to tell whether there was, or was not? We seem to have an embarrassing option on this matter, an option which may recur indefinitely many times.

There is at this point a sharp contrast with mechanics. For we do not have any option between different ways of identifying the forces exerted on billiards balls. In fact, there are three distinct contrasts here. First, the equations of mechanics are entirely general, whereas an action is explained by a psychological theory about the particular agent. Second, the best theory about the kind of thing that happens on the billiards table has already been discovered, so that it is no longer an open question which types of descriptions of such events yield the best theory; whereas much work remains to be done on the question which types of descriptions of the agent's desires need to be added to his own impromptu descriptions of them, and what are the criteria of application for these additional types of descriptions. Third, as has already been pointed out, if we do go into the details of a particular sequence of events on the billiards table, there is no limit to the number of factors which might be included in a full account of the cause; whereas, if we go into the details of an agent's motivation, there are some restrictions, but – this is the objector's point – they do not provide us with a firm way of answering the question, what should be included, and what excluded.

On the other hand, when we search for identifications of the agent's desires which will yield the most probable psychological theory about him, we are not in the position of the child watching the vitriol. For we do know that the agent's own sincere identifications are the right starting-point, and that they will often not need much qualification. It might, therefore, seem that the objector is exaggerating a small difficulty. But he has an answer to this. He can point out that, though the difficulty is small in cases like that of the man selecting personnel, it is much larger in another kind of case, where the situation is more open.

In a closed situation, like that of the selector, an agreed goal – in this case efficiency in a particular type of job – determines a fairly specific set of requirements. There may still be doubts about the completeness of the set, but such doubts will not put us in a very difficult position when we are testing the agent's statement of his reason. We will know the kind of addition that will have to be made to the agent's identification of his operative desires, if we want to get the most probable psychological theory, and so we shall not need to go back to first principles.

But in a more open situation, the objector may claim, the difficulty is much greater. Suppose, for example, that someone is asked why he chose to live in a particular house, or why he treated a friend in a particular way. Such questions do not expect answers restricted to a more or less agreed set of factors of a more or less agreed degree of specificity. In this kind of case, a fairly specific identification of the operative desire, 'Only because I wanted to achieve B', is quite likely to require qualification by the agent, and his qualification may mention a possible disadvantage which is not taken from a short list of agreed, relevant factors, as happened in the case of the man selecting personnel.

In fact, the qualification in this kind of case might go right back to first principles: he might say that, in general, he wants to achieve B – perhaps something in his own interest – only when it is morally permissible. Or he might move off in a different direction and add a suggestion about unconscious motivation.

In these open situations the task of formulating the most probable psychological theory about the agent often presents difficulties which are not marginal but substantial. The trouble is that a person's desires form a hierarchical system with the most general dominant one at the summit of the pyramid; or, if there are several very general, dominant desires, which are independent of one another, as is more likely, they will each occupy a high point on a more complicated diagram. Moreover, if unconscious motivation is brought in, it must be allowed that we do not command a clear view of the high points. This last difficulty is a general one. There will also be special difficulties of a somewhat similar kind in cases of pre-conscious motivation.

The theories of motivation put forward by Freud and by the nineteenth-century idealists have an important point in common. Both are opposed to the idea that we can always judge an agent's motivation by adding desire to desire in the atomistic way that is appropriate to a closed situation. Instead, we must often judge the tendency of the whole system of his relevant desires. Such judgments are intuitive and holistic, and, though they involve analytical descriptions of his motivation, they do not require the process of division and subdivision to be continued until we reach a set of independent co-ordinate desires. In an open situation, if we want to understand an agent's motivation, it is necessary to trace the connexions that he sees, or can be helped to see, between the objects of his desires. When we do this, it is essential to allow for the difference between those desires with which he identifies himself and those with which he does not identify himself, and, the objector will add, we must not use the word 'desire' in an extended way that obliterates this difference.

This is a powerful objection. It offers two separate explanations of the fact that we are often unable to use the method of falsification described in this paper. It also suggests that there is a different, more intuitive way of judging an agent's statement of his reason for an action. But how much damage does it do to the thesis that such a statement implies a general proposition through which it can be tested? There are several dimensions in which this thesis amounts to less than the whole truth, and the objection mentions some new and important ones. But, if the aim were to show that it is not wholly true, success would be more difficult.

First, there is nothing wrong with the extended use of the concept of a desire. It is true that an agent will not always identify himself with a desire that influences him, and this may (but need not) be connected with the morality of the action. In such cases his desires will exhibit a hierarchical structure. But our appreciation of this structure will not prevent us from formulating a psychological theory about his action, or relieve us of the necessity of formulating one. In fact, it will often allow us to formulate more than one theory through which his statement of his reason may be tested. For example, if he says that he did A only because he wanted B, and if we know that he prefers C to B, we can test his statement in two different types of situation. Or, if he wants B only because it is an instance of D, we can broaden the description of the object of his desire and increase the scope of the test. So the formulation of psychological theories is actually facilitated by the existence of this kind of hierarchical structure. Nor is this surprising. For the claim to have discovered the ranking of two of an agent's desires obviously implies a general proposition.

The problem about the formulation of a general proposition, which will cover not only the particular case but also all partially similar cases, is more formidable. Obviously we cannot formulate in advance a general theory which will mention, and allow for the effect of, all the desires which on future occasions might be opposed to those mentioned by the agent. He himself will often be unable to hazard answers to questions of the form, 'What would you have done if. . . ?' *A fortiori* we shall have to content ourselves with building up this very ambitious kind of theory as we find out more and more about him from his behaviour.

But this does not prevent us from using the simpler kind of theory which can be tested in situations which do not bring in new opposition from old desires. This is an important resource, and it is in no way affected by the difficulties that we encounter when we lift the restriction on testing situations, and try to extract information from situations in which there is new opposition from old desires.

However, these difficulties are real ones, and we might wonder how in fact we succeed in dealing with them. Part of the answer is that if an agent's statement of his reason is substantially false, that fact will be revealed by tests of the simpler kind of theory; and so, if it comes through those tests successfully, we may be reasonably confident that only relatively minor modifications will have to be made thereafter in the light of what happens when there is new opposition from old desires.

But when we look at this sort of evidence, and begin constructing the more ambitious kind of theory, how shall we know when we need to make consequential additions to the agent's original statement of his reason? The objector claimed that we would merely exercise an arbitrary option about this. But in fact we are not reduced to such straits. For in a problematical case we shall have discovered a new consideration – in the earlier example, the first candidate's lack of the defect – and we have a rough idea of the kind of consideration that would pass before the agent's mind if his deliberation were slow and full. So we ask ourselves whether the new consideration is of this kind, and, if it is, we add it to his original statement of his reason. No doubt, this is a rather rough and ready procedure, but it is reliable enough to justify us in attributing pre-conscious motives. The attribution of unconscious motives naturally depends on a more sophisticated procedure.

There remains the difficulty of establishing that the desires which, according to the agent, influenced him on the first occasion, have not subsequently changed in number or in strength. This requirement of constancy in the agent's desires is a special form of the more general requirement that their total contribution must not have diminished. The general requirement might be met even if the special form of it were not met: for example, one of the desires mentioned by the agent might have become stronger in the interim.

The objector rightly implies that these things must be established independently of what the agent does on the testing occasion, and his point is that this is not always possible. This is true. It is also true that in some of the cases in which we are unable to set up the test we are nevertheless able to judge the agent's statement of his reason in some other way. But what does this show? Are we to suppose that these judgments are unfalsifiable in practice but falsifiable in principle? Or should we conclude that they are not even falsifiable in principle, so that any general implicate would necessarily be an idle cog in the mechanism? This evidently depends on how our predicament should be interpreted. We naturally tend to think that the facts were there, if only we had been able to discover them. But it is possible that at a certain point this natural description ceases to fit our predicament.

Now if the objection is only intended as a mild one, insisting that something needs to be added to the thesis defended in this paper, it succeeds. But if the intention is to show that some of our judgments of agents' statements of their reasons are independent of any general implicate, success is more difficult. The objector would have to establish that we can make firm judgments about such statements not only when the general implicate is unfalsifiable in practice, but also when it is unfalsifiable in principle. For when we reach the point at which the natural description ceases to apply to our predicament, there will be no point in the general implicate, and it might as well be dropped.

First, we must be careful not to underestimate our actual resources. Before the agent finds himself in the testing situation, we can ask him to tell us honestly whether the desires, which, according to his own statement, influenced him on the first occasion, have changed in number or in strength, and, if so, how they have changed. We can also accumulate indirect evidence about these desires by examining his behaviour over a longer period both before and after the occasion on which he gives his reason for his action. This sort of evidence can be very impressive. If his later history agrees with his earlier history, leaving a putative decrease in the strength of a crucial desire isolated on the single occasion, we would be practically certain that his statement of his reason had been incomplete. When we cannot achieve such a high degree of certainty, we are content to balance one probability against another, and to choose the greater one. There is also a general consideration which often increases the probability of the hypothesis that the desires mentioned by the agent have remained constant: in important matters the desires of normal people do exhibit a high degree of constancy. The idea of an agent as an accountable person also exerts a force at this point. For some degree of this constancy is a prerequisite of the utility, and perhaps of the justice, of resentment, blame and punishment.

But what are we to say when these resources fail us? There are two kinds of cases of failure. First, we may merely happen to lack the requisite evidence. Yet, as the objector rightly observes, we may still be able to make a reasonably firm judgment about the agent's statement of his reason. However, it is obvious that this kind of case provides no support for the fiercer form of the objection.

The second kind of case is more interesting. The question, whether the agent's statement of his reason was true, may be too fine and subtle to be answered by the rather rough and ready method which has been described in this paper. There are several ways in which this might come about. It may be a marginal, and almost speculative question whether there is new opposition from an old desire on a testing occasion.

Or, if we know that there is, we may feel uncertain whether to add to the agent's original statement of his reason, because it is a borderline case. Or the agent may have only just brought himself to perform the action on the first occasion, so that the question, whether any of the desires mentioned by him have decreased in strength in the interim, is too fine to be answered by our crude methods. These are difficulties of a different order which cannot be attributed to lack of evidence. In such cases there is some plausibility in the view that it is in principle impossible to use the method described in this paper to test the agent's statement of his reason. This will mean that the question is so subtle that, in order to answer it, we should have to refine our system of measurement.

But is there any reason to believe that in such a case we could still make a firm judgment about an agent's statement of his reason? I think not. In fact, one would expect the agent himself to be equally hesitant. So though the objection points to some further ways in which my description of the structure of rational explanations falls short of the whole truth, it cannot rebut the claim that it is nothing but the truth.

VI

When we try to think of ways of removing these uncertainties, we naturally use determinism as the focal point which fixes the direction of the lines of improvement. If the trouble is that we cannot formulate completely general propositions, because we cannot measure the strengths of desires, like physical forces, we simply imagine ourselves discovering a method of measuring them. The complete elimination of the other difficulty is harder to imagine. Since most of an agent's desires can be identified in ways which connect them with other desires of his, we are not in a position to treat them atomistically, like billiards balls or objects in space. So, though we can imagine ourselves discovering new and perhaps more reliable ways of establishing that he has desires for certain goals, this would not put us in a position to produce an adequate atomistic theory, ignoring the holistic complications. That would be possible only if practical reasoning became simpler. To put the point the other way round, if practical reasoning retains its present complexity, and if we discovered a new method of establishing what goals a person desires, then this new method would have to yield results which more or less agreed with the complex inter-relations of the agent's desires as he saw them.

If we did discover new direct ways of ascertaining what a person's desires at a given moment are, and how strong they are, it seems almost certain that they would be neurological. Perhaps this would be a reason for refusing to call the new system 'psychological determinism'. But at least there would have to be general agreement between the results of the new tests and the established psychological facts. So, however we characterise this speculation, what it envisages is a refinement of our present rough and ready psychological system.

There is also another speculation which brings in determinism at a different point in order to produce an improvement in our system. When we ask ourselves whether the desires, which, according to the agent's own statement, influenced him on a given occasion, remain the same in number and strength on a later occasion, we have two ways of settling this question. We may ask the agent himself, or we may make some kind of inductive inference from his previous history. It is at this point that determinism is often brought in again in another, familiar speculation. We imagine ourselves making discoveries which would enable us to improve our indirect evidence of an agent's desires and their strengths on a given occasion: our inductive inferences might become cast-iron. But this speculation is subject to the same limitation as the last one. The improved indirect method would have to give results which more or less agreed with the inter-relations of the agent's desires, just as our rough and ready indirect method does at present.

These speculative improvements would make our system less loose and more closely articulated. But its over-all shape would remain the same. There would be the same re-identification of an isolated set of the agent's desires, and the same simple test after they had been re-identified. The complex feature of the improved system would be the elaborate inductive generalisations which we would need in order to infer his present psychological state from an earlier one. So, though the working of the isolated set of desires would be very like a calculable mechanical process, it would be set in the context of the agent's psychological history, which would not exhibit such a simple pattern. Half of our task could then be carried out neatly, but the untidiness would remain in the other half. One explanation of this division in our task is the complexity of the forces that act on a person throughout his life. It is as if there were frequent major changes in the forces exerted on the solar system from outside it. But that is not the complete explanation. It is also necessary to add that, if one of his desires is identified as a desire for a particular type of object, this will not give us as reliable a criterion of persistent identity for desires as the criterion that we use for heavenly bodies and billiards balls. We must also take account of the internal structure of the agent's system of desires.

Subject to this limitation, other improvements can be imagined. For example, a certain kind of measurement would make it unnecessary to find the same isolated set of desires at work on another occasion: it would be enough if we could establish that the total output was the same again. But there is no need to spin out any more speculations of this kind. It is clear that our system of rational explanation of actions might be tightened up in various deterministic ways. Why labour the point?

There are many ways of developing a more exact science out of a rough but serviceable system of thought. In this case, the simplest development would be to find a way of assigning exact values to the data which are the basis of our everyday judgments. But there is no reason to assume that science will develop in this way. There is a real danger that such speculations may turn into dogmatic pronouncements about its future development. However, provided that this sort of folly is avoided, they do serve several useful purposes.

First, such speculations compress a possible, lengthy, scientific development into a paragraph, and speeding up the sequence in this way helps us to overcome our natural conceptual conservatism. New criteria can be discovered for old concepts, and the conservative idea, that new criteria change the subject, is often mistaken. Second, these speculations produce a healthy scepticism about unverifiability and unfalsifiability in principle. Third, they may reveal a real obstacle lying in the way of a certain improvement. The requirement, that the internal structure of the agent's system of desires must be respected, is an obstacle of this kind. It does not make the imagined improvement impossible, but it does make it more complicated. Incidentally, this point provides part of the explanation of the idea that practical reasoning is autonomous. It is not that practical reasoning is independent, but, rather, that any satisfactory deterministic account of it must allow the 'natural relations' between desires to keep in step with their 'philosophical relations' (Hume's terminology).

Lastly, deterministic speculations of this kind do show very clearly at what point the importation of inappropriate ideas from classical mechanics begins. The description of the structure of rational explanation of actions which has been given in this paper makes no use of such imports. They begin to come in only when we follow a certain very natural line of speculation about possible ways of improving our system.

Christ Church, Oxford

Notes

1 Inaugural Lecture at Cambridge (Cambridge University Press, 1971).
2 Mr Robert Nozick pointed out to me in discussion the importance of examples of this type.

Freedom
to act
Donald Davidson

KEF

Freedom to act

The view that free actions are caused by states and episodes like desires, beliefs, rememberings and the promptings of passion comes under fire from two quarters. There are the broadsides from those who believe they can see, or even prove, that freedom is inconsistent with the assumption that actions are causally determined, at least if the causes can be traced back to events outside the agent. I shall not be directly concerned with such arguments, since I know of none that is more than superficially plausible. Hobbes, Locke, Hume, Moore, Schlick, Ayer, Stevenson, and a host of others have done what can be done, or ought ever to have been needed, to remove the confusions that can make determinism seem to oppose freedom.

The other attack is more interesting. It is aimed not at determinism as such but at the causal theory of action. If a free action is one that is caused in certain ways, then freedom to act must be a *causal power* of the actor that comes into play when certain conditions are satisfied. The champion of the causal theory cannot evade the challenge to produce an analysis of freedom to act which makes it out to be a causal power, or so at least it seems. Here the causal theorist has felt forced into a defensive stance, for no proposed analysis meets all objections. What is worse, the faults in known analyses show recurring patterns, suggesting the impossibility of a satisfactory solution. In brief outline, here is one familiar and disturbing difficulty.

It is natural to say that a person can do something (or is free to do it) if all that is required, if he is to do it, is that he *will* to do it. But does 'He would do it if he were to will to do it' express a causal disposition? If willing is an act distinct from doing, it might be a cause, but the question would then arise when an agent is free to will. If willing is not an act distinct from doing, then it cannot be a cause of the doing. The dilemma is not resolved by substituting choosing, deciding, intending or trying for willing; most of these alternatives merely make it more obvious which horn does the impaling. If this difficulty cannot be overcome, shouldn't we abandon the causal theory of action, even if it doesn't fall to frontal assault?

The particular dilemma just mentioned can, I believe, be resolved, and many other usual objections to a causal analysis of freedom also turn out not to be sound, or to have sound countermoves. A central difficulty nevertheless remains which permanently frustrates the formulation of a satisfactory analysis; but this fact ought not to persuade us that freedom to act is not a causal power. Broadly adumbrated, this is the view for which I shall now argue.[1] First, something more must be said about the idea of a causal power.

By a causal power, I mean a property of an object such that a change of a certain sort in the object causes an event of another sort. This characterization is, of course, much in need of clarification. The appeal to sorts of change, for example, invites discussion of causal laws, counterfactuals, and natural kinds. I hope to avoid the worst troubles that lurk here, however, by holding assumptions down. In particular, I shall not take it as given that causal powers can be analyzed by subjunctive conditionals, though much of the discussion will concern the propriety of proposed subjunctive conditional analyses.

The concept of a causal power is indifferent to the intuitive distinction between the active and passive. We may think of solubility as a passive characteristic, and of being a solvent as active. Yet they are logically on a par, the former being a property of things changes in which cause them to dissolve, and the latter being a property of things changes in which cause other things to dissolve. Both are equally causal powers.

Many attacks on the causal theory of free action fasten on powers like solubility as only analogs for being free to act. This puts an unwarranted strain on the theory. If a substance is soluble, certain eventualities cause it to dissolve; analogy suggests that a free action is one where the agent is caused to act by something that happens to him. Yet an equally good analogy would say that a free action is one where a change in the agent causes something to happen outside him. This would, in fact, be the natural meaning of 'causal power' attributed to a person: he has the power to cause things to happen. Again, however, the details of the parallel are wrong. It is true that a person is free to bring about whatever would be brought about by actions he is free to perform. But this concept of what an agent is free to bring about depends on a prior idea of what he is free to do. A man might have the power to destroy the world, in the sense that if he were simply to push a button before him, the world would be destroyed. Yet he would not be free to destroy the world unless he were free to push the button.

Another kind of causal power is such that an object that possesses it is caused to change in a certain way if a prior change takes place in the object. An example might be the property of a tank that is self-sealing. If the tank starts to leak, this causes the leak to seal. Similar properties are: being in equilibrium, unstable, homeostatic. If freedom to act is a causal power, it belongs to this category.

There is little difference, perhaps, between 'The heat caused the flower to wilt' and 'The heat caused the wilting of the flower.' But there can be a great difference between 'The heat caused Samantha to return to Patna' and 'The heat caused Samantha's return to Patna.' The former implies, or strongly suggests, a limitation on Samantha's freedom of action; the latter does not. In testing the plausibility of the claim that freedom to act is a causal power we should therefore bear in mind the neutral reading. An *action* may be caused without the *agent* being caused to perform it. Even when the cause is internal, we sense a difference. 'Desire caused him to do it' suggests a lack of control that might excuse because it made the act less than voluntary; 'Desire was the cause of his doing it' leaves the question of freedom open.

Turning from these preliminary matters, let us consider arguments designed to show that being free to perform an action cannot be a causal power. We may begin with some of the claims in J. L. Austin's 'Ifs and Cans'.[2] According to Austin, G. E. Moore suggested the following three propositions, the first two explicitly, and the third implicitly:

(1) 'Could have' simply means 'could have if I had chosen'.

(2) For 'could have if I had chosen' we may substitute 'should have if I had chosen'.

(3) The *if*-clauses in these expressions state the causal conditions upon which it would have followed that I could or should have done the thing different from what I did actually do.

Austin argues that (1) to (3) are false. I shall argue that for all Austin says they may be true (though there is an important point on which Austin is right: one of the disjuncts of (3) is false).

Let's suppose that Moore's basic view was that to say an agent could have done something, or can now do something (that is, that he was, or is, free to do it) means that if he had chosen to do it, he would have done it (or if he now chooses to do it, he does or will do it). I have transposed the thesis from the first to the third person in order to forestall irrelevant qualms over performatives, and I have generalized a bit on the tenses. (Difficulties over tense and time remain, but I do not believe we need to resolve them here.) To settle on one formulation, take Moore's thesis to be: 'A can ——' means 'If A chooses to ——, then he ——s.' (The 's' at the end is to be added to the main verb, even if it does not conclude the phrase substituted for the blank. Thus, 'Jones can anchor his boat in the channel' means 'If Jones chooses to anchor his boat in the channel, then he anchors his boat in the channel.') I shall examine Austin's attack on Moore in the light of this proposal.

If we accept the suggestion, then 'A can ——' does mean the same as (or anyway is logically equivalent to) 'A can —— if he chooses.' For given Moore's suggestion, 'A can ——' means 'A ——s if he chooses', while 'A can —— if he chooses' expands into 'A ——s if he chooses, if he chooses, and these last two sentences are logically equivalent.

Moore sees no important difference between 'A ——s if he chooses' and 'A can —— if he chooses.' And given his suggested analysis of 'can', he is surely right, for the second sentence becomes, as we just saw, 'A ——s if he chooses, if he chooses', which is logically equivalent to 'A ——s if he chooses.' Austin argues against this equivalence, but the argument is faulty. He assumes as obvious that if 'A ——s if he chooses' means the same as 'A can —— if he chooses', then '——s' and 'can ——' must mean the same; and this is patently false. But the assumption is wrong. '——s' and 'can ——' don't mean the same, and yet the sentences 'A ——s if he chooses' and 'A can —— if he chooses' are equivalent – granted Moore's suggestion that 'can ——' means '——s if he chooses'.[3]

Austin emphasizes the fact that not all *if* clauses introduce causal conditions; some sentences in which 'if' is the main connective are causal conditionals and some are not. Austin is obviously right in saying that 'A can —— if he chooses' is not a causal conditional, at least given Moore's analysis of 'can'. The reason is that 'A can ——' is itself (we are supposing) a conditional, the antecedent of which is 'He chooses'. So 'A can —— if he chooses' logically entails the consequent, which shows that the longer sentence can't be a causal conditional. It would be a blunder, however, to reason that since 'A can —— if he chooses' is logically equivalent to 'A ——s if he chooses' and the former is not a causal conditional, therefore the latter is not a causal conditional.

Austin seems to have thought that the word 'if' has a different meaning in causal conditionals than elsewhere, but the evidence for this is not very convincing. There is no good reason to say that 'if' has different meanings in 'If a number is divisible by four, it is divisible by two' and 'If you eat enough apple seeds you will get arsenic poisoning', though the latter is presumably a causal conditional and the former is not. The difference is not semantical but epistemological: the first sentence we hold to be true for logical or arithmetic reasons; the second sentence we would hold to be true only if we thought eating apple seeds *caused* arsenic poisoning.

The question of meaning is relevant to the next point. Austin says it is characteristic of causal conditionals that contraposition is a valid form of inference. This is surely right, and we can see that contraposition does work for 'A ——s if he chooses.' But are there any *if*-sentences for which contraposition does not work? (If there are, we must admit that 'if' is ambiguous.) I do not think so. We are not inclined to *reason* from 'A can —— if he chooses' to its contrapositive, but the reason is not, I think, because the formal entailment fails. A better explanation is this: on Moore's analysis, 'A can —— if he chooses' means 'A ——s if he chooses, if he chooses', which in turn is logically equivalent to its consequent. The question whether 'A can —— if he chooses' entails its contrapositive is therefore just the question whether 'A can ——' entails 'If A can't ——, then he doesn't choose to ——.' Of course it does entail it, in the formal and vacuous way a contradiction entails anything at all. This is not the kind of entailment that invites serious reasoning outside of logic. Austin's argument helps us see, once more, that 'A can —— if he chooses' isn't a causal conditional, but it doesn't show that a causal 'if' isn't in the offing – i.e. in the 'can'.[4]

In a review of Austin's papers,[5] Roderick Chisholm comes, by a somewhat different route, to essentially the same conclusion I have reached, that Austin has given no conclusive reason for rejecting Moore's analysis of 'can' in terms of 'does if he chooses', nor have the resulting sentences been shown not to be causal conditionals. Chisholm believes Austin has shown that 'He can —— if he chooses' is not a conditional, and that there are difficulties about 'choose' as the appropriate verb for the antecedent. I don't think Austin succeeds in demonstrating either of these things, but it doesn't matter so far as Chisholm's argument is concerned. For Chisholm's argument, if it is a good one, applies not only to 'choose', but also to many other verbs we might try in its place, like 'try'.

Chisholm's point is that while it might be true that if a man were to choose, or try, to perform some action, then he would perform that action, nevertheless he might be unable to choose or to try, in which case, he couldn't perform the action. So it might be true that a person would —— if he tried, yet false that he could ——.

I think Chisholm's argument is very important, and that he is right in saying that to overlook it is to make a 'first-water, ground-floor mistake' (Austin's words). What the argument shows is that the antecedent of a causal conditional that attempts to analyze 'can' or 'could' or 'free to' must not contain, as its dominant verb, a verb of action, or any verb which makes sense of the question, Can someone do *it*?

If I am not mistaken, M. R. Ayers[6] has supposed that because the antecedent of a causal conditional analyzing freedom to act cannot be dominated by a verb of action, no causal analysis is possible. His argument seems to be that in all other cases of causal conditionals, the antecedent is something we can make true independently of the supposed effect. But in the case of action, he says, 'that testing one's ability to do something is not the same kind of thing as testing the truth of a hypothesis, simply follows from the truism that in order to do something it is not always necessary to do something else first.' He concludes, 'Thus the possibility of any hypothetical analysis of personal power is ruled out' (p. 145).

The conclusion does not follow from the premise. What follows from the truism that 'in order to do something it is not always necessary to do something else first' is only that if a causal conditional is to analyze freedom to act, the antecedent cannot have as its main verb a verb of action. Of course, this does mean the agent himself cannot normally test the truth of the conditional by doing something else – by making such an antecedent true. It does not follow, however, that he cannot test in some other way whether he has the ability to do something, nor does it follow that the ability may not consist in a causal power. All we can conclude is that the test cannot (always, anyway) be performed by the agent's doing something to create the conditions for actualizing the power.

Keith Lehrer has urged, on far more general grounds, that no causal conditional can give the meaning of 'A is free to —— (or can ——).' He claims that 'A ——s if condition C obtains' is consistent with the following two statements: 'A cannot —— if condition C does not obtain' and 'C does not obtain.' Yet if these two last sentences *are* true A cannot ——. In Lehrer's words, 'it is logically possible that some condition which is a sufficient condition to cause a person to do something should also be a necessary condition of his being able to do it, and that the condition should fail to occur.'[7]

Although Lehrer does not seem to have noticed it, his argument has nothing in particular to do with action. If his line of reasoning is sound, it shows that no attribution of a power or disposition is ever equivalent to a conditional (whether the conditional is construed as causal law or subjunctive). Thus on Lehrer's argument, to say something is water-soluble can't mean it dissolves if placed in water, since it may now be soluble and yet placing it in water might make it insoluble.[8] There are various ways one may try to cope with this point. But for my purposes it will be enough to remark that even if Lehrer's argument showed that no disposition or power is correctly analyzed by a subjunctive conditional, the claim that being able to do something is to have a causal power would not be undermined.

There are, of course, cases where wanting, trying, choosing, or even intending, to do something prevents us from doing that very thing, even though there may be a sense in which we could have done it (if we hadn't wanted to, tried to, etc.). Moralists from Aristotle to Mill have pointed out that trying to be happy is unlikely to produce happiness, and Schlick was so convinced of this that he revised hedonism to read, not, 'Do what you can to be happy', but 'Be ready for happiness.' Austin gives a more pedestrian example: a man may try to (choose to, want to, intend to) sink a putt and fail, while not admitting that he couldn't. None of these cases is like Lehrer's, where trying (etc.) fixes it so one can't do the task. Rather they are cases where one can, and yet although one tries (chooses, intends, wants), one doesn't bring it off.

Chisholm proposes a way around this difficulty. He suggests that A can do something provided there is something (different or the same) such that if A tries (chooses, wants, intends) to do *it*, then he does do the first thing. In the case of the putt, this means the agent can sink the putt if there is something else, perhaps hit the ball an inch to the left of the cup, such that if he tries to do *it*, then he will sink the putt.

Neither Chisholm nor I thinks this is the correct analysis, only that it answers Austin's objection to Moore's proposal. But there is another fact (not given by Chisholm) that recommends Chisholm's revision of Moore. Our actions, the things we do, include not only what we do intentionally but also many things we do unintentionally. If one holds, as I do, that unintentional actions are intentional actions under other descriptions, then the point may be put by saying that action-descriptions include descriptions of actions as intentional, and certain other descriptions of those same events. For example, I may intentionally put down a coin on the counter of a newsstand in Paris, intending to pay for a purchase. Unintentionally, I put down a drachma instead of a franc, thus provoking some interesting argot. My one action can be correctly characterized as: putting down a coin, putting down a drachma, provoking some interesting argot. Only under the first characterization is my act intentional.

An important way of describing actions (and other events) is in terms of their effects or consequences. Provoking some interesting argot characterizes my act of putting down the coin in terms of a consequence, namely the provoked response. The provoked response is not, of course, *part* of my action, only part of its description. We may call the effect caused by my action the *completion* of the action. My actions include, then, what I do intentionally, and anything I do the completion of which is caused by an action. The second clause adds no new events, only new ways of describing the old.[9]

The analysis of the concept of an action comes, then, if I am right, in two stages; the first bringing in intention directly, and the second extending the concept to actions in the first sense redescribed in terms of unintended consequences or other unintended characteristics. Since what we do do is surely included in what we can do, the pattern of analysis that applies to the concept of action ought to work for the notion of what an agent can, or is free to, do. He is free to do those things he would do if he chose (wanted, tried) to do them; but he is also free to do those things whose completions would be caused by an action he is free to do in the first sense.

This is a very generous way of counting the things we can do – it includes all the things we could bring about through our intentional action, whether by plan or by accident, through blind luck, or masterful contrivance. In this broad sense of 'can' or 'could', every one of us could make a million dollars on the stock market, marry a movie star, or even bring an end to the war. If only we knew how.

For practical purposes we are often interested in more limited concepts of what we can do – what we do do if we want or intend or try to do *it*, for example, or what we can do reliably. But the broader concept I have introduced is basic, at least in the sense that the others could be defined in terms of it – assuming, of course, that we have things right so far. It is simply a more inclusive concept than we usually put to work, because it includes in the things we can do things we would do only by luck or if we knew more than we do. But it is not so broad as to include the merely possible, logically or physically – what someone could do for all that nature cares. This category would embrace things I could not do intentionally, and that would not be caused by any intentional act I could perform, like run a mile in four minutes.

We have now decided on a two-part theory of what a man can do: one part aims to explain what he can do intentionally, and the other part extends this to what the intentional would cause. I want to concentrate on the first part, and for the moment on the main verb of the antecedent. To say a man can do *x* intentionally is to say he would do it if – what?

The problem is the one we sketched at the beginning. In order to be eligible as a cause, the event mentioned must be separate from the action; but if it is separate from the action, there is, it seems, always the possibility of asking about *it*, whether the agent is free to do it. The objection applies to choosing, willing, intending and trying. None of these is plausibly the cause of an action, because normally these are ways of characterizing the action chosen, willed, intended or tried, not descriptions of further actions, events or states. Thus if a man tries to hit a home run and succeeds, his try *is* his success, and cannot be its cause. Sometimes choosing or willing to do something are mental acts performed prior to doing the things but in these cases the question does arise whether the agent is free to do them. The analysis fails for another reason, for a man may choose or decide on Monday to swallow a button on Tuesday and yet fail to do it, and this would not necessarily show that he could not swallow a button on either Monday or Tuesday – or even that he could not, on Monday, swallow a button on Tuesday. Finally, we should remember that a person may be able to do something, and may actually do it intentionally, and yet never have chosen, decided, tried or intended to do it.

The only hope for the causal analysis is to find states or events which are causal conditions of intentional actions, but which are not themselves actions or events about which the question whether the agent can perform them can intelligibly be raised. The most eligible such states or events are the beliefs and desires of an agent that *rationalize* an action, in the sense that their propositional expressions put the action in a favorable light, provide an account of the reasons the agent had in acting, and allow us to reconstruct the intention with which he acted. For example, suppose a man saws a piano in half because he wants to throw the piano out the window and he believes that sawing the piano in half will promote his enterprise. His reason for sawing the piano in half was that he wanted to throw the piano out the window – to which we may add that he believed he could do this if he first sawed the piano in half. Obviously his reasons, or the beliefs and desires that correspond to them, explain why he acted as he did. And we can see that the intention with which he sawed the piano in half was to get the piano out the window.

So now I suggest that we consider the following formulation of the first part of our theory of what a man can do:

A can do x intentionally (under the description d) means that if A has desires and beliefs that rationalize x (under d), then A does x.

A number of previous problems seem to be solved by this analysis. The antecedent condition (A has desires and beliefs that rationalize x) is prior to and separate from the action, and so is suited to be a cause (in this case, it is a state rather than an event – but this could be changed along these lines: 'coming to have desires and beliefs that rationalize x'[10]). The antecedent condition does not mention something that is an action, so the question whether the agent can do it does not arise. The point isn't that desires and beliefs aren't ever in an agent's control, but rather that coming to have them isn't something an agent does. I do not want to suggest that the nature of an agent's beliefs and desires, and the question how he acquired them, are irrelevant to questions of how free he, or his actions, are. But these questions are on a different and more sophisticated level from that of our present discussion.

By adding 'intentionally' to the definiendum, we have answered one of Austin's objections to a conditional analysis of 'can'. For one of his objections to 'I shall if I choose' was that the consequent alone entails 'I can.' Similarly, if we were to analyze 'A can do x' as 'If A has attitudes that rationalize x, then A does x', Austin would doubtless complain that 'A does x' again entails 'A can do x', showing that there is something odd about the conditional. The difficulty disappears when the definiendum is 'A can do x intentionally', for this *doesn't* follow from 'A does x.' But more important, the reason for the change shows that the objection was not valid in the first place. In fact, doing x *doesn't* entail that one can do x.[11] The word 'doing' suggests intention somewhere, but in the present context, it serves only as a blank to be filled by any verb whose subject can name or describe a person. It doesn't follow, from the fact that at noon today I became exactly 55 years, 72 days, 11 hours and 59 minutes old, that I was free to become this age (rather than another) on this date, or that I could do it. It simply wasn't in my power to do it – no desire or belief of mine played any causal role in my becoming this age on this date, nor could it have. If, on the other hand, rationalizing attitudes do cause an action of mine, then not only does the action occur, but it is, under the rationalized description, intentional. This is, of course, what we should expect: what an agent does do intentionally is what he is free to do *and* has adequate reasons for doing.

The discussion of the last few paragraphs may help to put another familiar puzzle in perspective. It is natural to suppose that an action that one is free to perform is an action that one is also free *not* to perform. Similarly, we find many philosophers maintaining that an action is freely performed only if the agent was, when he did it, free to abstain: he could have done otherwise. For suppose he could not have done otherwise; doesn't this mean he had no choice? If the causal theory drives us to this, why isn't the libertarian right when he denies that freedom can be reconciled with the causal theory? Or to take the merely potential case, isn't it an empty pretense to say a man is free to perform an action if he is not also free not to perform it? Surely, freedom means the existence of alternatives.

The difficulty (recently brought to the fore by Harry Frankfurt in 'Alternate Possibilities and Moral Responsibility'[12]) is that if we say a man is free to do x only if his doing x depends on whether or not the attitudinal condition holds (he chooses to do x, decides to, wills it, has rationalizing attitudes), then we find counter instances in cases of overdetermination. What a man does of his own free will – an action done by choice and with intent, caused by his own wants and beliefs – may be something he would have been caused to do in another way if the choice or motives had been lacking.

Two intuitions seem at war, and the territory that is threatened with destruction is occupied by the causal theory. The intuitions are, on the one hand, the view that we cannot be free to do what we would be causally determined to do in any case, and on the other hand, the feeling that if we choose to do something and do it because we chose it, then the action is free no matter what would have happened if we *hadn't* chosen.

The puzzle is resolved by a discovery we made in another context. What depends on the agent is the intentional performance of an act of a certain sort. It is true that it may sometimes be the case that what a man does intentionally he might have been caused to do anyway, by alien forces. But in that case what he would have done would not have been intentional. So even in the overdetermined cases, something rests with the agent. Not, as it happens, *what* he does (when described in a way

Donald Davidson

that leaves open whether it was intentional), but whether he does it intentionally. His action, in the sense in which action depends on intentionality, occurs or not as he wills; what he does, in the broader sense, may occur whether or not he wills it.

These reflections show, I think, that it is an error to suppose we add anything to the analysis of freedom when we say an agent is free to do something if he can do it *or not*, as he pleases (chooses, etc.). For if this means that he acts freely only if he would not have done what he did had the attitudinal conditions been absent, it is false. And if it means he would not have acted intentionally had the attitudinal conditions been absent, then this is true, but it is gratuitous to say it since it is a logical truth.

I have been examining the concept of what a person can do, or is free to do, when this concept is interpreted to include what he can do, whether he knows it or not, by doing something intentional. On the present proposal, a man is free to assassinate a future tyrant if he is standing next to the future tyrant, has a gun, and otherwise the opportunity, even if he has no reason for thinking the man next to him is the future tyrant. For *if* he believed the man next to him was the future tyrant and he wanted above all to kill the future tyrant, then, given the propitious circumstances, he would kill him. We get a more limited version of what he can do if we say he can kill the future tyrant only if, given that he wants to kill the future tyrant, he does. For then, since he will not do it intentionally unless he knows or believes the man next to him is the future tyrant, he is not free to do it unless he has the knowledge. Obviously this more restricted sense of being able to do something is important when it comes to holding a man responsible for failing to act.

My purpose in pointing out how we can adjust the conditions under which a man acts to accommodate various interpretations of freedom is to make plain the extent to which the problem of analyzing freedom to act is interlocked with the problem of defining intentional action (and with it, action in general, since non-intentional actions are intentional actions under other descriptions). The reason is obvious: to say when an agent is free to perform an action intentionally (i.e. with a certain intention) is to state conditions under which he would perform the action; to explain the performance of an action with a certain intention is to say that the conditions are satisfied. Of course, this style of analysis and explanation works only if the satisfaction of the conditions (which we are assuming are causal) always leads to the performance of the action. And so, if we can analyze either freedom to act (in our broad sense) *or* acting with an intention, we will be in command of a law saying that whenever certain conditions are satisfied, an agent will perform an action with a certain intention.

Since intentional action is, on the causal theory, defined by its causes, it should perhaps not surprise us that merely knowing the analysis of intentional action would put us in command of a law of behaviour. Still, how can what seems to be an empirical generalization emerge from wholly analytic considerations? I shall return to this question presently.

These things, then, stand together: a law stating conditions under which agents perform intentional actions; an analysis of freedom to act that makes it a causal power; and a causal analysis of intentional action. They stand together, or they fall together. In my opinion, they fall together if what we want are explicit, non-question begging analyses, or laws without generous caveats and *ceteris paribus* clauses.

A brief discussion of three recent attempts to provide the appropriate law or analysis will help me explain the difficulties. First consider the following law of action proposed by Paul Churchland:[13]

If A wants ϕ and believes x-ing is a way to bring about ϕ and that there is no better way to bring about ϕ, and A has no overriding want, and knows how to x, and is able to x, *then* A x's. [I have simplified Churchland's formulation.]

Clearly if this proposal were acceptable we could define being able to x as the state of an agent who, when the other conditions are satisfied, x's. But the 'law' is defective. For one thing, the notion of 'overriding want' is treacherous, since it is unclear how a want is shown to be overriding except by the fact that it overrides. The more general difficulty, however, is this: all the conditions may be satisfied, and yet they may fail to ignite an action. It might happen as simply as this: the agent wants ϕ, and he believes x-ing is the best way to bring about ϕ, and yet he fails to put these two things together; the practical reasoning that would lead him to conclude that x is worth doing, may simply fail to occur. There is no more reason to suppose that a person who has reasons for acting will always act on them than to suppose that a person who has beliefs which entail a certain conclusion will draw that conclusion.

Alvin Goldman illustrates the interlocking of the three enterprises I have been discussing in this way. First he defines a basic act-type as a kind of act an agent performs if no external forces prevent him and he wants to perform an act of that type. He goes on:[14]

> if x is a basic act-type for A at t, and if A is in standard conditions with respect to x at t, then the following causal conditional is true: 'If A wanted to do x at t, then A would do x at t.' This causal conditional statement . . . entails the statement that A is 'able' to do x at t. [I have altered the letter symbolism.]

Because Goldman makes wanting to do x the attitudinal cause of doing x, his analysis may seem to get around our difficulty. But in fact it does not, as we see when we clearly distinguish act-types and particular actions. Wanting to do x is, for Goldman, a desire for a type of action, not for a particular action. This is fine: the objects of wanting and desiring are propositional in character, and so cannot be particular actions. But then it is a mistake to say that wanting to do x (i.e. to perform an action of type x) causes x, since x, not being an event, but a type, cannot be caused. What can be caused is only some event that belongs to the type. Which one of these is to be caused? Goldman enunciates a law that, rephrased, would go like this: if a person is not restrained by external forces, then if he wants to do something of type x, he does something of type x. This is supposed to apply only to 'basic' acts, but in fact I do not believe it applies to any interesting class of actions. The trouble is that wanting to do something of type x, even if x-ing is completely in his power, and he knows it, may not cause an agent to do anything of type x. And a worse trouble is that wanting to do something of type x may cause someone to do something of type x, and yet the causal chain may operate in such a manner that the act is not intentional.

David Armstrong, in a recent paper called 'Acting and Trying',[15] comes closest to seeing the nature of the difficulty. He asks the question what we must add to 'A tried to do x' in order to have necessary and sufficient conditions for 'A did x intentionally.' Most of us would say – I certainly would – that trying itself isn't necessary in many cases, but this point, though at the heart of Armstrong's interest, is largely irrelevant to the present theme. According to Armstrong, A's doing x intentionally entails that A's trying to do x caused the occurrence of x, but A's trying to do x, even if it causes the occurrence of x does not prove that A did x intentionally. The difficulty is, that the attempt may bring about the desired effect in an unexpected or undesired way. Here is an example of Daniel Bennett's. A man may try to kill someone by shooting at him. Suppose the killer misses his victim by a mile, but the shot stampedes a herd of wild pigs that trample the intended victim to death. Do we want to say the man killed his victim *intentionally*? The point is that not just any causal connection between rationalizing attitudes and a wanted effect suffices to guarantee that producing the wanted effect was intentional. The causal chain must follow the right sort of route.

Armstrong tries to fill this gap by saying that the wanted effect must be produced by a causal chain that answers, at least roughly, to the pattern of practical reasoning. In Bennett's example, we must suppose the agent intended to kill the victim by pulling the trigger because he reasoned that pulling the trigger would cause the gun to fire, which would cause the bullet to fly, which would cause the bullet to penetrate the body of the victim, thus causing his death. But the pattern of events portrayed by the pattern of practical reasoning was not produced by the action of pulling the trigger. This throws in doubt the question whether the agent intentionally killed his victim.

I am not sure whether or not this difficulty can be overcome, but there is a related problem that Armstrong does not consider which seems to me insurmountable. This is the problem, not of quaint *external* causal chains, but of non-standard or lunatic *internal* causal chains. Armstrong, in trying to mend the trouble about unwanted external causal relations, was pushed into talking of the course of practical reasoning, the way in which beliefs and desires interact to produce action. (Given this, I doubt that there is any gain to him in the strained thesis that everything we do intentionally is caused by trying to do it. But never mind that.) And here we see that Armstrong's analysis, like the one I proposed a few pages back, must cope with the question *how* beliefs and desires cause intentional actions. Beliefs and desires that would rationalize an action if they caused it in the *right* way – through a course of practical reasoning, as we might try saying – may cause it in other ways. If so, the action was not performed with the intention that we could have read off from the attitudes that caused it. What I despair of spelling out is the way in which attitudes must cause actions if they are to rationalize the action.

Let a single example serve. A climber might want to rid himself of the weight and danger of holding another man on a rope, and he might know that by loosening his hold on the rope he could rid himself of the weight and danger. This belief and want might so unnerve him as to cause him to loosen his hold, and yet it might be the case that he never *chose* to loosen his hold, nor did he do it intentionally. It will not help, I think, to add that the belief and the want must combine to cause him to want to loosen his hold, for there will remain the *two* questions *how* the belief and the want caused the second want, and *how* wanting to loosen his hold caused him to loosen his hold.

Some distance back, I tried analyzing 'A is free to do x (or can do x)' in terms of the conditional 'He would do x intentionally if he had attitudes that rationalized his doing x.' Even if we read this subjunctive conditional as implying a causal relation, we can see now that it is not adequate. If the agent does x intentionally, then his doing x is caused by his attitudes that rationalize x. But since there may be wayward causal chains, we cannot say that if attitudes that would rationalize x cause an agent to do x, then he does x intentionally.

It is largely because we cannot see how to complete the statement of the causal conditions of intentional action that we cannot tell whether, if we got them right, the result would be a piece of analysis or an empirical law for predicting behavior. If we begin with the suggestion that if a man has beliefs and desires that rationalize an action of type x, then he intentionally performs an action of type x, it is easy to see that we improve matters if we add to the antecedent 'and those beliefs and desires, or the coming to have them, cause the agent to perform an action of type x'. To improve on this formulation in turn, in a way that would eliminate wrong causal chains, would also eliminate the need to depend on the open appeal to causal relations. We would simply say, given these (specified) conditions, there always is an intentional action of a specified type. This would be understood as a causal law, of course, but it would not need to mention causality. Necessary mention of causality is a cloak for ignorance; we must appeal to the notion of cause when we lack detailed and accurate laws. In the analysis of action, mention of causality takes up some of the slack between analysis and science.

If the finished formulation of the proposed law were produced, we could try to judge its character more accurately. If the terms of the antecedent conditions were to remain mentalistic (for example by using such concepts as those of belief and desire), the law would continue to seem constitutive or analytic. But the attempt to be more accurate, to eliminate appeal to question-begging notions like 'overriding' desires, would, I think, suggest that a serious law would have to state the antecedent conditions in physical, or at least behavioristic, terms. Then the law would be more clearly empirical. But the attempt to find such a law would also end in frustration, though for different reasons.[16]

We must count our search for a causal analysis of 'A is free to do *x*' a failure. Does this show that Austin was, after all, right? Well, he was right in rejecting Moore's analysis (though many of his reasons are, I have argued, defective). And he was right, I believe, in holding that no other causal conditional could analyze 'A is free to do *x*.' But Austin also believed, however tentatively, that he had shown that being free to perform an action cannot be a causal power at all, and hence that the causal theory of action is false (he calls it 'determinism', but I don't want to go into that). On this last, and important, point he was, I think, wrong. For although we cannot hope to define or analyze freedom to act in terms of concepts that fully identify the causal conditions of intentional action, there is no obstacle to the view that freedom to act is a causal power of the agent.

The Rockefeller University and Princeton University

Notes

1 I benefited from the advice and criticism of Michael Bratman, David Lewis, Mary Mothersill, Richard Reiss, Irving Thalberg, and David Wiggins.

2 'Ifs and Cans', *Proceedings of the British Academy*, 1956.

3 In 'If, Cans and Causes', *Analysis*, 20 (1960), pp. 122–4, Keith Lehrer notes the equivalence, on Moore's analysis, of 'I shall if I choose' and 'I can if I choose.' But then he follows Austin's *non sequitur*: ' "I can, if I choose" is clearly not equivalent to "I shall, if I choose" because "I can" is not equivalent to "I shall".'

4 For analogous reasons, I would maintain that 'There are biscuits on the sideboard if you want them' contains a normal 'if' and does entail its contrapositive. We miss this because we assume that mere wanting can't produce biscuits; therefore, 'There are biscuits on the sideboard if you want them' is true only if there are biscuits on the sideboard. This assumption contradicts the antecedent of the contrapositive, so instead of inferring the contrapositive, we are simply baffled by the question whether it is true.

5 'J. L. Austin's Philosophical Papers', *Mind*, LXXIII (1964), pp. 20–5.

6 *The Refutation of Determinism* (London: Methuen, 1968).

7 'An Empirical Disproof of Determinism', in K. Lehrer (ed.), *Freedom and Determinism* (New York: Random House, 1966), p. 196.

8 The point is made by Alvin Goldman, *A Theory of Human Action* (New York: Prentice-Hall, 1970), pp. 199–200.

9 See my 'Agency', in R. Binkley (ed.), *Agent, Action and Reason* (University of Toronto Press, 1971).

10 This idea is discussed at further length in 'Actions, Reasons and Causes', *Journal of Philosophy*, 60 (1963), pp. 685–700.

11 David Pears makes the same observation, though for somewhat different reasons, in 'If and Cans', *Canadian Journal of Philosophy*, 1 (1972), p. 382.

12 'Alternate Possibilities and Moral Responsibility', *Journal of Philosophy*, 66 (1969), pp. 829–39.

13 'Action Explanations', *Philosophical Review*, 79 (1970), pp. 221–2.

14 *A Theory of Human Action*, p. 199.

15 The paper was read at the Rockefeller University in the winter of 1971–72, and is forthcoming in the *Philosophical Review*.

16 I discuss why strict psycho-physical laws are impossible in 'Mental Events', in Lawrence Foster and J. W. Swanson (eds), *Experience and Theory* (University of Massachusetts Press, 1970).

Mechanism and
responsibility
D. C. Dennett

Mechanism and
responsibility

I

In the eyes of many philosophers the old question of whether determinism (or indeterminism) is incompatible with moral responsibility has been superseded by the hypothesis that *mechanism* may well be. This is a prior and more vexing threat to the notion of responsibility, for mechanism is here to stay, unlike determinism and its denial, which go in and out of fashion. The mechanistic style of explanation, which works so well for electrons, motors and galaxies, has already been successfully carried deep into man's body and brain, and the open question now is not whether mechanistic explanation of human motion is possible, but just whether it will ultimately have crucial gaps of randomness (like the indeterminists' mechanistic explanation of electrons) or not (like the mechanistic explanation of macroscopic systems such as motors and billiards tables). In either case the believer in responsibility has problems, for it seems that whenever a particular bit of human motion can be given an entirely mechanistic explanation – with or without the invocation of 'random' interveners – any non-mechanistic, rational, purposive explanation of the same motions is otiose. For example, if we are on the verge of characterizing a particular bit of human motion as a well-aimed kick in the pants, and a doctor can show us that in fact the extensor muscles in the leg were contracted by nerve impulses triggered by a 'freak' (possibly random?) epileptic discharge in the brain, we will have to drop the search for purposive explanations of the motion, and absolve the kicker from all responsibility. Or so it seems. A more central paradigm might be as follows. Suppose a man is found who cannot, or will not, say the word 'father'. Otherwise, we may suppose, he seems perfectly normal, and even expresses surprise at his 'inability' to say 'that word I can't say'. A psychoanalyst might offer a plausible explanation of this behavior in terms of unconscious hatred and desires and beliefs about his father, and a layman might say 'Nonsense! This man is just playing a joke. I suspect he's made a bet that he can go a year without saying "father" and is doing all this deliberately.' But if a neurosurgeon were to come along and establish that a tiny lesion in the speech center of the brain caused by an aneurysm (random or not) was causally responsible for the lacuna in the man's verbal repertory (not an entirely implausible discovery in the light of Penfield's remarkable research), both the analyst's and the layman's candidates for explanation would have the rug pulled out from under them. Since a mere mechanistic happening in the brain, random or not, was the cause of the quirk, the man cannot have had reasons, unconscious or ordinary, for it, and cannot be held responsible for it. Or so it seems.

The principle that seems to some philosophers to emerge from such examples is that *the mechanistic displaces the purposive*, and any mechanistic (or causal) explanation of human motions takes priority over, indeed renders false, any explanation in terms of desires, beliefs, intentions. Thus Hospers says, 'Let us note that the more *thoroughly* and *in detail* we know the causal factors leading a person to behave as he does, the more we tend to exempt him from responsibility.'[1] And Malcolm has recently supported the view that 'although purposive explanations cannot be dependent on non-purposive explanations, they would be refuted by the verification of a comprehensive neurophysiological theory of behavior'.[2] I want to argue that this principle is false, and that it is made plausible only by focusing attention on the wrong features of examples like those above. The argument I will unwind strings together arguments and observations from a surprisingly diverse group of recent writers, and perhaps it is fair to say that my share of the argument is not much. I will try to put the best face on this eclecticism by claiming that my argument provides a more fundamental and unified ground for these variously expressed discoveries about the relations between responsibility and mechanism.

II

The first step in reconciling mechanism and responsibility is getting clearer about the nature of the apparently warring sorts of explanations involved. Explanations that serve to ground verdicts of responsibility are couched at least partly in terms of the beliefs, intentions, desires, and reasons of the person or agent held responsible. There is a rough consensus in the literature about the domain of such explanations, but different rubrics are used: they are the 'purposive' or 'rational' or 'action' or 'Intentional' explanations of behavior. I favor the term 'Intentional' (from the scholastics, via Brentano, Chisholm, and other revivalists), and shall capitalize it to avoid confusion with 'intend' and its forms, thereby freeing the latter terms for more restrictive duty. *Intentional explanations*, then, cite thoughts, desires, beliefs, intentions, rather than chemical reactions, explosions, electric impulses, in explaining the occurrence of human motions. There is a well-known controversy debating whether (any) Intentional explanations are ultimately only causal explanations – Melden and Davidson[3] are the initial protagonists – but I shall avoid the center of this controversy and the related controversy about whether a desire or intention could be identical with a physical state or event, and rest with a more modest point, namely that Intentional explanations are at least not causal explanations *simpliciter*. This can best be brought out by contrasting genuine Intentional explanations with a few causal hybrids.

Not all explanations containing Intentional terms are Intentional explanations. Often a belief or desire or other Intentional phenomenon (Intentional in virtue of being referred to by Intentional idioms) is cited as a cause or (rarely) effect in a perfectly Humean sense of cause and effect.

(1) His belief that the gun was loaded caused his heart attack
(2) His obsessive desire for revenge caused his ulcers
(3) The thought of his narrow escape from the rattler made him shudder.

These sentences betray their Humean nature by being subject to the usual rules of evidence for causal assertions. We do not know at this time how to go about confirming (1), but whatever techniques and scientific knowledge we might have recourse to, our tactic would be to show that no other conditions inside or outside the man were sufficient to bring on the heart attack, and that the belief (however we characterize or embody it) together with the prevailing conditions brought about the heart attack in a law-governed way. Now this sort of account may be highly suspect, and ringed with metaphysical difficulties, yet it is undeniable that this is roughly the story we assume to be completable in principle when we assert (1). It may seem at first that (1) is not purely causal, for the man in question can tell us, infallibly or non-inferentially, that it was his belief that caused his heart attack. But this is false. The man is in no better position than we to say what caused his heart attack. It may feel to him as if this was the cause of the attack, but he may well be wrong; his only *knowledge* is of the temporal juxtaposition of the events. Similarly, (2) would be falsified if it turned out that the man's daily consumption of a quart of gin was more than sufficient to produce his ulcers, however strong and sincere his intuitions that the vengeful-ness was responsible. We are apt to think we have direct, non-inferential experience of thoughts causing shudders, as asserted in (3), but in fact we have just what Hume says we have: fallible experience over the years of regular conjunction.

These explanations are not Intentional because they do not explain by *giving a rationale* for the *explicandum*. Intentional explanations explain a bit of behavior, an action, or a stretch of inaction, by making it reasonable in the light of certain beliefs, intentions, desires ascribed to the agent. (1) to (3) are to be contrasted in this regard with

> (4) He threw himself to the floor because of his belief that the gun was loaded
>
> (5) His obsessive desire for revenge led him to follow Jones all the way to Burma
>
> (6) He refused to pick up the snake because at that moment he thought of his narrow escape from the rattler.

The man's heart attack in (1) is not made *reasonable* in the light of his belief (though we might say we can now understand how it happened), but his perhaps otherwise inexplicable action in (4) is. Sentence (5) con-spicuously has 'led' where its counterpart has 'caused', and for good reason. Doubts about (5) would not be settled by appeal to inductive evidence of past patterns if constant conjunctions, and the man's own pronouncements about his trip to Burma have an authority his self-diagnosis in (2) lacks.

The difference in what one is attempting to provide in mechanistic and Intentional explanations is especially clear in the case of 'psycho-somatic' disorders. One can say – in the manner of (1) and (2) – that a desire or belief merely *caused* a symptom, say, paralysis, *or* one can say that a desire or belief led a person to *want* to be paralyzed – to become paralyzed *deliberately*. The latter presumes to be a purely Intentional explanation, a case of making the paralysis – as an *intended condition* – *reasonable* in the light of certain beliefs and desires, e.g. the desire to be waited on, the belief that relatives must be made to feel guilty.

III

Intentional explanations have the actions of persons as their primary domain, but there are times when we find Intentional explanations (and predictions based on them) not only useful but indispensable for accounting for the behavior of complex machines. Consider the case of the chess-playing computer, and the different stances one can choose to adopt in trying to predict and explain its behavior. First there is the *design stance*. If one knows exactly how the computer's program has been designed (and we will assume for simplicity that this is not a learning or evolving program but a static one), one can predict the computer's designed response to any move one makes. One's prediction will come true provided only that the computer performs as designed, that is, without breakdown. In making a prediction from the design stance, one *assumes* there will be no malfunction, and predicts, as it were, from the blueprints alone. We generally adopt this stance when making predictions about the behavior of mechanical objects, e.g. 'As the typewriter carriage approaches the margin, a bell will ring (provided the machine is in working order)', and more simply, 'Strike the match and it will light'. We also often adopt this stance in predictions involving natural objects: 'When spring comes new buds will burst on these twigs'. The essential feature of the design stance is that we make predictions solely from knowledge of or assumptions about the system's design, often without making any examination of the innards of the particular object.

Second, there is what we may call the *physical stance*. From this stance our predictions are based on the actual state of the particular system, and are worked out by applying whatever knowledge we have of the laws of nature. It is from this stance alone that we can predict the malfunction of systems (unless, as sometimes happens these days, a system is *designed* to malfunction after a certain time, in which case malfunctioning in one sense becomes a part of its proper functioning). Instances of predictions from the physical stance are common enough: 'If you turn on that switch you'll get a nasty shock', and, 'When the snows come that branch will break right off' are cases in point. One seldom adopts the physical stance in dealing with a computer just because the number of critical variables in the physical constitution of a computer would overwhelm the most prodigious human calculator. Significantly, the physical stance is generally reserved for instances of breakdown, where the condition preventing normal operation is generalized and easily locatable, e.g. 'Nothing will happen when you type in your question, because it isn't plugged in' or, 'It won't work with all that flood water in it'. Attempting to give a physical account or prediction of the chess-playing computer would be a pointless and herculean labor, but it would work in principle. One could predict the response it would make in a chess game by tracing out the effects of the input energies all the way through the computer until once more type was pressed against paper and a response was printed.

There is a third stance one can adopt toward a system, and that is the *Intentional stance*. This tends to be most appropriate when the system one is dealing with is too complex to be dealt with effectively from the other stances. In the case of the chess-playing computer one adopts this stance when one tries to predict its response to one's move by figuring out what a good or reasonable response would be, given the information the computer has about the situation. Here one assumes not just the absence of malfunction, but the rationality of design or programming as well. Of course the stance is pointless, in view of its extra assumption, in cases where one has no reason to believe in the system's rationality. In weather predicting one is not apt to make progress by wondering what clever move the wise old West Wind will make next. Prediction from the Intentional stance assumes rationality in the system, but not necessarily perfect rationality. Rather, our pattern of inference is that we start with the supposition of what we take to be perfect rationality, and then alter our premise in individual cases as we acquire evidence of individual foibles and weaknesses of reason. This bias in favor of rationality is particularly evident in the tactics of chess players, who set out to play a new opponent by assuming that he will make reasonable responses to their moves, and then seeking out weaknesses. The opponent who started from an assumption of irrationality would be foolhardy in the extreme. But notice, in this regard, how the designer of a chess-playing program might himself be able to adopt the design stance and capitalize from the very beginning on flaws in rationality he knew were built into the program. In the early days of chess-playing programs, this tactic was feasible, but today, with evolving programs capable of self-improvement, designers are no longer capable of maintaining the design stance in playing against their own programs, and must resort, as any outsider would, to the Intentional stance in trying to outwit their own machines.

Whenever one can successfully adopt the Intentional stance toward an object, I call that object an *Intentional system*. The success of the stance is of course a matter settled pragmatically, without reference to whether the object *really* has beliefs, intentions, and so forth, so whether or not any computer can be conscious, or have thoughts or desires, some computers undeniably *are* Intentional systems, for they are systems whose behavior can be predicted, and most efficiently predicted, by adopting the Intentional stance toward them.[4]

This tolerant assumption of rationality is the hallmark of the Intentional stance with regard to people as well as computers. We start by assuming rationality in our transactions with other adult human beings, and adjust our predictions as we learn more about personalities. We do not *expect* new acquaintances to react irrationally to particular topics, but when they do we adjust our strategies accordingly. The presumption that we will be able to communicate with our fellow men is founded on the presumption of their rationality, and this is so strongly entrenched in our inference habits that when our predictions prove false we first cast about for external mitigating factors (he must not have heard, he must not know English, he must not have seen x, been aware that y, etc.) before questioning the rationality of the system as a whole. In extreme cases personalities may prove to be so unpredictable from the Intentional stance that we abandon it, and if we have accumulated a lot of evidence in the meanwhile about the nature of response patterns in the individual, we may find that the design stance can be effectively adopted. This is the fundamentally different attitude we occasionally adopt toward the insane. To watch an asylum attendant manipulate an obsessively counter-suggestive patient, for instance, is to watch something radically unlike normal interpersonal relations. It need hardly be added that in the area of behavior (as opposed to the operation of internal organs, for instance) we hardly ever know enough about the physiology of individuals to adopt the physical stance effectively, except for a few dramatic areas, like the surgical cure of epileptic seizures.

IV

The distinction of stance I have drawn appears closely related to MacKay's distinction between the 'personal aspect' and the 'mechanical aspect' of some systems. Of central importance in MacKay's account is his remarking that the choice of stance is 'up to us', a matter of *decision*, not discovery.[5] Having chosen to view our transactions with a system from the Intentional stance, certain characterizations of events necessarily arise, but that these arise *rightly* cannot be a matter of proof. Much the same distinction, I believe, is presented in a different context by Strawson, who contrasts 'participation in a human relationship' with 'the objective attitude'. 'If your attitude toward someone is wholly objective, then though you may fight him, you cannot quarrel with him, and though you may talk to him, even negotiate with him, you cannot reason with him. You can at most pretend to quarrel, or to reason, with him.'[6] Both MacKay and Strawson say a great deal that is illuminating about the conditions and effects of adopting the personal or participant attitude toward someone (or something), but in their eagerness to establish the implications for ethics of the distinction, they endow it with a premature moral dimension. That is, both seem to hold that adopting the personal attitude toward a system (human or not) involves admitting the system into the moral community. MacKay says, in discussing the effect of our adopting the attitude toward a particular animate human body,[7]

> At the personal level, Joe will have established some personal claims on us, and we on Joe. We shall not be able rightly to tamper with his brain, for example, nor feel free to dismantle his body. . . . He has become 'one of us', a member of the linguistic community – not, be it noted, by virtue of the particular *stuff* of which his brain is built . . . but by virtue of the particular kinds of mutual interaction that it can sustain with our own – interaction which at the personal level we describe as that of person-to-person.

MacKay is, I believe, conflating two choices into one. The first choice, to ascend from the mechanistic to the Intentional stance, as portrayed by our chess-playing designer, has no moral dimension. One is guilty of no monstrosities if one dismembers the computer with whom one plays chess, or even the robot with whom one has long conver-sations. One adopts the Intentional stance toward any system one assumes to be (roughly) rational, where the complexities of its operation preclude maintaining the design stance effectively. The second choice, to adopt a truly moral stance toward the system (thus viewing it as a person), might often turn out to be psychologically irresistible given the final choice, but it is logically distinct. Consider in this context the hunter trying to stalk a tiger by thinking what *he* would do if he were being hunted down. He has adopted the Inten-tional stance toward the tiger, and perhaps very effectively, but though the psychological tug is surely there to disapprove of the hunting of any creature wily enough to deserve the Intentional treatment, it would be hard to sustain a charge of either immorality or logical incon-sistency against the hunter. We might, then, distinguish a fourth stance, above the Intentional stance, called the *personal stance*. The per-sonal stance presupposes the Intentional stance (note that the Intentional stance presupposes neither lower stance) and seems to cursory view at least to be just the annexation of moral commitment to the Intentional. (A less obvious relative of my distinctions of stance is Sellars' distinction between the manifest and scientific images of man. Sellars himself draws attention to its kinship to Strawson: 'Roughly, the manifest image corresponds to the world as conceived by P. F. Strawson. . . . The manifest image is, in particular, a framework in which the distinctive features of persons are conceptually irreducible to features of non-persons, e.g. animals and merely material things.'[8] A question I will not attempt to answer here is whether Sellars' manifest image lines up more with the more narrow, and essentially moral, personal stance or the broader Intentional stance.)

Something like moral commitment can exist in the absence of the Intentional stance, as Strawson points out, but it is not the same; the objective attitude – my design or physical stances – 'may include pity or even love, though not all kinds of love'. The solicitude of a gardener for his flowers, or for that matter, of a miser for his coins, cannot amount to moral commitment, because of the absence of the Intentional. (Parenthetical suggestion: is the central fault in utilitarianism a confusion of gardener-solicitude with person-solicitude?)

Since the second choice (of moral commitment) is like the first in being just a choice, relative to ends and desires and not provably right or wrong, it is easy to see how they can be run together. When they are, important distinctions are lost. Strawson's union of the two leads him to propose, albeit cautiously, a mistaken contrast: 'But what is above all interesting is the tension there is, in us, between the participant attitude and the objective attitude. One is tempted to say: between our humanity and our intelligence. But to say this would be to distort both notions.'[9] The distortion lies in allying the non-Intentional, mechanistic stances with the coldly rational and intelligent, and the Intentional stance with the emotional. The Intentional stance of one chess player toward another (or the hunter toward his prey) can be as coldly rational as you wish, and alternatively one can administer to one's automobile in a bath of sentiment.

Distinctions are also obscured if one makes *communicating with* a system the hallmark of Intentionality or rationality. Adopting the Intentional stance toward the chess-playing computer is not necessarily viewing one's moves as *telling* the computer anything (I do not have to *tell* my human opponent where I moved – he can *see* where I moved); it is merely predicting its responses with the assumption that it will respond rationally to its *perceptions*. Similarly, the hunter stalking the tiger will be unlikely to try to *communicate* with the tiger (although in an extended sense even this might be possible – consider the sort of *entente* people have on occasion claimed to establish with bears encountered on narrow trails, etc.), but he will plan his strategy on his assessment of what the tiger would be reasonable to *believe* or *try*, given its perceptions. As Grice has pointed out,[10] one thing that sets communication as a mode of interaction apart from others is that in attempting a particular bit of communication with A, one intends to produce in A some response *and* one intends A to recognize that one intends to produce in him this response *and* one intends that A produce this response on the basis of this recognition. When one's assessment of the situation leads to the belief that these intentions are not apt to be fulfilled, one does not try to communicate with A, but one does not, on these grounds, necessarily abandon the Intentional stance. A may simply not understand any language one can speak, or any language at all (e.g. the tiger). One can still attempt to influence A's behavior by relying on A's rationality. For instance, one can throw rocks at A in an effort to get A to leave, something that is apt to work with Turk or tiger, and in each case what one does is at best marginal communication.[11]

Communication, then, is not a separable and higher *stance* one may choose to adopt toward something, but a type of interaction one may attempt within the Intentional stance. It can be seen at a glance that the set of intentions described by Grice would not be fulfilled with any regularity in any community where there was no *trust* among the members, and hence communication would be impossible, and no doubt this sort of consideration contributes to the feeling that the Intentional community (or at least the smaller *communicating* community) is co-extensive with the moral community, but of course the only conclusion validly drawn from Grice's analysis here is a pragmatic one: if one wants to influence A's behavior, and A is capable of communicating, then one will be able to establish a very *effective* means of influence by establishing one's trustworthiness in A's eyes (by hook or by crook). It is all too easy, however, to see interpersonal, convention-dependent communication as the mark of the Intentional – perhaps just because Intentional systems process information – and thus make the crucial distinction out to be that between 'poking at' a system (to use MacKay's vivid phrase) and communicating with it. Not only does this way of putting the matter wrongly confuse the system's perception of communications with its perception more generally, but it is apt to lead to a moralistic inflation of its own. The notion of communication is apt to be turned into something mystical or semi-divine – synonyms today are 'rap', 'groove', 'dig', 'empathize'. The critical sense of communication, though, is one in which the most inane colloquies between parent and teenager (or man and bear) count as communication. (MacKay himself has on occasion suggested that the personal attitude is to be recognized in Buber's famous I–Thou formula, which is surely inflation.) The ethical implication to be extracted from the distinction of stance is not that the Intentional stance is a moral stance, but that it is a precondition of any moral stance, and hence if it is jeopardized by any triumph of mechanism, the notion of moral responsibility is jeopardized in turn.

V

Reason, not regard, is what sets off the Intentional from the mechanistic; we do not just reason about what Intentional system will do, we reason about how they will reason. And so it is that our predictions of what an Intentional system will do are formed on the basis of what would be reasonable (for anyone) to do under the circumstances, rather than on what a wealth of experience with this system or similar systems might inductively suggest the system will do. It is the absence from the mechanistic stances of this presupposition of rationality that gives rise to the widespread feeling that there is an antagonism between predictions or explanations from these different stances. The feeling ought to be dissipated at least in part by noting that the absence of a presupposition of rationality is not the same as a presupposition of non-rationality.

Suppose someone asks me whether a particular desk calculator will give 108 as the product of 18 and 6.[12] I work out the sum on a piece of paper and say, 'Yes'. He responds with, 'I know that it *should*, but will it? You see, it was designed by my wife, who is no mathematician.' He hands me her blueprints and asks for a prediction (from the design stance). In working on this prediction the assumption of rationality, or good design, is useless, so I abandon it, not as false but as question-begging. Similarly, if in response to his initial question I reply, 'It's an IBM, so yes', he may reply, 'I know it's *designed* to give that answer, but I just dropped it, so maybe it's broken'. In setting out to make this prediction I will be unable to avail myself of the assumption that the machine is designed to behave in a certain way, so I abandon it. My prediction does not depend on any assumptions about rationality or design, but neither does it rescind any.

One reason we are tempted to suppose that mechanistic explanations preclude Intentional explanations is no doubt that since mechanistic explanations (in particular, physical explanations) are for the most part attempted, or effective, only in cases of malfunction or breakdown, where the rationality of the system is obviously impaired, we associate the physical explanation with a failure of Intentional explanation, and ignore the possibility that a physical explanation will go through (however superfluous, cumbersome, unfathomable) in cases where Intentional explanation is proceeding smoothly. But there is a more substantial source of concern than this, raised by MacIntyre.[13]

> Behaviour is rational – in this arbitrarily, defined sense – if, and only if, it can be influenced, or inhibited by the adducing of some logically relevant consideration. . . . But this means that if a man's behaviour is rational it cannot be determined by the state of his glands or any other antecedent causal factor. For if giving a man more or better information or suggesting a new argument to him is a both necessary and sufficient condition for, as we say, changing his mind, then we exclude, for this occasion at least, the possibility of other sufficient conditions. . . . Thus to show that behaviour is rational is enough to show that it is not causally determined in the sense of being the effect of a set of sufficient conditions *operating independently of the agent's deliberation or possibility of deliberation* [my italics]. So the discoveries of the physiologist and psychologist may indefinitely increase our knowledge of why men behave irrationally but they could never show that rational behaviour in this sense was causally determined.

MacIntyre's argument offers no license for the introduction of the italicized phrase above, and without it his case is damaged, as we shall see later, when the effect of prediction is discussed. More fundamental, however, is his misleading suggestion that the existence of sufficient conditions for events in a system puts that system in a strait-jacket, as it were, and thus denies it the flexibility required of a truly rational system. There is a grain of truth in this, which should be uncovered. In elaborating the distinction between stances, I chose for an example a system of rather limited versatility; the chess-playing system is un-equipped even to play checkers or bridge, and input appropriate to these other games would reveal the system to be as non-rational and unresponsive as any stone. There is a fundamental difference between such limited-purpose systems and systems that are supposed to be capable of responding appropriately to input of all sorts. For although it is possible in principle to design a system that can be guaranteed to respond appropriately (relative to some stipulated ends) to any limited number of inputs given fixed, or finitely ambiguous or variable, environmental 'significance', there is no way to design a system that can be guaranteed to react appropriately under *all* environmental conditions. A detailed argument for this claim would run on too long for this occasion, and I have presented the major steps of it elsewhere,[14] so I will try to establish at least comprehension, if not conviction, for the claim by a little thought-experiment about *tropistic behavior*. Wooldridge gives a lucid account of a tropism:[15]

> When the time comes for egg laying the wasp *Sphex* builds a burrow for the purpose and seeks out a cricket which she stings in such a way as to paralyze but not kill it. She drags the cricket into the burrow, lays her eggs alongside, closes the burrow, then flies away, never to return. In due course, the eggs hatch and the wasp grubs feed off the paralyzed cricket, which has not decayed, having been kept in the wasp equivalent of deep freeze. To the human mind, such an elaborately organized and seemingly purposeful routine conveys a convincing flavour of logic and thoughtfulness – until more details are examined. For example, the wasp's routine is to bring the paralyzed cricket to the burrow, leave it on the threshold, go inside to see that all is well, emerge, and then drag the cricket in. If, while the wasp is inside making her preliminary inspection the cricket is moved a few inches away, the wasp, on emerging from the burrow, will bring the cricket back to the threshold, but not inside, and will then repeat the preparatory procedure of entering the burrow to see that everything is all right. If again the cricket is removed a few inches while the wasp is inside, once again the wasp will move the cricket up to the threshold and re-enter the burrow for a final check. The wasp never thinks of pulling the cricket straight in. On one occasion, this procedure was repeated forty times, always with the same result.

The experiment unmasks the behavior as a tropism, rigid within the limits set on the significance of the input, however felicitous its operation under normal circumstances. The wasp's response lacks that freewheeling flexibility in response to the situation that Descartes so aptly honored as the infinity of the rational mind. For the notion of a perfectly rational, perfectly adaptable system, to which all input compatible with its input organs is significant and comprehensible is the notion of an unrealizable physical system. For let us take the wasp's tropism and improve on it. That is, suppose we take on the role of wasp designers, and decide to enlarge the subroutine system of the tropism to ensure a more rational fit between behavior and *whatever* environment the wasp may run into. We think up one stymying environmental condition after another, and in each case design subroutines to detect and surmount the difficulty. There will always be room for yet one more set of conditions in which the rigidly mechanical working out of response will be unmasked, however long we spend improving the system. Long after the wasp's behavior has become so perspicacious that we would not think of calling it tropistic, the fundamental nature of the system controlling it will not have changed; it will just be more complex. In this sense any behavior controlled by a finite mechanism must be tropistic.

What conclusion should be drawn from this about human behavior? That human beings, as finite mechanical systems, are not rational after all? Or that the demonstrable rationality of man proves that there will always be an inviolable *terra incognita*, an infinite and non-mechanical mind beyond the grasp of physiologists and psychologists? It is hard to see what evidence could be adduced in support of the latter conclusion, however appealing it may be to some people, since for every awe-inspiring stroke of genius cited in its favor (the Einstein-Shakespeare gambit), there are a thousand evidences of lapses, foibles, bumbling and bullheadedness to suggest to the contrary that man is only imperfectly rational. Perfection is hard to prove, and nothing short of perfection sustains the argument. The former alternative also lacks support, for although in the case of the wasp we can say that its behavior has been shown to be *merely* mechanically controlled, what force would the 'merely' have if we were to entertain the notion that the control of man's more versatile behavior is merely mechanical? The denigration might well be appropriate if in a particular case the mechanical explanation of a bit of behavior was short and sweet (consider explanations of the knee-jerk reflex or our hypothetical man who cannot say 'father'), but we must also consider cases in which the physiologist or cybernetician hands us twenty volumes of fine print and says, 'Here is the design of this man's behavioral control system'. Here is a case where the philosopher's preference for simple examples leads him astray, for of course any *simple* mechanistic explanation of a bit of behavior will disqualify it for plausible Intentional characterization, make it a mere happening and not an action, but we cannot generalize from simple examples to complex, for it is precisely the simplicity of the examples that grounds the crucial conclusion.

The grain of truth in MacIntyre's contention is that *any* system that can be explained mechanistically – at whatever length – must be in an extended sense tropistic, and this can enhance the illusion that mechanistic and Intentional explanations cannot coexist. But the only implication that could be drawn from the *general* thesis of man's ultimately mechanistic organization would be that man must, then, be imperfectly rational, in the sense that he cannot be so designed as to *ensure* rational responses to all contingencies, hardly an alarming or counter-intuitive finding; and from any *particular* mechanistic explanation of a bit of behavior it would not follow that that particular bit of behavior was or was not a rational response to the environmental conditions at the time, for the mere fact that the response *had* to follow, given its causal antecedents, casts no more doubt on its rationality than the fact that the computer *had* to answer '108' casts doubt on the arithmetical correctness of its answer.

What, then, can we say about the hegemony of mechanistic explanations over Intentional explanations? Not that it does not exist, but that it is misdescribed if we suppose that whenever the former are confirmed, they drive out the latter. It is rather that mechanistic predictions, eschewing any presuppositions of rationality, can put the lie to Intentional predictions when a system happens to fall short of rationality in its response, whether because of weakness of 'design', or physically predictable breakdown. It is the presuppositions of Intentional explanation that put prediction of *lapses* in principle beyond its scope, whereas lapses are in principle predictable from the mechanistic standpoint, provided they are not the result of truly random events.[16]

VI

It was noted earlier that the search for a watershed to divide the things we are responsible for from the things we are not comes to rest usually with a formulation roughly harmonious with the distinction drawn here between the Intentional and the mechanistic. Many writers have urged that we are responsible for just those events that are our intentional *actions* (and for their foreseeable results), and a great deal has been written in an effort to distinguish action from mere happening. The performing of actions is the restricted privilege of rational beings, persons, conscious agents, and one establishes that something is an action not by examining its causal ancestry but by seeing whether certain sorts of talk about *reasons* for action are appropriate in the context. On this basis we exculpate the insane, with whom one is unable to reason, unable to communicate; we also excuse the results of physical *force majeure* against which reason cannot prevail, whether the force is external (the chains that bind) or internal (the pain that makes me cry out, revealing our position to the enemy). This fruitful distinction between reason giving and cause giving is often, however, the source of yet another misleading intuition about the supposed antagonism between mechanism and responsibility. 'Roughly speaking', Anscombe says, 'it establishes something as a reason if one argues against it.'[17] One is tempted to go on: a reason is the sort of thing one can argue against with some hope of success, but one cannot argue against a causal chain. There is of course a sense in which this is obvious: one cannot argue with what has no ears to hear, for instance. But if one tries to get the point into a form where it will do some work, namely: 'the presentation of an argument cannot affect a causal chain', it is simply false. Presentations of arguments have all sorts of effects on the causal milieu: they set air waves in motion, cause ear drums to vibrate, and have hard to identify but important effects deep in the brain of the audience. So although the presentation of an argument may have no detectable effect on the trajectory of a cannonball, or closer to home, on one's *autonomic* nervous system, one's perceptual system is designed to be sensitive to the sorts of transmissions of energy that must occur for an argument to be communicated. The perceptual system can, of course, be affected in a variety of ways; if I sneak up behind someone and yell 'flinch, please!' in his ear, the effects wrought by my utterance would not constitute an action in obedience to my request, not because they were effects of a cause, but because the intricate sort of causal path that in general would have to have existed for an Intentional explanation to be appropriate was short-circuited. An Intentional system is precisely the sort of system to be affected by the input of information, so the discovery in such a system of a causal chain culminating in a bit of behavior does not at all license the inference: 'since the behavior was caused we could not have argued him out of it', for a prior attempt to argue him out of it would have altered the causal ancestry of the behavior, perhaps effectively.

The crucial point when assessing responsibility is whether or not the antecedent inputs achieve their effects as inputs of information or by short-circuit. The possibility of short-circuiting or otherwise tampering with an Intentional system gives rise to an interesting group of perplexities about the extent of responsibility in cases where there has been manipulation. We are generally absolved of responsibility in cases where we have been manipulated by others, but there is no one principle of innocence by reason of manipulation. To analyze the issue we must first separate several distinct excusing conditions that might be lumped together under the heading of manipulation.

First, one may disclaim responsibility for an act if one has been led to commit the act by deliberately false information communicated by another, and one might put this: 'he manipulated me, by forging documents'. The principle in such cases has nothing to do with one's Intentional system being tampered with, and in fact the appeal to the deliberate malice of the other party is a red herring.[18] The principle invoked to determine guilt or innocence in such cases is simply whether the defendant had reasonably good evidence for the beliefs which led to his act (and which, if true, would have justified it presumably). The plain evidence of one's senses is normally adequate when what is at issue is the presentation of a legal document, and so normally one is absolved when one has been duped by a forgery, but not, of course, if the forgery is obvious or one has any evidence that would lead a reasonable man to be suspicious. And if the evidence that misled one into a harmful act was produced by mere chance or 'act of God' (such as a storm carrying away a 'Stop' sign) the principle is just the same. When one is duped in this manner by another, one's Intentional system has not been tampered with, but rather exploited.

The cases of concern to us are those in which one's behavior is altered by some non-rational, non-Intentional interference. Here, cases where a person's body is merely mechanically interposed in an ultimately harmful result do not concern us either (e.g. one's arm is bumped, spilling Jones's beer, or less obviously, one is drugged, and hence is unable to appear in court). One is excused in such cases by an uncomplicated application of the *force majeure* principle. The only difficult cases are those in which the non-rational, non-Intentional interference alters one's beliefs and desires, and subsequently, one's actions. Our paradigm here is the idea – still fortunately science fiction

– of the neurosurgeon who 'rewires' me and in this way inserts a belief or desire that was not there before. The theme has an interesting variation which is not at all fictional: the mad scientist might discover enough about a man's neural *design* (or program) to figure out that certain inputs would have the effect of reprogramming the man, quite independent of any apparent sense they might have for the man to react to rationally. For instance, the mad scientist might discover that flashing the letters of the alphabet in the man's eyes at a certain speed would cause him (in virtue of his imperfectly rational design) to believe that Mao is God. We have, in fact, fortuitously hit upon such ways of 'unlocking' a person's mind in hypnotism and brain-washing, so the question of responsibility in such cases is not academic. Some forms of psychotherapy, especially those involving drugs, also apparently fall under this rubric. Again it should be noted that the introduction of an evil manipulator in the examples is superfluous. If I am led to believe that Mao is God by a brain hemorrhage or eating tainted meat, or by being inadvertently hypnotized by the monotony of the railroad tracks, the same puzzling situation prevails.

Philosophers have recognized that something strange is going on in these cases, and have been rightly reluctant to grant that such descriptions as I have just given are fully coherent. Thus Melden says,[19]

> If by introducing an electrode into the brain of a person, I succeed in getting him to believe that he is Napoleon, that surely is not a rational belief that he has, nor is he responsible for what he does in consequence of this belief, however convinced he may be that he is fully justified in acting as he does.

Why, though, is the man not responsible? Not because of the absurdity of the belief, for if a merely negligent evidence-gatherer came to believe some absurdity, his consequent action would not be excused, and if the electrode-induced belief happened to be true but just previously unrecognized by the man, it seems we would still deny him responsibility. (I do not think this is obvious. Suppose a benevolent neurosurgeon implants the belief that honesty is the best policy in the heads of some hardened criminals; do we, on grounds of non-rational implantation, deny these people status in the society as responsible agents?) The non-rationality, it seems, is not to be ascribed to the *content* of the belief, but somehow to the manner in which it is believed or acquired. We do, of course, absolve the insane, for they are *in general* irrational, but in this case we cannot resort to this precedent for the man has, *ex hypothesi*, only one non-rational belief. Something strange indeed is afoot here, for as was mentioned before, the introduction of the evil manipulator adds nothing to the example, and if we allow that the presence of one non-rationally induced belief absolves from responsibility, and if the absurdity or plausibility of a belief is independent of whether it has been rationally acquired or not, it seems we can never be sure whether a man is responsible for his actions, for it just may be that one of the beliefs (true or false) that is operative in a situation has been produced by non-rational accident, in which case the man would be ineligible for praise or blame. Can it be that there is a tacit assumption that no such accidents have occurred in those cases where we hold men responsible? This line is unattractive, for suppose it were *proved* in a particular case that Smith was led to some deed by a long and intricate argument, impeccably formulated by him, with the exception of one joker, a solitary premise non-rationally induced. Our tacit assumption would be shown false; would we deny him responsibility?

A bolder skepticism toward such example has been defended by MacIntyre: 'If I am right the concept of causing people to change their beliefs or to make moral choices, by brain-washing or drugs, for example, is not a possible concept.'[20] Hampshire, while prepared to countenance causing beliefs in others, finds a conceptual difficulty in the reflexive case: 'I must regard my own beliefs as formed in response to free inquiry; I could not otherwise count them as beliefs.'[21] Flew vehemently attacks MacIntyre's proposal:[22]

> If it did hold it would presumably rule out as logically impossible all indoctrination by such non-rational techniques. The account of Pavlovian conditionings in Aldous Huxley's *Brave New World* would be not a nightmare fantasy but contradictory nonsense. Again if this consequence did hold, one of the criteria for the use of the term *belief* would have to be essentially backward-looking. Yet this is surely not the case. The actual criteria are concerned with the present and future dispositions of the putative believer; and not at all with how he may have been led, or misled, into his beliefs.

Flew's appeal to the reality of brain-washing is misplaced, however, for what is at issue is how the results of brain-washing are to be coherently described, and MacIntyre is right to insist that there is a conceptual incoherency in the suggestion that in brain-washing one causes beliefs, *tout simple*. Elsewhere[23] I have argued that there *is* an essential backward-looking criterion of belief; here I shall strike a more glancing blow at Flew's thesis. Suppose for a moment that we put ourselves in the position of a man who wakes up to discover a non-rationally induced belief in his head (he does not know it was non-rationally induced; he merely encounters this new belief in the course of reflection, let us say). What would this be like? We can tell several different stories, and to keep the stories as neutral as possible, let us suppose the belief induced is false, but not wild: the man has been induced to believe that he has an older brother in Cleveland.

In the first story, Tom is at a party and in response to the question, 'Are you an only child?' he replies, 'I have an older brother in Cleveland.' When he is asked, 'What is his name?' Tom is baffled. Perhaps he says something like this: 'Wait a minute. Why do I think I have a brother? No name or face or experiences come to mind. Isn't that strange: *for a moment* I had this feeling of conviction that I had an older brother in Cleveland, but now that I think back on my childhood, I remember perfectly well I was an only child.' If Tom has come out of his brainwashing still predominantly rational, his induced belief can last only a moment once it is uncovered. For this reason, our earlier example of the impeccable practical reasoning flawed by a lone induced belief is an impossibility.

In the second story, when Tom is asked his brother's name, he answers 'Sam' and proceeds to answer a host of other obvious questions, relates incidents from his childhood, and so forth. Not *one* belief has been induced, but an indefinitely large stock of beliefs, and other beliefs have been wiped out. This is a more stable situation, for it may take a long time before Tom encounters a serious mismatch between this large and interrelated group and his other beliefs. Indeed, the joint, as it were, between this structure of beliefs and his others may be obscured by some selective and hard to detect amnesia, so that Tom never is brought up with any hard-edge contradictions.

In the third story, Tom can answer no questions about his brother in Cleveland, but insists that he believes in him. He refuses to acknowledge that well-attested facts in his background make the existence of such a brother a virtual impossibility. He says bizarre things like, 'I know I am an only child and have an older brother living in Cleveland.' Other variations in the story might be interesting, but I think we have touched the important points on the spectrum with these three stories. In each story the question of Tom's responsibility can be settled in an intuitively satisfactory way by the invocation of familiar principles. In the first case, while it would be *hubris* to deny that a neurosurgeon might some day be able to set up Tom in this strange fashion, if he can do it without disturbing Tom's prevailing rationality the effect of the surgery on Tom's beliefs will be evanescent. And since we impose a general and flexible obligation on any rational man to inspect his relevant beliefs before undertaking important action, we would hold Tom responsible for any rash deed he committed while under the temporary misapprehension induced in him. Now if it turned out to be physically impossible to insert a single belief without destroying a large measure of Tom's rationality, as in the third story, we would not hold Tom responsible, on the grounds of insanity – his rationality would have been so seriously impaired as to render him invulnerable to rational communication. In the second story determining responsibility must wait on answers to several questions. Has Tom's rationality been seriously impaired? If not, we must ask the further question: did he make a reasonable effort to examine the beliefs on which he acted? If the extent of his brainwashing is so great, if the fabric of falsehoods is so broad and well-knit, that a reasonable man taking normal pains could not be expected to uncover the fraud, then Tom is excused. Otherwise not.

With this in mind we can reconsider the case of the hardened criminals surgically rehabilitated. Are they responsible citizens now, or zombies? If the surgeon has worked so delicately that their rationality is not impaired (perhaps improved!), they are, or can become, responsible. In such a case the surgeon will not so much have implanted a belief as implanted a suggestion and removed barriers of prejudice so that the suggestion *will be* believed, given the right sort of evidential support. If on the other hand the patients become rigidly obsessive about honesty, while we may feel safe allowing them to run loose in the streets, we will have to admit that they are less than persons, less than responsible agents. A bias in favor of true beliefs can be detected here: since it is hard to bring an evidential challenge to bear against a true belief (for lack of challenging evidence – unless we fabricate or misrepresent), the flexibility, or more specifically rationality, of the man whose beliefs all seem to be true is hard to establish. And so, if the rationality of the hardened criminals' new belief in honesty is doubted, it can be established, if at all, only by deliberately trying to shake the belief!

The issue between Flew and MacIntyre can be resolved, then, by noting that one cannot directly and simply cause or implant a belief, for a belief is essentially something that has been *endorsed* (by commission or omission) by the agent on the basis of its conformity with the rest of his beliefs. One may well be able to produce a zombie, either surgically or by brainwashing, and one might even be able to induce a large network of false beliefs in a man, but if so, their persistence *as beliefs* will depend, not on the strength of any sutures, but on their capacity to win contests against conflicting claims in evidential showdowns. A parallel point can be made about desires and intentions. Whatever might be induced in me is either fixed and obsessive, in which case I am not responsible for where it leads me, or else, in MacIntyre's phrase, 'can be influenced or inhibited by the adducing of some logically relevant consideration', in which case I am responsible for *maintaining* it.

VII

I believe the case is now complete against those who suppose there to be an unavoidable antagonism between the Intentional and the mechanistic stance. The Intentional stance toward human beings, which is a precondition of any ascriptions of responsibility, *may* coexist with mechanistic explanations of their motions. The other side of this coin, however, is that we *can* in principle adopt a mechanistic stance toward human bodies and their motions, so there remains an important question to be answered. *Might* we abandon the Intentional stance altogether (thereby of necessity turning our backs on the conceptual field of morality, agents, and responsibility) in favor of a purely mechanistic world view, or is this an alternative that can be ruled out on logical or conceptual grounds? This question has been approached in a number of different ways in the literature, but there is near unanimity about the general shape of the answer: for Strawson the question is whether considerations (of determinism, mechanism, etc.) could lead us to look on everyone exclusively in the 'objective' way, abandoning the 'participant' attitude altogether. His decision is that this could not transpire, and he compares the commitment to the participant attitude to our commitment to induction, which is 'original, natural, non-rational (not *irrational*), in no way something we choose or could give up'.[24] Hampshire puts the point in terms of the mutual dependence of 'two kinds of knowledge', roughly, inductive knowledge and knowledge of one's intentions. 'Knowledge of the natural order derived from observation is inconceivable without a decision to test this knowledge, even if there is only the test that constitutes a change of point of view in observation of external objects.'[25] In other words, one cannot *have* a world view of any sort without having beliefs, and one could not have beliefs without having intentions, and having intentions requires that one view *oneself*, at least, Intentionally, as a rational agent. Sellars makes much the same point in arguing that 'the scientific image cannot replace the manifest without rejecting its own foundation'.[26] Malcolm says, 'The motto of the mechanist ought to be: One cannot speak, therefore one must be silent.'[27] But here Malcolm has dropped the ball on the goal line; how is the mechanist to *follow* his 'motto', and how *endorse* the 'therefore'? The doctrine that emerges from all these writers is that you can't get there from here, that to assert that the Intentional is eliminable 'is to imply pragmatically that there is at least one person, namely the one being addressed, if only oneself, with regard to whom the objective attitude cannot be the only kind of attitude that is appropriate to adopt'.[28] Recommissioning Neurath's ship of knowledge, we can say that the consensus is that there is at least one plank in it that cannot be replaced.

Caution is advisable whenever one claims to have proved that something cannot happen. It is important to see what does not follow from the consensus above. It does not follow, though Malcolm thinks it does,[29] and there are some things in the world, namely human beings, of which mechanism as an embracing theory cannot be true, for there is no incompatibility between mechanistic and Intentional explanation. Nor does it follow that we will always characterize some things Intentionally, for we may all be turned into zombies next week, or in some other way the human race may be incapacitated for communication and rationality. All that is the case is that we, *as persons*, cannot *adopt* exclusive mechanism (by eliminating the Intentional stance altogether). A corollary to this which has been much discussed in the literature recently is that we, as persons, are curiously immune to certain sorts of predictions. If I cannot help but have a picture of myself as an Intentional system, I am bound, as MacKay has pointed out, to have an *underspecified* description of myself, 'not in the sense of leaving any parts unaccounted for, but in the sense of being compatible with more than one state of the parts'.[30] This is because no information system can carry a complete true representation of itself (whether this representation is in terms of the physical stance or any other). And so I cannot even in principle have all the data from which to predict (from any stance) my own future.[31] Another person might in principle have the data to make all such predictions, but he could not tell them all to me without of necessity falsifying the antecedents on which the prediction depends by interacting with the system whose future he is predicting, so I can never be put in the position of being obliged to believe them. As an Intentional system I have an epistemic horizon that keeps my own future as an Intentional system indeterminate. Again, a word of caution: this barrier to prediction is not one we are going to run into in our daily affairs; it is not a barrier preventing or rendering incoherent predictions I might make about my own future decisions, as Pears for one has pointed out.[32] It is just that since I must view myself as a person, a full-fledged Intentional system, there is no complete biography of my future I would be right to accept.

All this says nothing about the impossibility of dire depersonalization in the future. Wholesale abandonment of the Intentional is in any case a less pressing concern than partial erosion of the Intentional domain, an eventuality against which there are no conceptual guarantees at all. If the growing area of success in mechanistic explanation of human behavior does not in itself rob us of responsibility, it does make it more pragmatic, more effective or efficient, for people on occasion to adopt less than the Intentional stance toward others. Until fairly recently the only well-known generally effective method of getting people to do what you wanted them to was to treat them as persons. One might threaten, torture, trick, misinform, bribe them, but at least these were forms of control and coercion that appealed to or exploited man's rationality. One did not attempt to adopt the design stance or the physical stance, just because it was so unlikely that one could expect useful behavioral results. The advent of brainwashing, subliminal advertising, hypnotism and even psychotherapy (all invoking variations on the design stance), and the more direct physical tampering with drugs and surgical intervention, for the first time make the choice of stance a genuine one. In this area many of the moral issues are easily settled; what dilemmas remain can be grouped, as MacKay has observed, under the heading of treating a person as less than a person *for his own good*. What if mass hypnosis could make people stop wanting to smoke? What if it could make them give up killing? What if a lobotomy will make an anguished man content? I argued earlier that in most instances we must ask for much more precise descriptions of the changes wrought, if we are to determine whether the caused change has impaired rationality and hence destroyed responsibility. But this leaves other questions still unanswered.

Tufts University, Medford, Mass.

Notes

1 J. Hospers, 'What Means This Freedom?' in S. Hook (ed.), *Determinism and Freedom in the Age of Modern Science* (New York: Collier, 1958), p. 133.
2 N. Malcolm, 'The Conceivability of Mechanism', *Phil. Review*, 1968, p. 51.
3 A. I. Melden, *Free Action* (London: Routledge & Kegan Paul, 1961); D. Davidson, 'Actions, Reasons and Causes', *J. Phil.*, 1963, pp. 685–700.
4 For a more detailed analysis of the concept, see my 'Intentional Systems', *J. of Philosophy*, 25 February 1971, pp. 87–106, where in particular the notions of rationality of design and Intentionality of information-processing systems are discussed at length.
5 D. M. MacKay, 'The Use of Behavioral Language to Refer to Mechanical Processes', *Brit. J. Phil. Sci.* XIII, 1962, pp. 89–103. See also H. Putnam, 'Robots: Machines or Artificially Created Life?', read at A.P.A. Eastern Div. Meeting, 1964, subsequently published in S. Hampshire (ed.), *Philosophy of Mind* (New York: Harper & Row, 1966), p. 91.
6 P. F. Strawson, 'Freedom and Resentment', *Proc. Brit. Acad.*, 1962, reprinted in Strawson (ed.), *Studies in the Philosophy of Thought and Action* (Oxford University Press, 1968), p. 79.
7 MacKay, *op. cit.*, p. 102.
8 W. Sellars, 'Fatalism and Determinism', in K. Lehrer (ed.), *Freedom and Determinism* (New York: Random House, 1966), p. 145. A Flew, 'A Rational Animal', in J. R. Smythies (ed.), *Brain and Mind* (London: Routledge & Kegan Paul, 1968), pp. 111–35, and A. Rorty, 'Slaves and Machines', *Analysis*, April 1962, pp. 118–20, develop similar distinctions.
9 Strawson, *op. cit.*, p. 80.
10 H. P. Grice, 'Meaning', *Phil. Review*, 1957; 'Utterer's Meaning and Intentions', *Phil. Review*, 1969.
11 J. Bennett, in *Rationality* (London: Routledge & Kegan Paul, 1964), offers an extended argument to the effect that communication and rationality are essentially linked, but his argument is vitiated, I believe, by its reliance on an artificially restrictive sense of rationality – a point it would take too long to argue here. See my 'Intentional Systems', *loc. cit.*, for arguments for a more generous notion of rationality.
12 Cf. L. W. Beck, 'Agent, Actor, Spectator, and Critic', *Monist*, 1965, pp. 175–9.
13 A. C. MacIntyre, 'Determinism', *Mind*, 2957, pp. 248f.
14 *Content and Consciousness* (London: Routledge & Kegan Paul, 1969).
15 D. Wooldridge, *The Machinery of the Brain* (New York: McGraw-Hill, 1963), p. 82.

16 In practice we predict lapses at the Intentional level ('You watch! He'll forget all about your knight after you move the queen') on the basis of loose-jointed inductive hypotheses about individual or widespread human frailties. These hypotheses are expressed in Intentional terms, but if they were given rigorous support, they would be in the process be recast as predictions from the design or physical stance.

17 G. E. M. Anscombe, *Intention* (Oxford: Blackwell, 1957), p. 24.

18 Cf. D. M. MacKay, 'Comments on Flew', in Smythies, *op. cit.*, p. 130.

19 Melden, *op. cit.*, p. 214.

20 Quoted by Flew, *op. cit.*, p. 118.

21 S. Hampshire, *Freedom of the Individual* (New York: Harper & Row, 1965), p. 87.

22 Flew, *op. cit.*, p. 120.

23 *Content and Consciousness*.

24 Strawson, *op. cit.*, p. 94.

25 This is of course an echo of Strawson's examination of the conditions of knowledge in a 'no-space world' in *Individuals* (London: Methuen, 1959).

26 W. Sellars, *Science, Perception and Reality* (London: Routledge & Kegan Paul, 1963), p. 21.

27 Malcolm, *op. cit.*, p. 71.

28 J. E. Llewelyn, 'The Inconceivability of Pessimistic Determinism', *Analysis*, 1966, pp. 39–44. Having cited all these authorities, I must acknowledge my own failure to see this point in *Content and Consciousness*, p. 190. This is correctly pointed out by R. L. Franklin in his review in *Austr. J. Phil.*, September 1970.

29 Malcolm, *op. cit.*, p. 71.

30 D. M. MacKay, 'On the Logical Indeterminacy of a Free Choice', *Mind*, 1960, pp. 31–40; 'The Use of Behavioral Language to Refer to Mechanical Processes', *loc. cit.*; 'The Bankruptcy of Determinism', unpublished, read June 1969, at University of California at Santa Barbara.

31 Cf. K. Popper, 'Indeterminism in Quantum Physics and Classical Physics', *Brit. J. Phil. Sci.*, 1950.

32 D. F. Pears, 'Pretending and Deciding', *Proc. Brit. Acad.*, 1964, reprinted in Strawson (ed.), *Studies in the Philosophy of Thought and Action, loc. cit.*, pp. 97–133.

One determinism
Ted Honderich

NEF

One determinism

States of the brain are, in the first place, *effects*, the effects of other physical states. Many states of the brain, secondly, are *correlates*. A particular state accompanied my experience the other moment of thinking about having walked a lot on Hampstead Heath, and a like state accompanies each like experience: each of my experiences of thinking of having walked a lot on Hampstead Heath. Given our present concern, it is traditional that the most important experiences are decidings and choosings. Some states of the brain, thirdly, are *causes*, both of other states of the brain and also of certain movements of one's body. The latter are actions. Some are relatively simple while others, such as speech acts and bits of ritual, depend on settings of convention and have complex histories. Simple or complex, however, all actions are movements, or of course stillnesses, caused by states of the brain. It follows from these three premises, about states of the brain as effects, as correlates and as causes, that on every occasion when we act, we can only act as in fact we do. It follows too that we are not responsible for our actions, and, what is most fundamental, that we do not possess selves of a certain character.

Determinism, one determinism, can be expressed in these sentences, the latter two of which contain belaboured terms that can be put to other uses. Fig. 1, an excessively schematic diagram which represents the premises of this determinism, may be useful in forestalling certain misunderstandings. A particular action, *A*, is shown in the diagram as the effect of two brain states and another physical state, which together are a sufficient condition of the action. Correlated with the brain states are conscious states, perhaps a desire and a perception. The three states which give rise to the action are themselves the effects of other physical states, some of them being brain states themselves. None of the initial array of states has a correlate in consciousness.

In what follows, incidentally, I shall speak in an ordinary way of causes. That is, a cause will be taken to be a chosen member of some set of conditions sufficient to produce an event or a state. To say of a

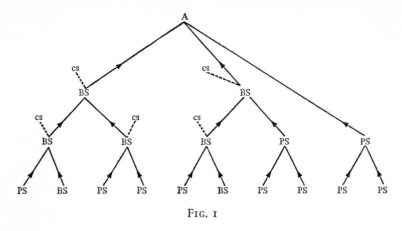

FIG. 1

state that it had a cause is to imply, rather than assert, that the state was the effect of some sufficient set of conditions. It will make no substantial difference if one understands sufficiency in terms of constant conjunction or in terms of some stronger notion. The latter course is taken when one understands the statement, say, that a particular brain state caused a movement, in some such a way as this: the brain state occurred, as did the movement, and the movement would have followed the state, given the other necessary conditions, whatever other logically consistent circumstances had obtained.

The conception that I have sketched, when it has been set out more fully, will go some way towards meeting the supposition that determinism is not in need of serious attention because it is irredeemably obscure or indeed incoherent.[1] Sometimes, although not always, the supposed obscurity has been thought to derive from the traditional philosophical pictures of mind. That is, determinism has been thought to be entangled with one or another of the traditional pictures, each of which, alas, has obscurity to spare. It is one of my particular intentions to state a determinism that commits one to as little as possible of the pictures, and indeed to tolerably little. My other particular intentions, in so far as clarification is in question, have to do with movement and action, the word 'can', and the idea of responsibility.

Arguments for the truth of the determinism in question are not to be construed as anything else, and in particular not as urgings of a kind of primacy. Determinism is but one characterisation of human existence. There are many others, and they are more enlightening.

With respect to the determinist characterisation, it is a travesty of empiricism to declare, as some too taken by science do, that when all is said and done, men are merely homeostatic machines. Appearances are otherwise, and here at least we may side with Wilde in the proposition that it is only shallow people who do not judge by appearances.

I The correlation thesis

It may be best to begin with the middle one of our three premises, which we may call the Correlation Thesis. It is to the effect that there exists, for each discriminable conscious state or occurrence, a theoretically discriminable brain correlate. This, like the diagram above, may be taken to imply something that I do not wish to maintain, and to which I shall not be committed. It would be natural, at any rate, to understand it to imply that there exist physical states of the brain and also, distinct from them, conscious states. It may seem, then, to rule out physicalism, the doctrine that conscious states in some sense *are* physical states. In fact, neither the denial nor the affirmation of physicalism is a part of the enterprise, or a consequence of it. The Correlation Thesis is consistent both with physicalism and with certain conceptions of mind, which I shall mention in a moment, that are opposed to it.

To make clearer that the proposed determinism does not require that we settle the central problem about mind, and also for other reasons, it will be best to state it formally in another way. Let us have the notion of *a description of consciousness*. Descriptions of consciousness typically are statements about persons to the effect that they are thinking or feeling. The statement that I am thinking about being home in England is one. So is the statement that a man is awake, or puzzled, doing this or that, or conscious. We might attempt a general analysis of descriptions of consciousness, which would of course depend on an analysis of consciousness. To do so would then bring us into consideration of precisely those dark propositions which I wish to avoid. For my purpose we need only the usual layman's understanding of descriptions of consciousness, a definition of an enumerative character which depends on a grasp of particular descriptions and their truth conditions. The Correlation Thesis, then, may be stated as follows.

Any particular description of consciousness D is true of an individual if and only if his brain or part of it is in one particular state or sequence of states S.

It is perhaps a touch contentious to label the physical correlates of descriptions of consciousness as states of a part or the whole *of the brain*. Given certain propositions in contemporary neurophysiology, and an inclination to caution, we might better talk of states of the central nervous system or a part of it. The term *part*, in any case, is no more than a stand-in for other more adequate descriptions. Nothing substantial hangs on these points and so I shall persist in a traditional usage. In what follows, too, I shall often take the convenience of referring to conscious states as the correlates of brain states. This is to be understood, of course, as not carrying any implication of the non-identity, or the identity, of brain states and conscious states. All that is to be understood concerns descriptions of consciousness and brain states. There are, of course, problems of several kinds concerning the individuation and the truth conditions of descriptions of consciousness. To my mind, they are not impediments to us, and I shall not discuss them in this essay.[2]

The Correlation Thesis, obviously, is not that physical states of the brain *cause* conscious states. This proposition is eschewed not because it is known to be false, or because it is obviously incoherent, but simply because of its obscurity and the perplexities it creates. A determinist does not need it, or them. The obscurity and the perplexities have to do in part with the very notions of conscious state and conscious event. It may be objected, mistakenly, that the thesis *is* tantamount to some assertion of causal connection between brain states and conscious states. Surely, it may be said, the thesis maintains the existence of a constant conjunction. On the contrary, what is being put forward does not even satisfy a minimal requirement for causal connexion, that of two logically independent entities. The thesis asserts no more than this, that if and only if a certain description of consciousness is true of a person, his brain or part of it is in a certain physical state.

The Correlation Thesis, then, is independent of physicalism, and also independent of three dualisms. The first is epiphenomenalism, construed as the proposition just noticed, that brain states cause conscious states. The second, sometimes called mentalism, is the proposition that conscious states cause brain states. The third, as shop-worn and as obscure as the others, is that there is interaction. Some brain states cause some conscious states, some conscious states cause some brain states. There is more to be said of these matters but I shall put it off for a time.

The thesis has been stated in an absolutely simple way. A neurophysiologist's version of it would be a much enlarged affair. Brain injuries and also a good deal of research have established that the normal brain possesses redundant capabilities. A particular function which ordinarily is that of one part of the brain can be taken over by another part. Indeed, it is clear that any adequate version of the Correlation Thesis would relate a certain disjunction about brain states to each of many descriptions of consciousness. The thesis as stated above, and mentioned in what follows, may be read in this way. That is, the term *brain state* may be so construed as to take as its referent either one state or one disjunctive set of states. This is not to say that in the thesis as stated, or in a developed version of it, any mentioned brain state would be related to a disjunction of descriptions of consciousness. The relation between descriptions of consciousness and brain states is not many-one. It is this that is of principal importance.

Ordinary brain function, further, is in a certain sense diffuse. There is no question of the entire physical correlate of, say, one thought, being found in one micro-locale of the brain. The thesis as stated should not be taken to imply any such thing. A developed version of the theory would take into account the true complication. Finally, it seems likely that further description of brain activity will require something other than an atomistic or reductionist model. What I have in mind is only that the further description will not be of elements all of which exist at some one level. There are, very likely, different properties at different levels. This too would enter into the Correlation Thesis in a developed form.[3]

Let us pass on to the question of truth, the truth of the thesis as stated. One can imagine a very stern objector who demands a confirmation beginning with a physical description of a really decent brain state: that one correlated, say, with liking Bertorelli's Restaurant, or that one for deciding not to pay taxes to a government waging an unjust war. Such demands, of course, cannot be met. Nor, even in the anticipated states of neurophysiology, are they likely to be met. This does not matter much. What is to be confirmed is that there exists, for each discriminable conscious state, a theoretically discriminable physical correlate. This generalisation can be confirmed without each or even many of its instances being confirmed.

On the basis of evidence of several kinds, one can extrapolate to the conclusion that there exists, for each and every occurrence of consciousness, a particular brain state. It would be jejune to suppose that either the data we can have, or the principles of non-deductive inference, are capable of such precise formulation that propositions of this character can be 'proved' or even in any precise sense 'confirmed'. What one can say is that the evidence is all one way and that an acceptance of the proposition in question is unavoidable. Since some will disagree, I shall sketch a part of the evidence.

One does not need neurophysiology in order to find in oneself a rational inclination towards belief in the Correlation Thesis. We share the conviction, almost all of us, that consciousness generally is correlated with the existence of a functioning brain. It requires no audacity to assert that all the evidence we have, at any rate Here Below, is in favour of this proposition. A denial of it is at about the level of belief in ghosts. Secondly, we accept many correlations of a more particular kind, or, at any rate, we will accept them after a bit of reflection. Suppose that two people are well placed to see the Empire State Building. One reports that he does, the other reports that he does not, and we believe both of them. We will readily and reasonably accept that the capabilities of the second man, probably his perceptual capabilities, are in some way impaired, and that if they were corrected, so as to be back in line with those of the first man, he would see the building. If we regard the claim that for a man to have the capability in question is for some physical sequence to occur, one which includes light transmission, events in the retina, and subsequent events in the central nervous system, we are led to the conclusion that a state of the brain is correlated with *the having of visual experience*. A particular state obtains if and only if the description of someone as having visual experience applies.

Perhaps it is worth noting that facts of this kind, of which there are many, also serve to support something other than our Correlation Thesis. That thesis, as stated, is about individual persons. It has the consequence that my brain is in state S if and only if I think of French beans. It does not have the consequence that your brain is in precisely the same state, S, if and only if you think of French beans. The rudimentary facts that have been mentioned also give support to this different thesis:

> *Some* descriptions of consciousness are true of all persons if and only if their brains or parts of them are in a certain state or sequence of states.

However, rudimentary correlations of the kind just indicated also support the Correlation Thesis. We believe not only that two persons have visual experience if and only if their brains are in some one state, but that *either* individual has such experience on different occasions if and only if *his* brain is in that state.

Evidence of a different character does come from neurophysiology, whose recent textbooks will have to go without recapitulation.[4] To have a reasonable grasp of the evidence, one must have some understanding of the theory's breadth and richness. I shall, as a poor substitute, give several unrelated instances in order to indicate that some physical description of some correlates of consciousness is available. Perhaps it is necessary, although it should not be, to remark that neurophysiology is a changing and progressing inquiry. It is no more a corpus of settled truths, no more devoid of dispute and speculation, than any other live science. However, if it would be absurd to see it as some finished work of indubitable truths, it would be equally absurd to regard it as a congeries of possibilities, some suitable for use no matter which way the mind of a philosopher may turn. Many of the propositions of neurophysiology are beyond question and their consequences are clear.

(1) It is possible, even in the present stage of research, to provide a considerable physical description of a physical state which obtains if and only if the owner of the brain satisfies the description of *being conscious*. An individual is conscious only if what is known as the reticular activating system is in a certain state, one that is open to physical description. What we have is something close to a locatable site of consciousness and an account of what electro-chemical states must obtain in this part of the brain for the person to be conscious. The system in question is the subject of many unanswered questions, and of many uneasinesses that are not yet clear questions. In this, I suppose, it is not unlike those other sources of mystery, physical states generally.

(2) It was supposed of early experiments in the electro-stimulation of

the hypothalmus in lower animals that all that was produced was 'sham' emotion. That is, implanted electrodes were thought to produce *only* what are taken to be, under ordinary conditions, the *behavioral manifestations* of emotion. Such resistance is no longer possible. Further investigation of lower animals, much of it morally offensive, has also produced very considerable findings. Treatment of mentally-ill persons has resulted in the identification of what are often called, if too loosely, the centres of pleasure and pain in the human brain. Electrical stimulation at various points produces satisfaction, relaxation, restlessness, fright and other discriminable emotional states. What we have, then, is something like an adequate identification of brain states correlated with fairly particular descriptions of consciousness.

(3) There are also Penfield's results having to do with the eliciting of past experiences.[5] Again as a result of exact electro-stimulation, subjects have experiences which are related to ordinary remembering but of a greatly more vivid nature. These are experiences which have precise conceptual content. As long as stimulation continues, thereby producing a certain electrical state, there occurs a sequential 're-experiencing' of a previously forgotten period of ordinary life. The 're-experiencing' ends with the ending of stimulation. It may begin again, where it began in the first instance of stimulation, if stimulation is begun again.

(4) Finally, there is absolutely no evidence to be found in neurophysiology that goes against the Correlation Thesis.

Despite all that can be said of this character, it remains a possibility for someone to maintain that the thesis is false, that there are *certain* descriptions of consciousness that lack physical correlates. In the past, even the recent past, candidates would have been drawn from moral experience, perhaps the experience of resolving a conflict of duty and desire. Today, some may be inclined to take a similar line with descriptions having to do with higher kinds of intellectual performance, or judgments that depend for their sense on institutions of a culture. It seems that a rational persistence in such a view is impossible. Who can believe, to take one consequence of denying the thesis, that one's judgment on some occasion, of *whatever* character, might have been different in some respect without one's brain having been in a different state? For my own part I am inclined to feel that I have already offended against Hume's dictum that next to the ridicule of denying an evident truth is that of taking much pains to defend it.

II The causation of brain states

We have so far looked at one premiss of the determinism being advanced. Another, to which we now turn, is the proposition that brain states are themselves the effects of other physical states. This is unlikely to be confused with other things and it is not, in itself, about consciousness. For these reasons we may proceed more briskly. I shall take it, as might have been mentioned above, that a physical state is one of which it is a conceptual possibility that it be completely described without recourse to descriptions of consciousness. This, which might be extended in several ways, is one of a number of possible definitions.

Those states which are causes of brain states fall into whole ranges of useful classifications. Let us notice only a taxonomy of three broad groupings. There are those causal states that are members of sets of conditions that are sufficient for the generation of a person with a functioning brain. Second, there are causal states of such a person which contribute to the ongoing sequence of brain states. Third, there are those causal states which are themselves brain states.

Examples of states of the first grouping, to begin at the beginning, can be had from a single human cell, whose structure is open to physical descriptions of different specificity and different degrees of confirmation. A particular effect already mentioned is that particular brain state correlated with consciousness generally, a state of the reticular activating system. An example of a state in the second grouping, or examples of several such states, can be had from an ordinary sequence beginning with a touch-receptor. Pressure on hair results in a change of orientation of appendages, the production of an electrical potential, and, in the end, certain events in the brain. These events are correlated with tactile awareness. There are a great many known connexions of this kind. An example of a causal state in the third grouping (those which are themselves brain states) is a state of the cortex, one which cannot be described except in the higher technicalities of neurophysiology and is correlated with learning. The effects in question are brain states correlated with certain performances.

We do not know what specific connexions hold between physical states and the brain states that are correlated with very specific higher mental events, such events as noticing the date or speculating that America is a plutocracy. The general thesis that each brain state is the effect of some set of sufficient conditions is the result of extrapolatory argument of several kinds. The premisses for the extrapolation come from ordinary belief, which is not to be disdained, and, as we have just seen, from neurophysiology. There are also premises of a certain character to be had from the history of the life-sciences, including such episodes as the defeat of vitalism. These premises, indeed, are of great importance. We may also add something that might have been included in the discussion of the Correlation Thesis, research in the mechanical simulation of intelligence. It is of considerable importance to our present concern, given our ignorance of the brain, which must not be minimised, and in particular our ignorance of the causal relations between brain states. The central point is that complex and sophisticated problem-solving, of a kind once thought to be exclusively a matter of competences associated with consciousness, is a function of physical states which indubitably are the effects of other physical states.

The thesis that all brain states are the effects of other physical conditions, unlike the thesis about correlation, runs up against a certain amount of philosophical and indeed ordinary inclination. It is here that one encounters both libertarianism and also something much more substantial, an ill-formed resistance on the part of philosophers and others. We are inclined to assign efficacy of some kind to mental states and events. We are wont to believe that thoughts and feelings, somehow or other, produce other thoughts and feelings.

There are three responses open to anyone who accepts both correlation and the thesis that brain states are effects of other physical states. It may be argued, first, that while relations between mental events of many kinds are undeniable, there is no point in assigning efficacy to them. We already have all we need of efficacy, and efficacy that can be understood. We may explain that one thought *appears* to give rise to another because the brain state correlated with the first thought stands in causal relation with the brain state correlated with the second thought. There is the appearance of efficacy because of correlation with that which is causally connected.

Second, there is the solution of physicalism. Brain states, in some sense, *are* mental states. If brain states are accepted as causes of other brain states, we have our thoughts and feelings, which are those states, efficacious in fact, and not merely appearance. On this view, there is one thing, A, that has certain electro-chemical properties and also has properties that are in question when we say, for example, that a man is thinking of a glass of wine. There are not two things, electro-chemical activity and thinking. What is A? One can describe it, partially, as electro-chemical activity in the brain. One can also describe it, partially, as thinking of a glass of wine. There is no more to it than properties that are brought in by these two descriptions.

There is also a third response, perhaps that one which is most uncomfortable. A determinist can allow the possibility of over-determination, in some enlarged sense, of the brain states correlated with descriptions of consciousness. That is, it can be allowed that these states are not only the effects of sufficient physical conditions but also, in some sense, the products of conscious states and events. There are problems about the very conception of over-determination, admittedly, and still more severe difficulties about the present use of the conception. We are offered the supposition that a certain physical state, a brain state, is the effect of a set of sufficient conditions of a physical nature and also has some other sufficient genesis in consciousness. The first of these propositions, by comparison, is a paradigm of clarity. The second is a matter of mystery, that same mystery that shrouds the three dualist pictures of mind mentioned above.

The main point upon which I wish to insist is that there is one ground rule in all of this. One must take it as true that brain states are effects of sufficient physical conditions. This second thesis of our determinism is not an attractive proposition, but a denial of it is quixotic. It is well confirmed, and, as I have indicated, it is in accord with whole bodies of established theory. I mean, of course, bodies of theory of the physical world and of persons as physical systems. The thesis that brain states are effects of a certain kind is as well supported as the Correlation Thesis. It is no surprise that many contemporary philosophers who wish to break a lance for responsibility do so in another field. Even in the absence of decently-articulated premises of determinism, they choose to offer resistance elsewhere instead, in the matter of conceptions of action and responsibility, to which we shall come. If the thesis that brain states are certain effects and the Correlation Thesis gave us *no* possibility of explaining the seeming efficacy of conscious states, the theses would be vulnerable. That there are possibilities of explanation, however uncomfortable, allows the theses to remain what they are: incontrovertible on the evidence that we have.

The Correlation Thesis, to recall, leaves open to us all the traditional pictures of mind. The addition of the second thesis excludes two pictures. As we noticed a moment ago, we remain free to choose a physicalism, which in some versions might have a less contentious name. We may also choose a kind of dualism. We are not prohibited from, or committed to, some assertions of the non-identity of the brain and mind. What must go is mentalism, construed as the conjunctive proposition that mental states have efficacy with respect to brain states *and* those brain states lack sufficient conditions of a physical nature. This loss, I take it, is not alarming. Our other loss, if it is such, is interactionism, construed in part as the proposition that *some* brain states derive from mental states and are not effects of sufficient physical conditions. This picture derives, no doubt, from the fact that some mental states or occurrents are customarily talked of as causes while others are talked of as effects. My deciding to avoid 42nd Street makes me think of other routes, but my seeing stars is made to happen by my bumping my head. One is tempted to feel that this particular picture is no more than an unnecessary state of philosophical dither, produced by paying too much attention to what we customarily say. A discontinuity of the supposed kind flies in the face of factual consistency.

Our two theses, then, leave us with a choice between physicalisms of several kinds and epiphenomenalisms of several kinds. We can, if we wish, make neither choice. If we wish to give a certain explanation of the appearance of efficacy of mental states, we may opt for a physicalism, but it may be maintained that the appearance can be explained by our two theses alone. If the inclination to separate brain and mind is overwhelming, we may opt for an epiphenomenalism. We can, if we want, also reflect on forms of mentalism and interactionism that allow for over-determination, a determination of brain states that includes sufficient conditions of a physical nature.

It is now clear how our determinism stands to the traditional pictures of mind. This is a matter of its first two premises. It is arguable, too, that it leaves open the only two options that on independent grounds are worth keeping open.

III Actions as effects of brain states

There remains to be considered the third and last premiss, that brain states cause certain body movements and stillnesses. Let us stick to movements. It is not true, obviously, even if we restrict ourselves to externally visible movements, that all of them are caused by brain states. This is so for several reasons. For example, it is well known that the nervous system includes what are called reflex arcs. Movements of the limbs, which usually have a different genesis, are sometimes 'reflexes': consequences of a sequence that begins in a receptor mechanism, ends in musculature, and does not get there by way of the usual brain functions.

It is equally certain that many movements, for example those of my fingers in typing this essay, are the effects of brain states. Any such assertion, at any rate in an essay on determinism, is bound to call up an anticipatory retort. It is commonplace to find it admitted that body movements of the kind in question are effects, products of sufficient conditions whose nature is left unclear. We are told, however, that this admission is of no use to the determinist. It is of no use because it itself is not, and it does not entail, the proposition that *actions* are caused. Determinism, it is supposed, requires the latter proposition. What I wish to suggest is that if certain movements are caused, then actions are caused, because the movements *are* the actions.

Why is it supposed that movements cannot be actions? One main reason can be brought out by noticing that *the same movement*, in one sense of those words, may occur both in the knee-jerk reflex and in the action of moving one's lower leg. Therefore, it is supposed, since there is no action at all in the first case but only a movement, it cannot be that the same movement which occurs in the second case is the action. All that needs to be said about this is that there is a perfectly clear sense in which *the same movement* does *not* occur in the two cases. It may be that the two movements are identical, that they are instances of the same movement-type, in that they would leave the same record on the film of a movie camera. They are not identical, or instances of the same movement-type, in that one does not *derive from intention* and one does. We need not pursue the analyses of what it is to *have an intention* and what it is for a movement to *derive from intention*. Having an intention appears to be a matter of wants and beliefs, including beliefs of several kinds. A movement, if it derives from an intention, falls under some description that is related to a description of an intention. Neither of these comments is near to being sufficient. What we do need, and what we have in sufficiency, is a grasp of ordinary truth-conditions governing the ascription of intentions and the description of movements as deriving from intention. We distinguish actions from those movements which are not actions.

The main point, that there is no difficulty in regarding actions as movements, can be made with respect to slightly more familiar examples. In one sense, *the same movement* can enter into these four actions: switching on the floor lamp, switching it from dim to medium, switching it from medium to bright, switching it off. The camera will record the same flick of the fingers on each occasion. These are, none the less, four different movements in the sense that each derives from a different intention. That it makes sense to say they are not different as movements does not affect the issue. That two 1967 Dodge Coronets are said to be not different as cars does not prevent us from distinguishing them. They can be distinguished as the one that is yours and the one that is mine.

It can certainly be granted that it would be mistaken to identify the class of actions with any class of movements whose selection did not bring in intention. It would be equally mistaken, obviously, to suppose that one could conclude, from such properties of a particular movement as those that might appear on film, that it was a particular action. This is nothing to the point.

What I wish to maintain, then, is that actions, which *are* certain movements, are caused by brain states. Given the amount of consternation about action in the philosophy of mind, it will be as well to rule out some possible confusions. (1) It is not being maintained, certainly, that we ordinarily individuate actions by first picking out movements and then by finding out if they are effects of brain states. It can be granted that we never individuate actions in such a way. Nor, obviously, is any such thing required for the argument. (2) Nor is it important that in order to provide evidence for the contention that actions are effects of brain states, a neurophysiologist must begin by picking out actions in the ordinary way. This is not denied. Having done so, he can proceed to establish that the movements in question, while in some way intentional, are also effects of states of the brain. (3) It is not being supposed, either, that the determinist argues in this way: movement M, identified only by such as its film properties, has a cause, and therefore action A is caused. If only because of the one-many relation between movements with those film properties, on the one hand, and actions, this would be difficult. All that is supposed is that there are movements which derive from certain intentions, and are individuated in this way, and that they have certain causes.[6]

As for the truth of the causal claim about actions, what we have is an evidence-situation very much of the kind mentioned in connection with previous propositions. Again, we lack knowledge of precisely what particular conditions give rise to particular actions, such actions as giving a hopeful answer, buying a ticket, pressing the button to explode the charge. The evidence we do have, which is of several kinds, is sufficient for a general conclusion. Neurophysiology, as many will be aware, has passed well beyond the stage of the familiar maps of the brain which assign kinds of motor function to particular parts. I take it that no serious question can be raised about the truth of our third premiss. Each and every action is a movement, or a stillness, or of course a sequence of movements or stillnesses, caused by states of the brain.

None the less, this discussion of action may be taken by some to be paradoxical. Surely, it may be said, it is eccentric to reduce the complexity of action to the simplicity of movement, eccentric to reduce the experiential character of action to the facts of matter in motion. Signing a contract, uttering a supplication, making love, putting on the brakes, committing an offence – surely it must be distortion to see these actions and activities merely as matters of movement. It must then be entirely mistaken to conclude from the premiss of caused movements that actions too are caused.

The correct response is that it would be more than eccentric to reduce action and its character to the simplicity of matter in motion. Nothing of the sort has been attempted. It can certainly be granted that one could give only the most impoverished account of human existence, or that existence of which action is a part, if one fastened on only such features of certain movements as those which turn up on film. These movements have their place in our attitudes by virtue of what precedes and accompanies them, and does not turn up on film: the complex processes of consciousness, the correlates of certain physical states. A determinist, furthermore, if he were to content himself with the proposition that actions are effects, would fail to direct his guiding principle to that which is of greatest importance. He would fail, indeed, to state a determinism. This would be so for the reason that it would remain possible to give something other than a deterministic account of the occurrence of the *causes* of action.

The determinism that has been advanced here is not in this way incomplete. (1) Actions are movements caused by states of the brain. (2) These latter, the physical correlates of consciousness, are themselves the effects of other physical states, many of which are likely to be correlates themselves. The propositions expressed in these two sentences have as their subject-matter the whole of human experience. They do not pertain only to a reduced subject-matter. To think that they do, at this point, can only be the consequence of fixing attention on the first proposition to the exclusion of the second.

IV 'Can'

Let us turn to what follows from the premisses of this determinism. The first conclusion, if it is such, is that whenever we decide or act, we can only decide or act as we do. Initially, let us consider actions alone. There are, certainly, uses of 'can' such that it does *not* follow from the premisses that one can only act as one does. What I wish to assert at this juncture, if only for purposes of clarification, is that there is one use of 'can' such that it does follow from the premisses that one can only act as one actually does.

The relevant use is bound up with causation, and it is 'cannot', rather than 'can', that is of the greater pertinence. To say that something, *A*, cannot happen in a given situation is to say that something else, *not-A*, is caused to happen. To say that something, *B*, can happen in a given situation is to say that something else, *not-B*, is not caused to happen. It is to be noticed that in asserting that *B* can happen in a given situation we are not asserting that *B* is caused to happen. We may indeed believe just that, but it is not a part of our assertion. If we do assert our further belief, that *B* is caused to happen, then it follows that what can happen is what does happen. It follows, in a related sense of the word 'possible', that what is possible is only what becomes actual.

We can enlarge on these accounts of 'cannot' and 'can' in several ways. We may write in either of the two accounts of causation mentioned at the beginning of this essay. Let us take the stronger one, where to say that one thing caused another is to say that the second thing would have happened, given the first and its accompanying necessary conditions, whatever other logically consistent circumstances had obtained. The second enlargement of our accounts has to do with what may be called the scope of 'cannot' and 'can'. What *cannot* happen, given attention to a part of a sequence of events, is something that *can* happen, given attention to more of the sequence. Suppose that *not-G* is the effect of *F*. We may say that G cannot happen. The statement takes into its scope, in so far as causal antecedents are concerned, only *F*. Suppose, however, that we go further back prior to *F*, and accept that *F* was not caused to happen. We may then say, despite the fact that *not-G* is the effect of *F*, that G can happen. Alternatively, if we believe that *F* was caused to happen, we may again say G cannot happen, in this case taking into account the longer sequence.

Consider, then, a man's action of signing a petition on a particular occasion, and the assertion that he cannot do other than sign it. The assertion advances or presupposes two propositions. (1) Given certain brain states which are correlated with descriptions of consciousness related to his action, and certain other conditions, he would have signed it as he did whatever other consistent circumstances had obtained. (2) Given certain earlier physical states, the mentioned brain states would have obtained whatever other consistent conditions had obtained. The assertion that he *can* do other than sign it, if the assertion is made, means or presupposes the falsehood of (1) or (2) or both.

The determinism that has been advanced includes generalisations of the two propositions. These generalisations are, respectively, the third and the first thesis. It follows from these two theses, then, that a man cannot ever do otherwise than he does. It would be patently mistaken, of course, to suppose that the given usage of 'cannot' and 'can' are our only usages. We sometimes say that *B* can happen in a certain situation and mean, essentially, that *B* will happen if some further condition is satisfied. This is not, as in the first usage, a denial that *not-B* will be caused to happen. Indeed, something that *cannot* happen, in the first usage, will be something that *can* happen, in the second usage.

It is not only that our chosen usage of 'cannot' and 'can' is not the only one. It may well be that it is not *all* of *any* ordinary usage. It is a part, however, of one very ordinary usage of the words when persons are under discussion. When we say that a man can do *G* we mean or presuppose, I think, that he is not compelled to do *not-G* and also that he is not caused to do *not-G*. If he is caused to do *not-G*, then he cannot do *G*. These contentions, or contentions of this general character, have often been opposed by philosophers, notably those of the British empirical tradition. It is denied that our chosen usage of 'cannot' and 'can' enters into *any* ordinary usage. I shall take up oppositions of this kind at a later stage, in connection with responsibility.

It may be thought at this point, reasonably enough, that nothing much has been gained by giving only this much attention to 'cannot' and 'can' as used of actions. The propositions expressed by the sentence that we cannot act otherwise than we do, with 'cannot' used in the given way, are no more than the first and third theses. It is misleading, even, to talk of a conclusion being derived from two premisses. I have in fact included what has been said about 'cannot' and 'can' only to make clear what I am not claiming. What I am not claiming, of course, is that the premisses of our determinism generate conclusions about what one cannot and can do, where these are understood in any but the given way. A number of philosophers have paid enough attention to 'cannot' and 'can' to make a certain caution irresistible.

For the same reason, I should like to look briefly at the pair of terms as used of decisions and choices. When they are so used, for obvious reasons, a different account must be given. What is to be understood, to go over to the past tense, by the claim that I *could not* have decided to look at something else in the gallery yesterday, when in fact I decided to look at Seurat? What is in question here is what many would call a mental act, an event of consciousness. Our determinism, it will be remembered, does not assert that such things are caused, or even that such things are not identical with events or states of the brain. All that is asserted in this area is that a certain description of consciousness, perhaps 'He is deciding to look at Seurat', which was true of me, stands in correlation with a certain brain state. We cannot take it, then, that to say I could not have looked at something else is to be understood, even in part, as the proposition that my deciding to look at Seurat was caused to happen.

If we allow ourselves the convenience of talk about mental events and states, however, we are not barred from assigning to this statement, 'He could not have decided to look at something else', this force: the different choice he did make was a correlate of a state of the brain that obtained at that time, which state was an effect of other physical states. More strictly, we may assign this force: the different description of consciousness which was true of him was a correlate of a state of the brain that obtained at that time, which state was the effect of other physical states.

It may be objected that while 'cannot' is capacious, it is not so capacious as all that. Its meaning, it may be objected, does not allow for any ordinary use which is near to, or includes, the use that has just been made of it. I think that an opposing case can be made out, but I shall not try to do so. Let me say only that ordinary users of English, whatever definition can be attached to their use of 'cannot', would say, if they accepted the Correlation Thesis and the prior thesis about causation, that we cannot decide in ways other than we do. My concern at the moment, as in the case of actions, is only to make clear all that is to be understood by the claim that a man cannot decide in ways other than he does. Neither the statement that we cannot *do* other than we do, nor the statement that we cannot *decide* other than we do decide, is needed for what follows. These are, in fact, no more than expressions of the premisses that have been set out.

V Responsibility

At this point, we might attempt to establish that it follows from these premisses that our actions are never *free* or *voluntary*. The argument would have to do, centrally, with accounts of voluntariness or freedom. As may be anticipated, I think we could succeed in this argument. A second option is to consider instead whether it is true, given the three premisses, that we are ever responsible for our actions. The two questions are intimately related, and I am inclined to think that the second takes one more directly to the answer to both.

What we must do is settle on the truth or falsity of several propositions, and, quite as important, fix their place in human life. Precisely what propositions they are is a matter of some difficulty. What is clear enough is that they can be expressed by this sentence: 'We are sometimes responsible for our actions.' The determinist will assert that there is one false proposition that can be expressed by the sentence. He will assert, too, that the proposition and its falsehood are not irrelevant to our attitudes and concerns. There are other propositions that can be expressed by the sentence, propositions whose truth is not put in jeopardy by the theses that have been advanced. It has been maintained of these propositions about responsibility that they are, in effect, the only ones which need be paid attention by anyone with a grasp of the real world.

I shall not attempt to supply anything like an exhaustive survey of the many notions of responsibility, each of which gives rise to one of the propositions that can be expressed by the sentence given above. All of these notions, I think, can be separated into one of two categories. The categories can be indicated by reference to two uses of ordinary forms of speech. We often speak, with a particular intention, of persons *being responsible* for this or that. We also speak of *holding persons responsible* for this or that. In the second class of cases it is often natural to talk of a man's liability. Although we can use these two labels, it must be admitted that there are no sure-fire inscriptional criteria which enable us to distinguish these two classes of ascriptions of responsibility. It is ordinary to talk of someone's being responsible for something and to mean what would be expressed more consistently by saying that he is being held responsible.

This does not prevent us from making the distinction. Let us first consider ascriptions where it is most natural to speak of *holding someone responsible.* (a) We may begin with a divide in the law. (a) For the most part, statutes require for conviction that it be established that a man intended to perform a prohibited action or at least was negligent about avoiding it. Other statutes, notably those which are interpreted as imposing what is called strict liability, do not require for conviction that it be established that a man intended to perform a prohibited action or even that he was negligent. It is enough that he did the thing. It is enough, in order to establish his responsibility, so-called, that he did perform an action which falls under a certain description. One such action, briefly described, is the selling of whisky to a man who is already intoxicated. It is ascriptions of responsibility of this second kind, where it is enough to have done a certain action, to which I wish to draw attention.

(b) In the history of philosophical reflection on the freedom of the will, secondly, one can find a related characterisation. Its simplest version is to the effect that a man is responsible for an action if his future behaviour can be affected by punishment. Proponents of the view typically have it in mind that a man is responsible for an action if punishment will make it probable that he will not repeat the action. Those who are not responsible for their actions are those whose future conduct cannot be affected in this way. It is notable, to say nothing else, that one abuses language if one wishes to convey only that a man may effectively be punished, and one attempts to do so by saying, merely, that he is or was responsible for some action. Not even a description of the man as being held responsible for the action is tolerable. Still, we may admit this as a stipulated usage.

(c) There are related conceptions of responsibility, considerably more suited to the name, which fasten on those conditions of persons which may be thought to make punishment reasonable. Some of these conceptions do derive from reflection on punishment. Here, a man may be described as responsible for an action if his performance of it was uncompelled. That is, the action was in accordance with his desires or intentions and these were not forced upon him. A man is *not* responsible for an action if its performance *was* compelled: if, that is, it was in some way in conflict with his desires, his intentions or indeed his true personality. Conceptions of this kind, which have a beginning with Aristotle, have been usefully developed in several ways.

What is to be noticed is that we have three instances of talk, strained or otherwise, such that it does *not* follow from the determinist premisses that there are no actions for which a man may be held responsible. Very clearly, that an action of mine was in a certain way an effect does not entail, given the rules of strict liability, that I cannot be held legally responsible for it. That an action of mine was in this way an effect does not entail that I cannot be held responsible, where that means something about the efficacy of punishment. It is not entailed, finally, by the fact that my action was in a certain way an effect, that I cannot be held responsible for it, where that means, roughly, that it was not in accord with my own uncoerced intentions.

So much for one category of notions of responsibility, those that may be labelled as notions of a person's *being held responsible*. They give rise to propositions, all of them open to expression by the sentence, 'We are sometimes responsible for our actions'. These propositions are not vulnerable to the three theses. The determinist must admit the existence of such notions of responsibility, and this he will do without reluctance. In fact, he will regard at least the last of the three notions as of great consequence. If his enterprise is successful, it will be first among the admissible notions of responsibility.

What seems to me to be our ordinary conception of responsibility falls into the other category and pretty well exhausts it. It is here that we can most naturally speak of a man being, rather than being held, responsible. Given this conception, it is a requisite that if a man is responsible for his action, he has not been forced into it. It *is* in accordance with his uncoerced intentions. This is the requisite which provides the whole of the limited conception just mentioned. However, our ordinary conception includes another feature as well. I shall look at this conception in several of its most familiar settings. What I shall consider are *not* those occasions, perhaps mercifully rare, when we do in fact declare that someone is responsible for this or that, using the very word.

If a man to whom I am talking is persisting, as I think, in a refusal to recognise a distinction that he does in fact see, I may feel a certain irritation. I am irritated, too, if my chosen projects are frustrated because the car does not accelerate properly, or the elevator ignores my signal and does not stop at the right floor, or the corkscrew does not draw the cork cleanly. One can be irritated, however, in different ways. I may, to choose one of several locutions, *hold it against* the man that he is being mulish. I do not hold it against the corkscrew that it obstructed me, or against the car, or the elevator. If I do find such a feeling in myself, I am sufficiently aware that it is out of place. It is, at best, a kind of self-indulgence. If, to take another example, someone passes lightly over one of my mistakes, or takes a special care to remember my vulnerabilities, my response may be one of relief or pleasure. I may also be pleased to discover that the record-player now works adequately or that the typewriter doesn't skip. I shall not, however, *be grateful to* either machine. So with certain other related responses.

All of them are in place only as responses to persons, and they rest on tacit ascriptions of a responsibility. To ascribe this responsibility is to have certain beliefs about persons. I wish for the moment to single out one of these beliefs and to describe it in an introductory way. I cannot hold it against the corkscrew that it did what it did, because that was all it could have done. There was, from the point of view of its contribution, no other possibility. That is, its not drawing the cork cleanly was a simple effect of forces applied to it. I can hold it against the man that he refused to recognise the distinction if I believe, among other things, that he had a certain possibility of doing so. If I believe that his action was an effect of such a causal sequence as the one we have sketched, I cannot hold it against him. At best, I can enter into a kind of feigning. So with gratefulness. I can be grateful to a man for a particular action only if some other action was possible. In general, the involved ascriptions of responsibility depend on the assumption, which is very nearly universal, that the actions which evoke them are not the only possibilities.[7]

What is true of responses of this kind to other persons is also true of certain moral attitudes, of certain related practices, and of certain attitudes to oneself. However, I shall not consider any of these.

VI Responsibility and explanation

All of this, predictably, will call up agreement and disagreement. There are those, surely a majority, who will readily accept that their conception of responsibility is of the kind that I have just described and called our ordinary one. They will have no doubt that the theses of determinism that have been advanced are incompatible with the existence of this responsibility. They will resist any suggestion that one can accept the theses while persisting in holding things against people and being grateful to people in the way we are. They will not mean that a psychological obstruction to certain responses is raised up by the claim that actions are effects of a certain kind. Rather they will suppose that there exists an inconsistency in accepting the claim that actions are such effects and also persisting in tacit ascriptions of responsibility of the kind involved.

There are others, surely a minority, who will maintain that *their* distinction between responsible and non-responsible actions, the distinction that enters into such responses as gratefulness, is only a distinction between actions of different causal ancestries. They may accept as true that actions are effects of a certain kind, and conjoin with that view an account of responsibility (c) mentioned above. That is, they may say that responsible actions are those caused by brain states with which there are correlated certain uncoerced intentions or desires. This, they will say, is entirely sufficient. Causality and correlation, by themselves, are in no way inconsistent with the existence of such actions. It will be maintained that gratitude and the other responses are in no way put in question by the fact that actions are in a certain way effects.

It would seem absurd for members of the majority party to deny the existence of conceptions of responsibility which are thought to be (as indeed they are) consistent with the premisses of our determinism. It would seem as mistaken for members of the minority party to deny the existence of conceptions of responsibility that are thought to be inconsistent with the premisses. This amounts to the denial that there are any significant number of people who actually possess a belief which is fundamental to such of their attitudes as gratitude and which they take to be inconsistent with the premisses. The denial is no more than a piece of audacity, owed in the main to Hume. It is falsified, even, by the relevant part of the written history of philosophy, which does not falsify very much. The belief in question, as must be admitted despite my attempt at general description, is in an essential respect obscure. That philosophers and many others *have had it* is a truism.

There are two other responses that may be made by the members of the minority party, and both are more interesting. They are inclined to believe that what I have called the ordinary conception of responsibility is a mess. They would say, I think, that the conception is such that it cannot possibly be *shown* that there exists an inconsistency between the relevant ascriptions of responsibility and the given theses. They would maintain that this statement, 'You have reason for gratefulness to him on account of his action', cannot be shown to be inconsistent with the statement that his action was an effect of a certain kind.

I am inclined to agree, in a way, that the inconsistency cannot be made perspicuous. It seems impossible first to give a characterisation of the responsibility in question which is independent of the statement about the action's being an effect, and then to proceed to display an inconsistency with that statement. Rather, a characterisation of the responsibility in question *is* essentially a characterisation of something *as* inconsistent with actions being effects. In the end the responsibility is described as that which cannot exist given certain causal sequences. Still, it may be that something can be done to make things clearer.

What is wrong with what I have called our ordinary conception of responsibility is that it contains what some of its defenders have called a primitive or irreducible element. It contains, one might better say, a blank where an essential element ought to appear. It is not a matter of importance, but it is worth notice that to accept determinism is not to be deprived of a satisfactorily articulated conception of responsibility. The blank occurs at that point where one should have an account of the non-causal agency that is ordinarily supposed to enter into responsible action. No one has ever offered more, by way of explanation, than a certain amount of dubious machinery, notably the 'Creative Self'. It is pretty hard to maintain the required suspension of disbelief in such items, or rather, it is hard to see what it is that one is trying not to disbelieve.

Despite this unintelligibility, let us make the attempt to shed some light on the conflict between the given conception of responsibility and the theses of determinism. Suppose that Tom Green performs an action and we accept that it was the effect of a set S of antecedent physical conditions, some of them being brain states correlated with descriptions of consciousness mentioning certain choices or decisions. We accept, furthermore, that all of these conditions were themselves effects of earlier sets of sufficient physical conditions. Let us call the group of sets R. What is implied by this, whatever tolerable analysis of causation one takes up, is that *all* R-like groups of conditions are followed by S-like sets of conditions. And, similarly, *all* S-like sets are followed by actions like that one performed by Tom Green. It does not matter that as a matter of fact neither S nor R are likely to recur. It is true, of course, that subsets of both R and S do in fact recur.

The central point is that *anyone* in an R-like state would come to be in an S-like state, and, furthermore, would perform an action like Tom Green's. Our propositions, then, imply a denial of individuality. This claim can certainly be understood in such ways as to make the implication fail. What I have in mind is only this, that what Tom Green did is *explained*, if one accepts the causal propositions, by something that is not individual to, or peculiar to, Tom Green. More precisely, it is explained by properties of his, which, no matter who else had them, would issue in an action like his.

The point is the simple one that causal explanations of particular conditions or events are implicitly general in that they rest on invariable connexions. Certainly it is true that to explain *B* by the proposition that *A* caused it is to cite some feature of *A*. The feature does any work in the account, however, only in virtue of being an instance of a type. The same point, incidentally, can be made about statistical explanations, as distinct from traditional causal explanations.

What remains to be said can be anticipated. To regard a man as responsible for an action, in the ordinary sense, *is* to make an assertion of individuality. It is to take the position that the action has not got a general explanation. I do not intend, of course, the truth that anyone who says that Tom Green was responsible for his action has in mind intentions or whatever which were those of Tom Green and nobody else. This *is* a truth, and is one condition that must be satisfied if Tom is to be regarded as responsible for the action. What I do intend is that anyone who says he was responsible, in the given sense, takes it that his action *cannot* be explained in such a way that all of his features cited in the explanation are explanatory in virtue of being instances of a type.

There is, I feel, no more than that to be said about what might be called individual explanation, and thus about the ordinary conception of responsibility. Any attempt to give a fuller account of the actions which have such explanations, if they can be called such, will result in vagaries about the Self or the Will, or in more ordinary talk which has even less utility. These melancholy facts, it seems, do not put in question what I wish to maintain. An ordinary ascription of responsibility, tacit or otherwise, rests on a belief or an attitude to the effect that an action cannot be explained in an essentially general way. It is unimportant that this belief or attitude is rarely articulated, even to the extent that it can be, but rather is a matter of unreflective commitment.

One can take different views of this state of affairs. It is a mistake, first of all, to suppose that the given conception of responsibility is not even coherent. What *is* true of it is that it is exceedingly thin. In a word, responsible action is characterised by what it is not. This is not to say that it is not characterised at all. If one is asked to display the inconsistency of such action and causation, it is not as if one had *nothing* of a literal character to offer. Such action is that which is inconsistent with causation.

There are, I suggested, two responses of interest that may be made by those who maintain that their conception of responsibility is not in conflict with the theses of determinism, and who wish to question the alternative conception. We have looked at one. The other response has as its burden that a general acceptance of the theses could not possibly issue in the disappearance of fundamental human attitudes. It could not possibly issue in the disappearance of such attitudes as are claimed to enter into the majority party's conception of responsibility. These attitudes, one of which is gratitude, are constitutive of any recognisably human existence. They constitute, anyway, what is a large part of human existence, interpersonal relationships.

One thing to be said about this is that it rests on over-statement. This is not the place for a general survey of human attitudes but surely it is clear that many of one's attitudes to others which are the substance of relationship are *not* attitudes which depend on ordinary ascriptions of responsibility. Nonetheless, it must be granted that many of our present attitudes of relationship do depend on such ascriptions. Can it be that all of these must go, given the coming of a new Enlightenment produced by the determinist?

The answer is far from easy. Let us concern ourselves for a moment with gratitude alone. When we feel it, we feel several things. There is, typically, that satisfaction which derives from a happy event, an event of benefit. This satisfaction is not necessarily connected with the actions of others, let alone assumptions about the nature of such action. If I need money then a loan, a win in the lottery or my own successful counterfeiting will all do something for my state of mind. Second, gratitude certainly involves a less contingent satisfaction, that satisfaction which derives from an awareness of the goodwill of another person. Beyond any doubt, this is one thing that is at the foundation of the experience of gratitude. Third, when I am grateful for an act, it appears that I take satisfaction from the supposition that the person to whom I feel grateful could have done something else, and did not. I take satisfaction, if that is not too crude a description, from a belief in responsibility or individual explanation, a belief which conflicts with the theses of our determinism.

There is no reason to think, obviously, that an acceptance of the theses would undermine the first two satisfactions or perhaps others. To accept them *would* undermine the third satisfaction. Because of this loss, or, more precisely, because of the accompanying change in belief about persons, one's state of feeling could not be described as gratitude. It would fail to satisfy one condition which governs our present concept of gratitude, that condition which has to do with individual explanation or responsibility. To say this, obviously, is not to admit that a general conversion to determinism would leave nothing where gratitude was before.

In the history of reflection on our problem, both too little and too much have been made of the fact of causation. One can make too little of it by supposing, as did Hume, that it has consequences only for the fantasies of metaphysicians and divines. It has, on the contrary, consequences for beliefs and attitudes which are very general and which enter into small and large practices. We have seen one way in which too much can be made of the fact of causation. A general acceptance of it would not be so destructive of attitudes as to transform human life. In the past there have been revisions of attitude of as substantial a nature.

There is, as always, more to be said, but I shall finish with three remarks.

(1) A good deal has been suggested about responsibility and action, but nothing about responsibility and decisions or choices. If it is accepted that actions have the character that has been claimed for them, and that there cannot be a certain responsibility for them, the matter of decisions and responsibility will have little interest. An assertion of responsibility for decisions and choices, whatever it might amount to, would not secure that reassurance to which proponents of free will aspire. They wish, principally, to have the reassurance that men are responsible for their actions. They have in mind that responsibility that I have denied. It should be clear enough, in any case, that the Correlation Thesis, together with the thesis about the physical causation of physical correlates, issues in a denial of responsibility for decisions. Again, this is the responsibility which is a matter of individual explanation. The argument is not precisely the same as with actions, but I shall not set it out.

(2) That it is actions that are important, given the view that has been advanced, may give rise to the question of why I have given attention to the Correlation Thesis. It may appear, that is, that the conclusion of my reflections, that we are in one way not responsible for our actions, might have been derived from the two theses that physical states are sufficient conditions of brain states and that these latter states, with

Ted Honderich

other conditions, are sufficient for actions. It is essential, however, to any determinism of a forceful kind, that it give an account of the place of decision, choice, and consciousness generally. It is these that have been in the forefront of both philosophical and ordinary reflection on our subject.

There is also a better reason. It is impossible to escape the conviction that choices and decisions, and also intentions and a good deal else, are in some way bound up with the genesis of action. Any account of the genesis of action that is not very clearly in line with this conviction will certainly fail. If, in the given account, the brain states that are said to cause actions were not intimately connected with choices and decisions and the rest, hardly any amount of empirical evidence would bring us to accept the causal claim. The Correlation Thesis, then, is essential to the determinism that has been advanced. It is essential to an acceptance of the truth, if it is such, that actions are effects of a certain kind. As we saw earlier, it is also essential to one explanation of the relation of efficacy that seem to hold between mental events.

(3) Finally, a word on our view of ourselves. That view, which seems doomed always to be inchoate, is closely connected with the given conception of responsibility and hence the individual explanation of actions and also decisions, reflections and the like. If it is accepted that these have the character that has been claimed for them, that they are not open to individual explanation, then we must revise our view of ourselves. It seems evident that it is here that the theses of determinism may have the greatest consequence for our attitudes. Again, however, it is far from being a consequence that is unthinkable.[8]

University College London

Notes

1 J. L. Austin was 'inclined to think that determinism . . . is a name for nothing clear', and that it 'has been argued for only incoherently' ('Ifs and Cans', *Proceedings of the British Academy*, 1956). P. F. Strawson aligns himself with 'the party of those who do not know what the thesis of determinism is', although, as he says, he has 'some inkling—some notion of what sort of thing is being talked about' ('Freedom and Resentment', *Proceedings of the British Academy*, 1962). It is noteworthy that both of these distinguished essays arrive at substantial conclusions about what was thought to be unclear. A good many subsequent essays have made something like the same assumption about the condition of determinism.

2 The confirmation of descriptions of consciousness rests on (1) a person's reports, (2) his situation, and (3) his behaviour. This, and the related matter of the individuation of descriptions of consciousness, is considered in my forthcoming book. With respect to the policy of withdrawal from problems about the traditional philosophical pictures of mind, see D. C. Dennett, *Content and Consciousness* (London, 1969).

3 Any 'emergent' properties will, of course, be physical properties. I do not have in mind unrestrained speculations that emerge from time to time about properties of a non-physical nature. Cf. R. W. Sperry, 'A Modified Concept of Consciousness', *Psychological Review*, 1969.

4 A very useful layman's guide to neurophysiology is given by Dean E. Wooldridge, *The Machinery of the Brain* (New York, 1963). See also, for example, Peter M. Milner, *Physiological Psychology* (New York, 1970); Sidney Ochs, *Elements of Neurophysiology* (New York, 1965); Peter Nathan, *The Nervous System* (Philadelphia, 1969); J. Z. Young, *A Model of the Brain* (Oxford, 1964); A. R. Luria, *Higher Cortical Functions in Man* (London, 1966); J. C. Eccles, *The Neurological Basis of Mind* (Oxford, 1953).

5 Wilder Penfield and Lamar Roberts, *Speech and Brain Mechanisms* (Princeton, 1959).

6 Some further reflections on action and movement, germane to the foregoing discussion, and also an argument about movement and responsibility, may be found in my essay, 'A Conspectus of Determinism', *Proceedings of the Aristotelian Society*, Supplementary Volume, 1970.

7 Cf. P. F. Strawson, 'Freedom and Resentment', *op. cit.*

8 My thanks for comments on this essay are due to G. A. Cohen, A. R. Jonckheere, John Odling-Smee, Timothy Shallice, John Watling, J. Z. Young, and philosophers to whom it was read at University College London, Princeton, Columbia, Yale, Pennsylvania, Connecticut and Swansea. None, I think, has agreed with all of it.